Abuse of Minors in Clinical Studies

A Worldwide Ethical Challenge for the 21st Century

By

Klaus Rose

Abuse of Minors in Clinical Studies: A Worldwide Ethical Challenge for the 21st Century

By Klaus Rose

This book first published 2023

Ethics International Press Ltd, UK

British Library Cataloguing in Publication Data

A catalogue record for this book is available from the British Library

Print Book ISBN: 978-1-80441-135-3

eBook ISBN: 978-1-80441-136-0

Table of Contents

Foreword

In this book I address very controversial issues and make statements critical of many traditional teachings. These thoughts could not have been formed without the internet, its search engines, the existence of clinicaltrials.gov (the largest and most user-friendly registry of clinical trials), many other tools that allow research of the literature, of regulatory decisions, and other information from a single laptop. Internet sources are very practical to get concise information for everyday issues. We cannot understand the world with Wikipedia alone, but we need to use all the information that is available.

The internet and its tools reflect a world that is developing at a rapid pace and does not allow an easy overview. I can read the international English language literature. I am a physician with a solid medical background and have worked in drug development for decades in a position that gave me access to decision makers in very different institutions and companies.

When we were preparing a conference on "pediatric drug development" in London almost twenty years ago, we tried to organize a pro and contra debate. We were unable to find a respectable opinion leader willing to play the devil's advocate. Everybody believed that it was a wonderful thing to let children participate in pharmaceutical progress. At the time I could not have imagined that many years later I would be the person to fundamentally criticize what is touted as pediatric drug development. Such is life.

The modern world offers new tools and it has become more complex, with institutions, illusions and doctrines that can only be understood with a broad look on the one hand, digging deeply on the other hand, and never stop asking critical questions. Much is said about "Big Data" in modern research. Fear of artificial intelligence is raised. My thoughts needed less "Big Data" and more my background in languages and the history of culture.

"Pediatric drug development" is a matter at the interface of medicine and law. With this, forces flow in such as politics, traditions, science, pseudoscience, junk science, self-interests of institutions and professional organizations, a negative image of the pharmaceutical industry in the public, and much more. I relied in my analyses on common sense and appeal to the readers' common sense as well.

Chapter 1
Introduction

Without modern medicine we would not live as long; many children with congenital defects would not survive; we would not have effective surgical care after accidents. Many formerly lethal diseases are now chronic challenges that you would rather not have but you can live with quite well. One key component of the ongoing development of medical care is the development of new drugs. Today, both the United States (US) Food and Drug Administration (FDA) and the European Medicines Agency (EMA) demand separate pediatric development plans before they approve new drugs. These plans consist mostly of clinical studies with minors, justified by the claim that without them child healthcare could not progress. Altogether, this is called "Pediatric Drug Development",[1,2] in the European Union (EU) also "Better Medicines for Children."[3] Only a scoundrel would speak out against better medicine for children - true? And what if most of these studies are pointless or even harm? If they are not being done for any real medical or scientific purpose, but to allow pseudo-scientific careers? If empty promises are made and someone addresses them? Who is then the scoundrel? This book explains how a broad systematic abuse of humans has slipped worldwide into medical research, much larger than the ones reported by Beecher in 1966 and the Tuskegee Study terminated in 1972.[4,5]

A hundred years ago, infant mortality was still high. This improved with better hygiene, housing, clothing, vaccinations, and effective medicines. The cause of death of most children had been infectious diseases. Today we prevent most and can treat many. Today's most frequent cause of death in young people is accidents, followed by suicide. Pediatric oncologists emphasize that cancer in children is the most frequent cause of death in children "by disease".[6] Not true, but good marketing to mobilize sympathy and funds for pediatric cancer research. The underlying cause of many suicides is depression, which is definitely a disease.[7,8]

Historically, the discipline of pediatric medicine emerged late. Today it is a respected medical specialty. Extraordinary gains were achieved in the health of children under 5 years. In developed countries, the burden of disease in children and adolescents is increasingly characterised by complex non-infectious diseases including chronic physical disorders, neurodevelopmental disabilities, and behavioural & mental challenges.[9] Most children with cancer survive. Antisepsis, anesthetics, and antibiotics allowed pediatric surgery to correct malformations such as congenital heart defects and disfiguring challenges such as cleft lips. Better nutrition, hygiene, healthcare, mental stimulation and improved general living conditions also accelerated the process of puberty that transforms the child's body into a mature body, allowing the unfolding of sexual activities.[10-12]

Drug development is complex and expensive. To develop a new drug costs today two to three billion $ US.[13,14] Two different institutions control their use. They must be approved by the regulatory authorities, they are prescribed by officially trained, recognized and registered medical doctors, and they are dispended by pharmacists. All these institutions are governed by special laws. Drugs are approved for specific indications, such as gastric ulcer. The clinical studies account for the lion's share of the costs of drug development. Once a drug is approved, the production costs are comparatively low. This has led to the pharmaceutical industry being criticized for excessive prices, comparing the low production costs of drugs with the high market prices. People who do not know (or do not want to know) the complexity of drug development conclude that the pharmaceutical industry primarily only enriches itself from the patients. An army of authors has established an entire industry that condemns the pharmaceutical industry.[15-17]

Initially companies developed and sold medicines without major supervision. This changed with two major catastrophes. The first, still "local" in the US only, occurred by a liquid form of the early antibiotic sulphanilamide. The used solvent diethylene glycol was toxic; about 150 people died.[18] The second disaster was already global. A German company developed thalidomide and sold and marketed it as a tranquilizer, also for pregnant women. Worldwide, it caused massive malformations in thousands of babies.[19] These disasters led to a new role for the regulatory authorities. In 1962, the US gave the Food and Drug Administration (FDA) the authority to only approve drugs whose safety and efficacy had already been proven, resulting in today's drug approval processes based on laboratory, animal, and human studies. Over the ensuing decades, the rest of the world followed the US. Drug development has progressed phenomenally.[20]

Prescription of drugs according to their approval/ label is called "on-label". The regulatory authorities have no right to tell doctors what to prescribe and what not. Once drugs are approved, doctors can prescribe them beyond their label. This is called "off-label" prescription. On one hand, it is correct to avoid that companies develop a drug in a tiny indication, market it after approval in different, larger areas, compromise safety, save development costs, and make higher profits. On the other hand, off-label prescribing is an integral part of medical work and contributes continuously to fine-tuning medical care and the use of existing drugs. The debate about on-label/off-label use is complex, goes on since decades, and keeps US lawyers and courts busy since many years.[21] There is no miracle recipe in this question. We will not resolve it here with a few lines. Anyway, a reasonable balance is crucial.

The on-label/off-label debate has taken on a special dimension with children. From 1962 on, companies inserted pediatric warnings into drug labels that the respective drug had not been tested in children. This was triggered by toxicities of antibiotics in preterm newborns reported in the 1950s.[22-24] These warnings had a *legal* purpose, reflecting the frequent lawsuits in the US for alleged damage. But Dr. Shirkey, first chairman of the American Academy of Pediatrics (AAP) Committee on Drugs, interpreted these warnings *medically*. He claimed they discriminated children and deprived them of the access to new, effective medicines. He coined the term of children as "therapeutic orphans",[25] which became extraordinarily successful. The AAP, the FDA, and pediatric researchers soon called for separate pediatric studies to end this alleged discrimination.[24,26] Eventually, this concept led to US pediatric laws from 1997 on, followed by an even more ambitious law of the European Union (EU), in force since 2007. Both demand separate proof of safety & efficacy in the "pediatric population", defined as younger than 18 years.[7,27] Industry must pay for these studies. In compensation, the US law initially rewarded such studies with a six months patent extension ("pediatric exclusivity"), allowing longer high-price sales. In the EU, there is also a reward at the end of patent life, but compared to the US it is negligible. In the EU, companies must commit to pediatric studies in a "pediatric investigation plan" (PIP) much earlier than in the US, years before marketing authorisation application. PIPs must be negotiated with the EU pediatric committee, coordinated by the European Medicines Agency (EMA).[7,27]

There is a catch in the concept of children as "therapeutic orphans", the consequences of which we see today. Of course, children were always treated with new effective drugs. Should doctors let have children die of infections because the new antibiotics were not approved in children? Apart from being murderous, such a logic did not even exist at the time. Children, adolescents and adults were taken for granted as human beings. The administrative distinction between adults and minors is old on the one hand, as we see from the documentation of medieval court discussions about heritage and/or caregiving of orphaned minors from wealthy families. One the other hand, much less was known about the physiology of the developing body. Furthermore, today's complex administrative structures that affect more and more details of our daily life did not yet exist. The term "off-label" appeared decades after the 1962 introduction of US pharmaceutical law, in 1988.[28] Without new drugs, pediatric surgery, neonatology and all other pediatric sub-disciplines could not have developed. But a new dimension had entered the debate. From the beginning, the AAP defined children *legally* by their *legal* incapacity to consent to clinical studies before they reached adulthood. Developmental physiology and developmental pharmacology had emerged, showing fundamental differences between babies and adults. Not only in the size of organs (you do not need to be a scientist to know that the baby and its organs are smaller), but in the function of the organs that run absorption, distribution, metabolism and excretion (ADME) of food and drugs, including liver and kidneys. A premature baby's kidneys are much less efficient than those of a six-month-old, and the enzyme composition of the liver is still different. Pediatricians had used formulas and dosing tables, which on the whole served their purpose. But in very young premature babies and newborns formulas and tables were often too mechanical and led to incorrect – and hence dangerous - dosage recommendations. The fact that special caution is indeed needed in premature babies turned into the warning that all drugs posed a great risk for all children if they were not tested separately. Massively exaggerated, but it hit successfully a nerve of the time.

When the US & EU regulatory authorities request or demand pediatric studies and the companies commit to these studies, patients are recruited worldwide. When the lawmakers enacted pediatric laws, they were told by the scientific community that these studies would be essential to further improve the medical care of children. In its 2001 report to Congress, the FDA stated: "The incentives provided by the newly authorized pediatric exclusivity should lead to significant advances in pediatric medicine. Superior drug treatment information is expected to permit quicker recoveries from childhood illnesses, with fewer attendant hospital stays, physician visits and parental work days lost".[29] These expected improvement were reasonable and would have been measurable. No such results have ever been published, neither by the FDA, the EMA, or academic publishers. Instead, later reports by FDA and EMA describe other types of "successes": number of pediatric patients recruited, number of pediatric studies performed, number of pediatric label changes, etc. Not real clinical successes, but administrative reports about bureaucratic activism.[30-32] The one truly important question is never asked and never answered: did all these activities improve hands-on child healthcare? To put it even more bluntly: did and do they make any scientific and/or medical sense?

Medical research has enormously advanced our therapeutic ability. During the years of preparation and enactment of pediatric legislation, there was much debate about the ethical justification of clinical research involving children. In all these discussions it was taken for granted that the studies to obtain separate drug approvals for minors were in their interest. But this assumption is flawed. The term "child" has different legal/administrative and physiological meanings. Blurring these different meanings attributes nonexistent bodily changes to a chronological age limit. By using the chronological age limit of initially 17, later 18 years, the demand for "pediatric" studies included adolescents that bodily are already mature. Drugs treat the body, not the administrative status. In itself, this blur is just semantic. But it has resulted and continues to result in thousands of pointless or massively exaggerated clinical studies that in many cases are even harmful. Individual clinical areas are discussed in later chapters of this book.

Society and humanity are changing rapidly. A century ago, there were only a few effective drugs, including strong painkillers (opiates), alcoholic beverages, laxatives, quinine, and topical wound remedies. Acetylsalicylic acid (aspirin) had just reached the market. The prerequisites for the societal changes had been profound intellectual changes in the Renaissance, the printing press, industrialization, the worldwide expansion of European states with large, cannon-equipped ships, and many other factors. The two world wars accelerated these changes, both on a technical and on a human level - for those who survived. Word War I brought tanks, chemical warfare, air warfare, hand grenades, flame throwers, submarines, and more useful inventions. World War II brought the radar, antibiotics, and the atomic bomb. Both wars broke down traditional mental structures and led to the collapse of many monarchies. The role of the state in directing societal efforts has two sides. The state can help to advance new inventions that otherwise would take longer to be developed, such as the industrial development of penicillin during World War II that was supported by US governmental institutions. But such advances come at a price, paid by those who are killed or maimed in a war, and all the human suffering that is inseparable from war.

Modern technology, academic research and the world wars developed in competition. States wanted to dominate. Individuals wanted to get to the top. This basic mechanism will never change, just that in different societies the rules for advancement are different and open competition is not always accepted. One strategy for getting to the top as a scientist consisted a century ago of unleashing the resources of the human body and mind. The world wars were marked on all sides by research in human capacities. American psychiatrists helped to select recruits for the armed forces. Nazis like

Mengele hoped to be rewarded after the war with academic honors for their horrifying "research". But the Nazis and Japan lost. After the war, criminal experiments of German and Japanese researchers were rightly condemned worldwide. For a long time, crimes against humanity were thought a peculiarity of the Nazis and the Japanese unit 731.[33-36] But in 1966 Beecher described how US researchers had carried out questionable experiments in humans and published them in recognized scientific journals.[4] By today's standards these experiments were criminal and inhuman. Then the Tuskegee study was brought to light in 1972. It was terminated within days after it had been published in a national US newspaper. In this study, African American men with syphilis had been observed since decades and had not been given antibiotics when these became broadly available from World War II on. Syphilis can be treated by antibiotics.[5,37]

"Pediatric" studies in adolescents that are bodily already mature are pointless, as the investigated subjects are physiologically no longer children. They are based on an artificial classification of these people as belonging to the "pediatric population". The researchers in developmental physiology and pharmacology know well that the major changes in the child's body occur during the first days and weeks after their birth.[38] Furthermore, the changes are more relevant in premature newborns. Pediatric researchers also know that the bodily maturation has accelerated during the last century.[10-12] But they refuse to apply these learnings to reality. Also in younger children, separate proof of efficacy is pointless. An antibiotic will work before and after the 12th birthday. Of course, toxicities must be avoided. But not by multicenter international studies, as the EU PIPs demand them for many or even most new drugs.[7] One group profits mainly from these studies: the researchers themselves and their institutions. But the entire issue is more complex. One essential condition for this spook to continue is that scientific journals publish reports about "pediatric" studies that violate the most elementary condition of the Declaration of Helsinki: that research on humans must be medically meaningful.[39] Nowhere does the Declaration of Helsinki justify conducting pointless studies to meet dogmatic regulatory requirements. These studies would not be performed if scientific journals would refuse to publish banal studies that for example confirm that insulin works also in "children",[7,40,41] or if peer reviewers, Institutional Review Boards (IRBs) and Ethics Committees (ECs) would be more careful in assessing study rationales. The FDA rewarded a "pediatric" study in nasopharyngeal carcinoma (cancer of the throat and larynx). The study was performed and published,[42] and the sponsoring company got its patent extension. But nasopharyngeal carcinoma is not a pediatric disease. It occurs in patients of all ages. Today, in hindsight, we can see the chain of sloppiness that triggered this study: the flawed assessment of a disease as "pediatric"; the offered reward for this "pediatric" study; the pseudo-scientific justification for the study; the acceptance of the justification and the study rationale by all clinicians that were happy to participate in an international study; the approval of the study by the responsible IRBs/ECs; the acceptance of the publication by the editor-in-chief of the journal that accepted the study; and the lack of criticism from the scientific world.

Before World War II, there had been no internationally accepted code of conduct of research in humans. After the defeat of Nazi Germany, the Nuremberg code was created in the verdict of one of the Nuremberg trials that dealt with various war crimes committed by Nazi Germany. It was a set of ethical research principles for human experimentation, articulated as part of the court's verdict.[43] It later became significant together with the Declaration of Helsinki, enacted by the World Medical Association in 1964, which is now widely regarded as the cornerstone document on human research ethics. It has been updated and fine-tuned several times since 1964.[39] The Declaration of Helsinki defines as the primary purpose of medical research in humans to understand the causes, development and effects of diseases and improve preventive, diagnostic and therapeutic interventions. It emphasizes that even the best proven interventions must be evaluated continually through research for safety, efficacy, and quality. Furthermore, it emphasizes that medical research is subject to high ethical standards.[39,43] Both the Nuremberg Code and the Declaration of Helsinki emphasize as one of the key requirement for human research the voluntary consent of the trial participant.

Consent requires that the individual is legally capable, which is not the case with minors, where parents or caretakers are responsible for giving permission to participate.

Coordinated by regulatory authorities, scientifically supported by academic researchers, and codified by "pediatric" laws, "pediatric drug development" is numerically the largest abuse of patients in medical research in history. It is not openly cruel "research" like the Mengele twin studies,[32,45] or the atrocities of the Japanese unit 731.[35,46,47] The concept began in the US probably with the best intentions. But it contained from the start the semantic blur that equated administrative/legal definitions of children with an alleged physical difference between adults and "children". The caution that is undoubtedly warranted in the case of premature infants is misplaced in the case of adolescents. A publication by FDA employees shows that for practically all drugs the doses determined in "pediatric" studies for adolescents from the age of 12 on were identical to the adult doses.[48] Not a surprise. Adolescents are already physically mature, even if legally/administratively they are still children. That they are mentally not yet mature is another story. Also the separate testing of the efficacy of drugs in school children is massively exaggerated. Medicines have to be dosed correctly. But large international multicenter studies are not necessary for dose finding.

The AAP and developmental pharmacologists have been central to the call for "pediatric" studies. Several myths have been built up over time. One such myth is that approved drugs are safer for children. But the entire discipline of pediatrics evolved without regulatory influence, "off-label," decades before the term "off-label" was first used in 1988.[7,28]

Research in developmental pharmacology and specialized branches of pediatrics needs funding. While industry had poured a lot of money into developing drugs to tackle serious problems in adults, such as high blood pressure, strokes, or gastric ulcers, representatives of pediatric research complained that hardly any money came from industry. That changed abruptly with the first US pediatric law in 1997.

A second factor was the aforementioned negative characterization of the pharmaceutical industry. It now came handy to justify the enforcing of "good" studies from the "bad" industry.[7]

While the FDA is in close contact with academic research and in many areas has waived the requirement for separate "pediatric" studies, at least in adolescents, the EMA is much more isolated from the general public. Its working language is English, which at its inception was widely spoken only in England and Ireland. The EMA demands are dogmatic and stick to the demand for "pediatric" studies, even where they are now rejected by relevant sections of academic research.[7] On the other hand, the EMA and the FDA together adhere to the fundamental justification of "pediatric drug development", see the recent jointly published position paper on "pediatric" studies in the development of vaccines against COVID-19.[49]

We live in an era of good sanitation, nutrition, and housing. That plus effective vaccines and medicines have significantly changed the composition of humanity in developed countries. Few children still die from infectious diseases. Many diseases that were once overlooked in the deluge of infectious diseases have become the subject of own pediatric disciplines. For a while it was thought that malignancies only existed in old people. In the mid-20th century, with improved communication, transportation, and the scientific literature, it became clear that, in rare cases, young people could also contract malignancies. The first children's cancer wards were established in the middle of the 20th century. At the same time, rare forms and sub-types of rheumatic diseases became known which can also affect minors. For a while, it had been thought that adolescents and children could not get depressed;[50] we know today that this is the case. Chronic diseases that primarily affect adults can also appear in minors, such as multiple sclerosis, an autoimmune disease of the central nervous system that leads to muscle weakness, abnormal sensations, poor eyesight, blindness and more. And so on. The myth that adults only get adult diseases and children only childhood diseases is flawed, as is the belief that any disease detected in somebody before his 18th birthday is therefore a "pediatric" disease. But with precisely this logic the EMA has meanwhile defined diseases such as amytrophic lateral sclerosis (ALS/ Lou Gehrig disease), hepatic cancer, malignant melanoma, Parkinson disease, and others as "pediatric" diseases and demands for drugs that target these diseases "pediatric" studies in those unfortunate few patients in which such a disease is diagnosed before the 18th birthday.[51]

There are serious and massive conflicts of interest behind "pediatric drug development" beyond the mere semantic blur described above. But these conflicts of interest have so far been overlooked by the system of precautions society has built against abuse in human research. This abuse has the official blessing by mainstream science, the regulatory authorities, and representatives of major life science companies.[52-56] In publications that are on a regular base published in high-ranking peer reviewed journals the principles of "pediatric drug development" are outlined and justified, however, without addressing the difference between the legal and the physiological meaning of the term "child".[52] Several myths outlined above are taught as mantras to generations of scientists, including that only drugs that are officially approved are allegedly safe and effective. Children-are-no-small-adults is a mantra which is correct for premature newborns, but not for all legally/administratively defined "children" until they come of age.

The administrative side of medicine has increased in importance. Several decades ago, a conference discussed the efficacy of antiepileptic drugs in minors.[57] The participants reported no problems with the payment by reimbursement institutions for antiepileptic drugs not approved in minors. Today, this has changed. Modern drugs can be very expensive, and the treatment of one single patient can put financial strain on any reimbursement institution. With increased complexity, procedures have also become more bureaucratic. If the computer reports a specific drug as not approved in minors, the administrator might demand justification from the treating doctor or, worse, might simply refuse to reimburse the costs.

There is the feeling of academic researchers and clinicians that they are morally superior to people working in for-profit companies. Such thoughts have been and are expressed in numerous medical publications,[14-16,58,59] but often such thoughts are elusive. The EU pediatric regulation explains in the preamble that the forces of the market are not sufficient to ensure enough pediatric research to meet the medical needs of the "pediatric population".[60] To correct this, the EU created the pediatric committee with the authority to enforce pediatric studies from pharmaceutical companies. Few academic researchers are aware of the "pediatric" debate between industry and EMA with its pediatric committee. So far, more than two thousand pediatric investigation plan (PIP) procedures have been performed, including many discussions about PIP modifications.[61] We should remember at this point that mankind has seen other experiments where a central bureaucracy, instead of the market, dictates what is to be produced. Ultimately, the Soviet Union perished because of its inability to meet the needs of its citizens.[62-64] The same inability to adapt to reality has happened and continues to happen to the EMA and its pediatric committee. There are not enough underage patients worldwide for the many "pediatric" studies.[7,65] Anybody who visits the sales exhibitions of a conference on neonatal care can see how the range of products in neonatology has expanded over the last few decades. This market is represented by the feedback of neonatologists that tell others, including sales representatives, what they need. Furthermore, they publish. The scientists that develop and produce drugs for neonatal care read these publications and recommend new developments. But in drugs, the EMA has established a position where it proudly knows better what the neonatal community needs. It acts accordingly and tells pharmaceutical companies which clinical studies are needed. They have allies in the neonatal clinical world and can, to some extent, influence the allocation of funding. They control the EnprEMA network where bona fide clinicians discuss access to funds for research projects and share experiences.[66] The EMA officials do not control neonatal research as a whole. But it is sufficient to show the support of individual clinicians in case of doubt.

Distrust in the market is another underlying factor resonating in "pediatric drug development". The demonization of the pharmaceutical industry is not only a favorite topic of industry haters.[14-16,58,59] The belief that business is too independent and should be controlled more by the state is quite strong among academics. We can call this the academic flirting with socialist ideas. Behind this flirtation are fundamental philosophical ideas about the desirable structure of our society. Again, we come back to the chilling historical examples of command economies that ultimately culminated in the collapse of the Soviet Union, the Holodomor in Ukraine,[67] and Stalinist mass murder.[68] All, of course, with reference to noble higher purposes.

There are multiple ethical challenges of "pediatric drug development". Patients are exposed to pointless and even harmful studies. The public has been and is being systematically deceived. Publications appear in reputable journals that report banal results such as that certain medications also work in minors. Why should they not work? All "pediatric" studies required by the FDA and EMA go through approval procedures by Institutional Review Boards (IRBs) and ethics committees (ECs). The International Committee of Medical Journal Editors (ICMJE) has not yet spoken out against the pseudo-scientifically justified "pediatric" studies.[69] It would be desirable if the Declaration of Helsinki would address "pediatric drug development" in its next update.

A challenge that appeared as highly ethical and noble half a century ago has developed an ugly face behind the shiny surface. Medieval stonemasons depicted the devil above the portals of cathedrals as a sympathetic young man. You had to step to the side of this portal figure to see toads and snakes crawling on his back.[70,71] It is not new in history that perspectives change. The discovery of the Americas is no longer celebrated as just a great discovery. But only blaming their negative consequences is just as wrong. We cannot turn back the wheel of history. Everything and every institution that dogmatically attempts to maintain mechanical formulas beyond their time is doomed to perish in the long run. It is time for a critical revision of the ethical challenges of "pediatric drug development".

The treatment of malignancies in minors is a very special case. When child mortality by infectious diseases had substantially declined, childhood diseases that had been overlooked so far began to come to the attention of scientific and medical research. One such area was malignancies in children, another one rheumatic diseases that begin early in childhood. There are many more, but we will address them later. Previously it had been assumed that cancer and other malignancies existed in adults only. In the 1940/50s, attention began to be given to malignancies in children. Malignancies are much less common in children, but when a child develops it, the whole family is devastated. This family will not be interested in hearing that this is just exceptionally bad luck. They want help for their child, period. The peculiarity of the fight against childhood cancer was that the progress up to around the year 2000 was not due to new drugs,[6,72,73] but by drugs used and approved since decades for adult cancer: chemotherapeutic agents. There were encouraging early results in the treatment of leukemia, particularly the most common childhood malignancy, acute lymphoblastic leukemia (ALL). Up until around the year 2000, chemotherapy for childhood cancer was continuously refined to e.g., 90% survival rate for ALL. Only with the surmounting of the plateau that had been reached in 2000, pediatric oncology returned, so to speak, into the mainstream development course of medical development: real new drugs and treatment methods were now required for further advances. The first successful new approach occurred with CAR-T cell therapy, which saved the life of Emily Whitehead who was with 6 years the youngest patient to participate in the pivotal trial of tisagenlecleucel.[74-77] It is crucial to emphasize here that the entire discipline of pediatric oncology emerged "off-label", decades before this term even began to exist. During the first decades of pediatric oncology, the regulatory authorities had no active role in its emergence. Today, as the mentioned peculiarity is over, there are attempts by regulatory dogmatists to criticize the merits of pediatric oncology to the effect that its emergence and development did not lead to the approval of the developed treatment schemes.[72,73] The purpose of medicine is to treat people, not to approve drugs. A dogmatic over-regulatory approach wants to impose retrospectively a process that exists today on the past, distorting what really happened at the time.

A central element of "pediatric drug development" is the desire to accelerate the fight against childhood cancer. In the early decades of pediatric oncology, the use of chemotherapy agents was switched from adult to childhood cancer. The regulatory authorities had no part in the original development of pediatric oncology. But they dream of achieving a successful repetition of the mentioned switch with new targeted anticancer drugs. Aside from criticizing the fact that pediatric oncology has not led to the regulatory approval of treatment regimes,[72] they now coerce the industry to clinically test new targeted adult anticancer drugs in different types of pediatric cancer. In this they are supported by a group of pediatric oncologists who profit from the studies industry is coerced to commit to. Fifteen years of such pediatric childhood cancer studies enforced by the EMA has not yielded clinical success.[7] It is psychologically understandable that under pressure of affected parents in the US, too, the FDA can now force the industry to carry out such pediatric cancer studies with the RACE for children act.[78-81] In addition to parents' associations, institutions that are active in child cancer research were particularly involved in the demand for this law.[82,83] Emily Whitehead was healed by advances in real, innovative research, not by coerced regulatory studies. Two schools have emerged in pediatric oncology and many other pediatric research areas: those that benefit from studies enforced by the regulatory authorities, and those that conduct real, meaningful, and innovative research.

Another layer of conflict of interest is the self-interest of the EMA, a powerful institution established in 1995.[84] The concept of "pediatric drug development" originated in the US, but has been dogmatically augmented and sharpened by the EMA. Supported by academic scientists who benefit materially from "pediatric" research studies, the EMA has even set up an own "pediatric" research structure, the

"European Network of Paediatric Research at the European Medicines Agency"(Enpr-EMA).[66] Many pediatricians participate in Enpr-EMA in the hope to find funds for their research activities. EMA employees are invited to prestigious academic conferences where they praise the purported contributions of their institution for the further development of pediatric medicine.

We see here a new type of conflict of interest that could only emerge in today's complex society. It could not exist without the framework that justifies "pediatric" research as if children were another species, demanding mostly pointless "pediatric" studies from pharmaceutical industry that banally repeat what we know already: that compounds such as insulin, antibiotics or chemotherapeutic agents work the same before and after the 12th or 18th birthday. Currently, the "Recommendations for the Conduct, Reporting, Editing, and Publication of Scholarly Work in Medical Journals" published by International Committee of Medical Journal Editors (ICMJE) represent the internationally accepted gold standard in the documentation of potential conflicts of interest by authors in scientific medical publications.[69] The structural conflict of interest in "pediatric drug development" is not well captured by these recommendations. With thousands of "pediatric" studies enforced by PIPs,[7] the relevance of studies in chronologically defined "children", which often also include physically adult young people, such pointless and often harmful studies deserve a strong mention in the ICMJE recommendations.

Readers may have wondered why there are no comparable initiatives to develop safer medicines for young animals. Pets living with humans often develop comparable diseases, including obesity, high blood pressure, rheumatic diseases and more. Animal rights activists are very resourceful when it comes to demanding more government protection for animals. But demands for the development of safer medicines for young animals have not emerged. The reason is simple: in the extended animal kingdom, humans are the only species that uses a legal definition of minority for young members.

This introduction gives a high-level overview. The blind enforcement of "pediatric" studies for all newly developed drugs not only results in pointless studies. In many medical fields, such studies have also directly harmed young people. These will be discussed in later chapters. Not all involved scientists will welcome a critical debate. Numerous critical assessments of harmful "pediatric" studies have been published in international peer-reviewed journals,[85-90] and in two medical textbooks.[7,91] Here we focus on the ethical evaluation of the entire initiative of alleged "pediatric drug development".

If we put "pediatric drug development" in historical perspective, it has certainly served a useful function. The recognition of rapid development processes in the body of the newborn and especially the premature baby were elementary scientific advances. But they encountered a new societal framework, represented by new institutions with massive self-interests, including the regulatory authorities, the professional representations of developmental pharmacology, academic research institutions that needed funding, the prosperous life science industry and its critics that appeal to protective instincts against injustice, and more. In a few hundred years, "pediatric drug development" will be just a spot on the historical map that will be smiled at in hindsight. When this debate started, there was no internet. Doctors had to refer to the printed labels for dosing recommendations for minors. The date of birth played a lesser role than today. Anybody who was physically mature was given medications at the usual adult dosage. All other methods to retrieve information, including asking advice from colleagues, correspondence, or search through the libraries would have taken days, weeks, or even months. Life-threatening situations do not allow a generous delay in decision making. Today the internet allows worldwide access to information with a few mouse clicks, provided you know where to look. In the advancing 21st century, the regulatory authorities argue with a century-old logic. Administration of drugs to special patients requires continuous adjustment. For premature babies who weigh just half a kilogram, fixed dosage recommendations for medicines are hardly possible. It may be the case that in the evening the dose that was correct early in the morning is already too high or too low.

In this introduction I give an overview and first idea how the drug treatment of children, a perfectly reasonable issue, has fallen into a framework that has turned it into an administrative nightmare, resulting in thousands of pointless and often even harmful studies with young people. Many of these studies are ongoing. It is time to separate meaningful studies with young people from pointless or exaggerated studies, or even worse. Young people need scientifically founded dosing recommendation, not dogmatically enforced, medically pointless regulatory studies. It is a challenge at the interface of medicine and law, involving ethical questions that have so far only been marginally addressed in the literature. Hopefully, this book will contribute to tackle and master this fundamental ethical challenge of the 21st century. In history, science and ethics had to overcome many obstacles on their zigzag path to intellectual, technical, and social progress. This entire issue is highly controversial.

It is unusual in our time that mainstream science supports a flawed concept. But it is not entirely new in history. For many centuries science was firmly convinced that the sun revolves around the earth and that we see stars in the sky. Today we know that the earth revolves around the sun and that most stars we see with the naked eye are actually distant galaxies. The Catholic Church, which for centuries represented the highest moral and scientific authority in Europe, has done everything in its power to halt the advance of science. At the end, she failed. That controversial positions can be expressed at all is a privilege of our time and of our free world.

I have worked in the pharmaceutical industry for decades. That does not mean that I liked everything I saw. The pharmaceutical industry, today also called the life science industry, is closely linked to the academic world. Advances in drug development mirror newest academic learnings, such as first the understanding of monoclonal antibodies, then their industrial production, the growing understanding of the body's mechanisms of inflammation, defense against pathogens, today's armamentarium of anti-inflammatory treatments, and last not least the development of an effective vaccine against the corona virus based on messenger RNA (mRNA) technology by a company that planned to use this technology to develop therapeutic vaccines against cancer.[92] Working in large pharmaceutical companies brings the convenience of being able to seek out, meet and interact with the world's leading specialists. I have always appreciated the relaxed and free nature of debate in the academic world, but I have also seen how determined project management allows successful product development, which then has a lasting impact on medical treatment worldwide, far beyond what a single clinician could achieve. It would be pointless to start a discussion about what is more important: clinical work or drug development. Both have become part of healthcare. What we have yet to achieve is to ensure that the clinical medical profession's high level of self-awareness gives way to a real team spirit. Drug development is complex and full of contradictions. Science, market research, marketing, competitive intelligence, and much more are included. No one can understand all of this alone. But that is not even necessary. It is teamwork.

Bleeding from gastric ulcers was a frequent cause of death half a century ago. Over time, it became preventable and treatable with a sequence of discoveries and increasingly powerful medications. It started with antacids; followed by the discovery of histamine H_2-receptors and the development of histamine H_2-receptor antagonists; then the identification of H^+K^+-ATPase as the parietal cell proton pump and the development of proton pump inhibitors; and finally the identification of Helicobacter pylori as the major cause of gastric & duodenal ulcer and esophagitis, and the development of effective eradication regimens.[93] Communication and leadership in industry is different from that in science. People do not remain in positions they will hold for decades. That alone makes the competition tougher. Decades of work in the industry does not mean that one fully identifies with the respective company. That definitely did not happen to me. I have had the privilege of being involved in the emergence and development of "pediatric drug development" in a leading position that allowed me to observe things for decades. Furthermore, I had access to the generation of key representatives in developmental pharmacology that had contributed to the emergence of the entire concept. Then the years of being self-employed and consulting a multitude of small, medium, and large companies opened my eyes to the conflicts of interest described in this book. Beyond realizing the blur of the various meanings of the term "child" were the discussions about European Union (EU) "pediatric investigation plans" (PIPs) and FDA pediatric requirements that finally resulted in my conclusions. Many examples I give about pointless, exaggerated, and/or harmful clinical studies in minors might be dismissed as isolated cases. What I then realized over the last few years was that there is a pattern that logically explains all of the seemingly isolated flaws in these studies.

The pharmaceutical industry is not a monolithic bloc. The research-based companies are represented by organisations that represent their interests to regulatory authorities, to the public, and to other institutions.[94-97] Many people who work in industry and manage after many years to advance to a senior rank where they can represent their company in a large and/or international organization are often content with this career move. They earn well, fly business class, and exchange high level ideas with authorities and scientists. So far, the principles of "pediatric drug development" are undisputed at this level. An additional thought that came to me in a discussion of this was the concern that too much criticism might lead the authorities to call for even more nonsensical studies and other "pediatric" measures.

To sum up my potential personal conflicts of interest, the positions in this book are not sanctioned, paid, or supported by any pharmaceutical company, nor by any regulatory agency, nor by any academic group. I managed to get my thoughts published in many peer-reviewed journals and was able to get enough academic support to be accepted as a medical textbook author. I managed to develop and maintain my own opinion in a demanding professional environment. I never had to deal with a university bureaucracy. In the industry, once things are approved, they are done without much frills. I understand medical terminology by having studied medicine and through my knowledge of classical Latin and Greek. And I have been outside of the direct medical clinical sphere of power long enough to be critical of its side effects as well. Not being operationally blind has its advantages.

In addition, our first daughter had Sturge-Weber-Syndrome, a very rare condition in which causal treatment will probably never be possible.[98-104] However, symptomatic treatment is available, including drug treatment of epilepsy, surgical treatment of congenital glaucoma, laser treatment of portwine stains, and much more. Our first daughter passed away when she was 27 years old. These years have shaped me at least as much as my studies and my professional experience.

There are many more challenges of our time. One of them is that the times when basic and applied science were sharply separated are over. The universities have preserved and advanced the scientific knowledge of mankind for centuries. But that role is not set in stone. A lot of knowledge only comes from putting principles into practice. With the scientific penetration of more and more areas of industry and business, there is a growing challenge to the academic world to encourage feedback in the composition of the academic teaching staff. This cannot work where academic positions are guaranteed lifetime jobs. In this regard, this introduction touches on further questions about what professional conflicts of interest are. I made some further reflections on this in the final chapter of this book. For now, I hope you will enjoy reading it.

References

1. Mulberg AE, Silber SA, van den Anker, JN (Eds). Pediatric Drug Development – Concepts and Applications. Wiley-Blackwell, Hoboken, NJ, USA, 2009

2. Mulberg AE, Murphy MD, Dunne J, Mathis LL (Eds). Pediatric Drug Development: Concepts and Applications. 2nd ed., John Wiley & Sons, Chichester, UK, 2013.

3. European Medicines Agency (EMA) 2015. Better Medicines for Children https://www.ema.europa.eu/en/documents/leaflet/better-medicines-children_en.pdf

4. Beecher HK. Ethics and clinical research. N Engl J Med. 1966 Jun 16;274(24):1354-60. https://www.observatoriobioetica.org/wp-content/uploads/2016/09/Beecher_Ethics_and_Clinical_Research_1966.pdf

5. Brandt, Allan M. 1978. Racism and research: The case of the Tuskegee Syphilis study. The Hastings Center Report 8(6): 21-29. https://dash.harvard.edu/handle/1/3372911

6. Adamson PC. Improving the outcome for children with cancer: Development of targeted new agents. CA Cancer J Clin. 2015 May-Jun;65(3):212-20. https://acsjournals.onlinelibrary.wiley.com/doi/epdf/10.3322/caac.21273

7. Rose K. Considering the Patient in Pediatric Drug Development. How good intentions turned into harm. Elsevier, London, UK, 2020

8. American Academy of Child & Adolescent Psychiatry (AACAP).Suicide in Children and Teens. AACAP 2021. https://www.aacap.org/AACAP/Families_and_Youth/Facts_for_Families/FFF-Guide/Teen-Suicide-010.aspx

9. Sawyer SM, McNeil R, Francis, KL, et al. The age of paediatrics. The Lancet Child & Adolescent Health 2019 Nov;3(11):822-830

10. Komlos J, Lauderdale BE. The mysterious trend in American heights in the 20th century. Ann Hum Biol. 2007;34(2):206–215.

11. Cone TE Jr. Secular acceleration of height. J Pediatr 1961 Nov;59:736-40.

12. Beunen GP, Rogol AD, Malina RM. Indicators of biological maturation and secular changes in biological maturation. Food Nutr Bull. 2006;27(4 Suppl Growth Standard):S244–S256. https://journals.sagepub.com/doi/pdf/10.1177/15648265060274S508.

13. DiMasi JA, Grabowski HG, Hansen RW. Innovation in the pharmaceutical industry: New estimates of R&D costs. J Health Econ. 2016 May;47:20-33.

14. DiMasi JA. Research and Development Costs of New Drugs. JAMA. 2020 Aug 4;324(5):517.

15. Goldacre B. Bad Pharma: How drug companies mislead doctors and harm patients. HarperCollins Publishers, London, UK, 2012

16. Angell M. The Truth about the Drug Companies: How They Deceive Us and What to Do about It. Random House Publishers, New York, USA, 2004

17. Gøtzsche P. Deadly Psychiatry and Organized Denial. People's Press, København, Denmark 2015. https://www.deadlymedicines.dk/wp-content/uploads/2014/10/G%C3%B8tzsche-Deadly-Psychiatry-chapter-1.pdf

18. Wax PM. Elixirs, Diluents, and the Passage of the 1938 Federal Food, Drug and Cosmetic Act. Ann Intern Med 1995 Mar 15;122(6):456-61 http://citeseerx.ist.psu.edu/viewdoc/download?doi=10.1.1.733.2602&rep=rep1&type=pdf

19. Vargesson N. Thalidomide-induced teratogenesis: History and mechanisms. Birth Defects Res C Embryo Today. 2015 Jun; 105(2): 140–156.

20. Rägo L, Santo B: Drug Regulation: History, Present and Future. In: Drug Benefits and Risks: International Textbook of Clinical Pharmacology, revised 2nd edition, van Boxtel CJ, Santo B & Edwards

IR (editors). IOS Press & Uppsala Monitoring Centre, Uppsala, Sweden, 2008, chapter 6, pp. 65-77
https://www.who.int/medicines/technical_briefing/tbs/Drug_Regulation_History_Present_Future.pdf

21. Janssen WM. A Historical Perspective on Off-Label Medicine: From Regulation, Promotion, and the First Amendment to the Next Frontiers. Food and Drug Law Institute, Levy MC (Editor). First Washington, D.C., USA Off-Label Communications (2008)

22. Silverman WA, Andersen DH, Blanc WA, Crozier DN. A difference in mortality rate and incidence of kernicterus among premature infants allotted to two prophylactic antibacterial regimens. Pediatrics. 1956;18:614

23. Burns LE, Hodgman JE, Cass AB. Fatal circulatory collapse in premature infants receiving chloramphenicol. N EngI 1 Med. 1959;261:1318-1321

24. AAP 1995: Guidelines for the Ethical Conduct of Studies to Evaluate Drugs in Pediatric Populations, Committee on Drugs. American Academy of Pediatrics, Pediatrics, 1995 Feb;95(2):286-94

25. Shirkey H. Therapeutic Orphans. J Pediatr 1968 Jan; 72 (1), 119-120. https://pdfs.semanticscholar.org/f1cb/acdbac19fa56236b919fb7799eaacaa10c77.pdf

26. Hirschfeld S. History of Pediatric Labeling. https://www.slideserve.com/marlin/history-of-pediatric-labeling; 2012

27. Hirschfeld S, Saint-Raymond A. Pediatric Regulatory Initiatives. Handb Exp Pharmacol 2011;205,245-68

28. Plate V. The Impact of Off-Label, Compassionate and Unlicensed Use on Health Care Laws in preselected Countries. https://bonndoc.ulb.uni-bonn.de/xmlui/bitstream/handle/20.500.11811/4152/1936.pdf

29. FDA 2001. The Pediatric Exclusivity Provision. January 2001. Status Report to Congress. https://www.fda.gov/downloads/Drugs/DevelopmentApprovalProcess/DevelopmentResources/UCM049915.pdf

30. FDA 2016. BPCA and PREA Status Report to Congress July 9, 2012 – June 30, 2016.
https://www.fda.gov/media/99184/download

31. FDA 2020. BPCA and PREA Status Report to Congress July 1, 2015 – June 30, 2020.
https://www.fda.gov/media/157840/download

32. EMA 2017. 10-year Report to the European Commission General report on the experience acquired as a result of the application of the Paediatric Regulation.
https://health.ec.europa.eu/system/files/2020-06/paediatrics_10_years_ema_technical_report_0.pdf

33. Mozes-Kor E. The Mengele twins and human experimentation. In: Annas G, Grodin M, editors. The Nazi Doctors and the Nuremberg Code. New York, NY, USA: Oxford University Press; 1992.

34. Wikipedia, Josef Mengele
https://en.wikipedia.org/wiki/Josef_Mengele

35. The Doctors Trial: The Medical Case of the Subsequent Nuremberg Proceedings. United States Holocaust Memorial Museum.
https://encyclopedia.ushmm.org/content/en/article/the-doctors-trial-the-medical-case-of-the-subsequent-nuremberg-proceedings

36. Lord of Liverpool Russell. The Knights of the Bushido (A Short History of Japanese War Crimes). Cassell & Co, London, UK, 1958

37. Wikipedia, Tuskegee Syphilis Study.
https://en.wikipedia.org/wiki/Tuskegee_Syphilis_Study

38. Kearns GL, Abdel-Rahman SM, Alander SW, Blowey DL, Leeder JS, Kauffman RE. developmental pharmacology - drug disposition, action, and therapy in infants and children. N Engl J Med 2003 Sep 18;349(12):1157-67

39. World Medical Association (WMA), Declaration of Helsinki, adopted by the 64th WMA General Assembly, Fortaleza, Brazil, October 2013
https://www.wma.net/policies-post/wma-declaration-of-helsinki-ethical-principles-for-medical-research-involving-human-subjects/

40. Thalange N, Deeb L, Iotova V, et al. Insulin degludec in combination with bolus insulin aspart is safe and effective in children and adolescents with type 1 diabetes. Pediatr Diabetes 2015 May;16(3):164-76. https://www.ncbi.nlm.nih.gov/pmc/articles/PMC4413367/pdf/pedi0016-0164.pdf

41. Robertson KJ, Schoenle E, Gucev Z, et al. Insulin detemir compared with NPH insulin in children and adolescents with Type 1 diabetes. Diabet Med 2007 Jan;24(1):27-34. https://onlinelibrary.wiley.com/doi/epdf/10.1111/j.1464-5491.2007.02024.x

42. Casanova M, Enis Özyar E, Patte C, et al. International randomized phase 2 study on the addition of docetaxel to the combination of cisplatin and 5- fluorouracil in the induction treatment for nasopharyngeal carcinoma in children and adolescents. Cancer Chemother Pharmacol 2016 Feb;77(2):289-98.

43. Wikipedia, Nuremberg Code. https://en.wikipedia.org/wiki/Nuremberg_Code

44. Wikipedia, Declaration of Helsinki. https://en.wikipedia.org/wiki/Declaration_of_Helsinki

45. Spellecy R, Busse K. The History of Human Subjects Research and Rationale for Institutional Review Board Oversight. Nutr Clin Pract. 2021 Jun;36(3):560-567

46. Gold H, Totani Y. Japan's Infamous Unit 731: Firsthand Accounts of Japan's Wartime Human Experimentation Program. Tuttle, Clarendon VT, USA, 2019

47. Wikipedia, Unit 731. https://en.wikipedia.org/wiki/Unit_731

48. Momper JD, Mulugeta Y, Green DJ, et al. Adolescent dosing and labeling since the Food and Drug Administration Amendments Act of 2007. JAMA Pediatr. 2013 Oct;167(10):926-32.

49. FDA/EMA 2020: FDA / EMA Common Commentary on Submitting an initial Pediatric Study Plan (iPSP) and Pediatric Investigation Plan (PIP) for the Prevention and Treatment of COVID-19.

https://www.fda.gov/media/138489/download and https://www.ema.europa.eu/en/documents/other/fda/ema-common-commentary-submitting-initial-pediatric-study-plan-ipsp-pediatric-investigation-plan-pip_en.pdf

50. Varley CK. Treating depression in children and adolescents: what options now? CNS Drugs. 2006;20(1):1-13

51. EMA 2015. European Medicines Agency (EMA). EMA/PDCO summary report on the review of the list of granted class waivers. 2015. https://www.ema.europa.eu/en/documents/other/ema/pdco-summary-report-review-list-granted-class-waivers_en.pdf

52. Ward RM, Benjamin DK Jr, Davis JM, Gorman RL, Kauffman R, Kearns GL, et al. The Need for Pediatric Drug Development. J Pediatr. 2018 Jan;192:13-21.

53. Rocchi F et al. 2011. The European paediatric legislation: benefits and perspectives. https://www.ncbi.nlm.nih.gov/pmc/articles/PMC2933611/pdf/1824-7288-36-56.pdf

54. Bucci-Rechtsweg C. Enhancing the Pediatric Drug Development Framework to Deliver Better Pediatric Therapies Tomorrow. Clin Ther. 2017 Oct;39(10):1920-1932 https://www.clinicaltherapeutics.com/action/showPdf?pii=S0149-2918%2817%2930832-9

55. Thomsen MDT. Global Pediatric Drug Development. Curr Ther Res Clin Exp. 2019 Feb 13;90:135-142. https://www.ncbi.nlm.nih.gov/pmc/articles/PMC6677570/pdf/main.pdf

56. Severin T, Corriol-Rohou S, Bucci-Rechtweg C, et al. How is the Pharmaceutical Industry Structured to Optimize Pediatric Drug Development? Existing Pediatric Structure Models and Proposed Recommendations for Structural Enhancement. Ther Innov Regul Sci 2020 Feb 6. https://link.springer.com/article/10.1007/s43441-020-00116-4

57. Sheridan PH, Jacobs MP. The development of antiepileptic drugs for children. Report from the NIH workshop, Bethesda, Maryland, February 17-18, 1994. Epilepsy Res. 1996 Feb;23(1):87-92.

58. Angell M. I academic medicine for sale? New Engl J Med. 2000 May 18;342(20):1516-8

59. Angell M. Industry-sponsored clinical research. A broken system. JAMA 2008 Sep 3;300(9):1069-71

60. Regulation (EC) No 1901/2006 of the European Parliament and of the Council of 12 December 2006 on Medicinal Products for Paediatric Use. https://ec.europa.eu/health//sites/health/files/files/eudralex/vol-1/reg_2006_1901/reg_2006_1901_en.pdf

61. EMA 2022. Opinions and decisions on paediatric investigation plans. https://www.ema.europa.eu/en/medicines/ema_group_types/ema_pip

62. Wikipedia, Dissolution of the Soviet Union https://en.wikipedia.org/wiki/Dissolution_of_the_Soviet_Union

63. Walker EW. Dissolution: Sovereignty and the Breakup of the Soviet Union (The Soviet Bloc and After) Rowman & Littlefield, Lanham, Maryland, 2003

64. Harari YN. Sapiens. A Brief History of Humankind. Vintage Classics, New York, NY, USA, 2019

65. Hwang TJ, Tomasi PA, Bourgeois FT. Delays in completion and results reporting of clinical trials under the paediatric regulation in the European Union: a cohort study. PloS Med 2018;15(3):e1002520 Mar 1 https://www.ncbi.nlm.nih.gov/pmc/articles/PMC5832187/pdf/pmed.1002520.pdf

66. European Network of Paediatric Research *at the* European Medicines Agency (Enpr-EMA). EMA 2022. https://www.ema.europa.eu/en/partners-networks/networks/european-network-paediatric-research-european -medicines-agency-enpr-ema

67. Wikipedia, Holodomor https://en.wikipedia.org/wiki/Holodomor

68. Jones, A. Genocide: A Comprehensive Introduction (3rd ed.). Routledge London, UK, 2016

69. International Committee of Medical Journal Editors (ICMJE), May 2022. Recommendations for the Conduct, Reporting, Editing, and Publication of Scholarly Work in Medical Journals. Updated May 2022 https://www.icmje.org/icmje-recommendations.pdf

70. Page H. Why the Winds Blow Furiously at Strasbourg Cathedral. Travel signposts, 2017 https://www.travelsignposts.com/France/sightseeing/strasbourg-cathedral-legend

71. Moral RP Aesthetics of Evil in Middle Ages: Beasts as Symbol of the Devil. Religions 2021;12:957. https://doi.org/10.3390/rel12110957

72. Saint-Raymond A, Brasseur D. Development of medicines for children in Europe: ethical implications. Paed Resp Rev 2005;6:45–51

73. Conroy S, Newman C, Gudka S. Unlicensed and off label drug use in acute lymphoblastic leukaemia and other malignancies in children. Ann Oncol 2003 Jan;14(1):42-7 https://www.annalsofoncology.org/action/showPdf?pii=S0923-7534%2819%2963921-9

74. Maude SL, Laetsch TW, Buechner J, et al. Tisagenlecleucel in Children and Young Adults with B-Cell Lymphoblastic Leukaemia. N Engl J Med 2018;378:439-448.

75. First Child To Receive CAR T-Cell Therapy Is 10 Years Cancer-Free. https://www.youtube.com/watch?v=0ei1yRxbdfU

76. 7 Year Old Girl Beats Acute Lymphoblastic Leukaemia: Emily Whitehead's Immunotherapy Story. https://www.youtube.com/watch?v=Sz11e0r2L_s

77. New Cancer Cure: World's First Child Treated with Immunotherapy Is Cancer-free 10 Years Later. https://www.youtube.com/watch?v=DP7fFoKPWcM

78. H.R.1231 . RACE for Children Act 115th Congress (2017-2018) https://www.congress.gov/bill/115th-congress/house-bill/1231

79. Reaman GH. FDARA 2017 and the RACE for Children Act: Implications for Pediatric Cancer Drug Development. Available online:

https://www.accelerate-platform.eu/wp-content/uploads/sites/4/2018/02/1640-REAMAN.pdf

80. Curesearch of children's cancer. The RACE for Children Act: A Game Changer for Children's Cancer. https://curesearch.org/The-RACE-for-Children-Act-A-Game-Changer-for-Childrens-Cancer

81. Pearson ADJ, Karres D, Reaman G, et al. The RACE to accelerate drug development for children with cancer. Lancet Child Adolesc Health. 2020 Oct;4(10):714-716.

82. Endorsements of RACE Act. The RACE for Children Act Coalition. https://www.kidsvcancer.org/race-for-children-act/endorsements-for-race-act/

83. Rose K. Pediatric Oncology At The Crossroads: A Call for Change. Editorial. Pharmaceut Med 2020 Oct 7. https://rdcu.be/b8drm

84. EMA 2015. History of EMA https://www.ema.europa.eu/en/about-us/history-ema

85. Rose K, Grant-Kels J, Striano P, Oishi T, Neubauer D. Paediatric Allergen-Specific Immunotherapy Studies Required by the European Medicines Agency: Is It Time for a Reassessment? Europ Med J Allergy Immunol 2022. https://emj.emg-health.com/wp-content/uploads/sites/2/2022/06/Paediatric-Allergen-Specific-Immunotherapy-Studies-Required-by-the-European-Medicines-Agency.pdf

86. Rose K, Ettienne EB, Grant-Kels JM, Striano P, Neubauer D, Oishi T. Neurology's vital role in preventing unnecessary and potentially harmful pediatric studies. Expert Review Neurotherapeutics 2022, https://doi.org/10.1080/14737175.2022.2045953

87. Rose K, Neubauer D, Grant-Kels JM. Ethical Issues in Pediatric Regulatory Studies Involving Placebo Treatment. J Pediatr Epilepsy 2020; 9(03): 073-079 DOI: 10.1055/s-0040-1712147

88. Rose K, Neubauer D, Grant-Kels JM. Rational Use of Medicine in Children – The Conflict of Interests Story. A Review. Rambam

Maimonides Med J. 2019 Jul 18; 10(3): e0018. Review. doi:10.5041/RMMJ.10371.
https://www.rmmj.org.il/userimages/928/2/PublishFiles/953Article.pdf

89. Rose K. The Challenges of Pediatric Drug Development. Curr Ther Res Clin Exp. 2019, https://www.sciencedirect.com/science/article/pii/S0011393X18300353

90. Rose K, Grant-Kels JM. Pediatric Melanoma – The Whole (Conflicts Of Interest) Story. Int J Womens Dermatol 2018,Nov 19;5(2):110-115. doi: 10.1016/j.ijwd.2018.10.020
https://www.ncbi.nlm.nih.gov/pmc/articles/PMC6451736/pdf/main.pdf

91. Rose K. Blind Trust - How parents with a sick child can escape the labyrinth of lies, hypocrisy and false promises of researchers and regulatory authorities. Hammersmith, London, UK, 2022.

92. Rose K. The COVID-19 Pandemic: A Global High-Tech Challenge at the Interface of Science, Politics, and Illusions. Elsevier, London, UK, 2022 https://www.elsevier.com/books/the-covid-19-pandemic/rose/978-0-323-99149-0

93. Schubert ML, Peura DA. Control of Gastric Acid Secretion in Health and Disease. Gastroenterology 2008;134:1842–1860

94. Pharmaceutical Research and Manufacturers of America (PhRMA) https://phrma.org

95. European Federation of Pharmaceutical Industries and Associations (EFPIA) https://www.efpia.eu/

96. Japan Pharmaceutical Manufacturers Association (JPMA) https://www.jpma.or.jp/english/

97. International Federation of Pharmaceutical Manufacturers and Associations (IFPMA) https://ifpma.org

98. Higueros E, Roe E, Granell E, Baselga E. Sturge-Weber Syndrome: A Review. Actas Dermosifiliogr. 2017 Jun;108(5):407-417. https://www.actasdermo.org/es-pdf-S1578219017300975

99. Comi AM. Sturge-Weber syndrome. Handb Clin Neurol. 2015;132: 157-68.

100. Yeom S, Comi AM. Updates on Sturge-Weber Syndrome. Stroke. 2022 Dec;53(12):3769-3779.

101. Breit Compton D. Sturge-Weber Syndrome. Independently published, USA, 2021

102. Bodensteiner JB, Roach ES (Eds.) Sturge-Weber Syndrome. The Sturge-Weber Foundation; 2nd edition, Sticklerville, NJ, USA, 2010

103. The Sturge-Weber foundation. https://sturge-weber.org/

104. Wikipedia, Sturge-Weber syndrome https://en.wikipedia.org/wiki/Sturge-Weber_syndrome

Chapter 2

Care of Children in History

Medicine and pediatrics are not pure sciences comparable to sciences that explore inanimate nature such as physics or chemistry. Medicine and pediatrics evolved in a balance of power between the medical profession and other healthcare professions which either remained a pillar of healthcare, such as pharmacies, were pushed aside to a large extent, such as barbers, midwives, wet-nurses and the apothecaries of the Middle Ages, were successfully integrated into the medical profession such as surgeons, or emerged anew and became recognized auxiliary sciences, such as physiology, pharmacology, developmental pharmacology, and more. Medicine today is official and state-sanctioned. It claims to be based on science, but as we shall see throughout this book, there are many biases that can only be explained by an understanding of the economic, political and cultural framework in which healthcare, medicine, its institutions, and the professional associations that officially represent it emerged and developed. These developments emerged on the background of the unfolding world of written communication, somewhat later printing, and eventually the transformation of society through the Renaissance, the scientific revolution, industrialization, the weakening of traditions by two world wars, and more.

The development of modern healthcare and medicine occurred during the emergence of a new industrialized world with all the internal changes in European states and societies, the colonial expansion of Europe, the associated changes and developments first in colonial North America and later the entire world. We focus here on elements that are not so easily accessible to the naked eye and furthermore were rather irrelevant at the time. But they bore the roots of developments that are becoming increasingly relevant today. There were endless technical inventions and innovations, but also fundamental social upheavals. We discuss all of this to show that the myths and illusions of the past, which we can correctly identify as myths and illusions today, were not simply directly superseded by rational thought and action. That would have been too easy. Rather, new myths and illusions emerged. One such new modern myth is the concept of "evidence-based medicine," which not only includes evidence. Another sphere of consideration is the tension between the self-image of health care and health care professions and their self-interest which is expressed less in noble and noble words and more in actions - if you have the patience to look closely.

Yet another aspect is the growing permeability of social structures in the course of the emergence of the new, industrialized world. For centuries, one of the few avenues for people who had not inherited land and farms from their parents was to go abroad and work as mercenaries, go to sea, or take up other risky trades. A few have always been successful. The vast majority perished, returned crippled, or disappeared forever. Industrialization changed the world not only because more and more was now being produced and the country could feed more and more people, but also because the old traditional structures were softening. In the colonies there were more opportunities for advancement. Modest prosperity could be achieved in the factory by honest work. The downside of all these developments was the growing concentration of people in the cities with today unimaginable dirt, stench, cramped houses, and an adventurous tension between the official self-image of society and the brutal reality of life. Women were portrayed in literature as noble, admirable beings, but in the 19th century, a fourteen year old girl could be bought for a few shillings. More churches were built in England than in its entire previous history, yet one in sixty houses in London was a brothel. Chastity was proclaimed in public but scandalous lives were normal in private. Children were now increasingly protected by new laws from mistreatment at home, in the factory and in the public, but foundling homes offered a simple way to deposit offspring anonymously. Movements against vices of all sorts were parallel with a huge spread of pornography.[1,2] In this imbroglio, men and women had to struggle through and could only hope that they would survive. The old, traditional frameworks in which one felt secure, but which also set narrow limits to personal development, became softer and gradually disappeared. The professional world gradually opened up to women and people of colour. Women who somehow became pregnant gave birth to their children. Medicine as a professional institution had to assert itself and survive in this white water. There was no fair, state-controlled competition between different service providers. There was an uncontrolled supply of quacks and ineffective and harmful medicines. Today, in hindsight, it is just as easy to praise the medicine of the time and the doctors who practiced this profession, or to do the opposite, to blame them for the fact that they too had to survive. Very gradually and slowly, quality standards prevailed. We are trying less to judge in retrospect. Instead, we try to show how hard and merciless the times were. And yet, very slowly, more and more people were given the opportunity to create their own lives through honest work. The evolving framework incorporated the ideas people had about the origin of diseases and the possible means of preventing them through prevention.

Midwifery, classical academic medicine, and medicine's ancient roots

Since prehistory, men and women (and our animal and later semi-animal ancestors) had sex. Women conceived and gave birth to children. During those millions and millennia, pregnancy was not seen as a disease, but as a natural process. The birth of a child and the child's first hours, days and weeks are precarious moments, a span of time in which mother and child are dependent on the support from others. Whether this support always came from the immediate family or from women with special skills depended on the structure of the respective society and on the social position of the respective woman and her family. Before the unfolding of the scientific revolution and European expansion, this hands-on care was provided predominantly by female family members and midwives. Midwifes did not have a strictly formalized training in the modern sense, but they had experience and knowledge by having given birth to own children and/ or having been apprenticed by an experienced midwife. They worked in an oral tradition that prepared them well for this task within the framework and the limits of the respective historical conditions.

Midwifes in antiquity and in early societies were able to roughly estimate the future date of birth; they explained the basics of the birth process to the unexperienced future mother; they assisted hands-on in preparing the mother and the birthing process; they assisted during the birth by calming down, comforting, giving instructions on breathing, relaxing and pushing; they assisted after the birth, including eliciting a first cry from the baby, cutting the umbilical cord, washing & cleaning the baby, returning it to the mother, helping the mother to clean herself, helping the newborn to suck a first amount of mother's milk, reassuring the child's father, & more. They often also helped with other medical problems. They were an elementary support when the mother-to-be went through the process of birth which is controlled to a relevant extent by the body itself and not by voluntary acts. Giving birth is first painful to the mother and scary, but then turns into deep feeling of joy and happiness when things went well, which fortunately is mostly the case. The value of this psychological support is immense and has been massively undervalued for many years in early modern times. Midwifes existed in many forms worldwide in prehistorical societies under many different names.[3-11] In most countries and cultures, they were a respected profession.

In antiquity and throughout pre-modern times child mortality was high. To understand the history of child care, we need to recap some key elements of societal development. In traditional agrarian communities, children were born within the family, perhaps assisted by a midwife. Ideas about the cause of diseases existed, but these ideas were mostly simply wrong. If babies were well fed, the most frequent cause of death of children were infectious diseases based on a lack of hygiene that we today know how important it is. During famines, which were common throughout history, children were often among the most common victims.

In the history of midwifery we can trace the transition from a predominantly oral, pre-modern, non-scientific tradition towards today's world of obstetrics & gynecology where midwifery has meanwhile found a new role. This transition included the gradual establishment of the medical profession as the doctrine that today has the lead also in the process of giving birth.

Several key dimensions merged. The first dimension was the transition from non-literate societies to a society in which the written word played an increasing role by written records and literature, a transition that took several thousand years. There had been a wide medical literature from antiquity to ancient Egypt and other even earlier advanced civilizations that used various methods of writing, but the most systematic medical literature emerged in ancient Greece. These medical writings included many texts on midwifery. Greek classical medical writings described anatomical details, described and named many diseases and their symptoms, speculated about their causes, and gave hands-on recommendations for treatment. In these writings we see today, in hindsight, a tension between what people saw and described, and how they interpreted their observations and put them into context. While the Greek culture had produced the first systematic literature on medical issues (and more), the center of civilization at the time shifted to the

Roman Empire. Rome conquered and ruled all of the lands that bordered the Mediterranean Sea and vast lands beyond, including parts of Germania, the British Island, the Balkans including Greece, Asia Minor, and more. The Roman Empire focused on its military and political might. Medicine in ancient Rome was initially in rather low regard, based on a combination of religious and magic thinking. The first professional physicians were Greek medical doctors, initially mostly Greek slaves, but their status improved gradually. Famines and plagues were usually attributed to divine powers. Appeasement of the gods by rituals was believed to alleviate and help. The Romans established high level systems of public hygiene with many aqueducts that transported fresh water for drinking, bathing and washing into the city from far away. Many of these ancient aqueducts are still preserved and visible today in Rome and other earlier cities of the Roman Empire. On the other hand, water pipes were made of lead, which lead to a systematic, slow poisoning of the entire population, especially since lead also played an important role in Roman cuisine and drinking culture. However, the ancient Romans were not yet able to analyze this problem, nor did the glorification of ancient Rome help to take a sober look at this aspect of Roman health care.[12-14] We cannot know to what degree there was an understanding of the importance of public health in ancient Rome. The dead were buried outside the city walls; large supplies of fresh water were available through aqueducts; there were public bathing areas and public sewage systems. Rome also began draining swamps in close proximity to cities, something that was completed only in the 20th century.[15-20]

The medical literature used increasingly a Latin in which partly Greek words were adopted, partly were translated into Latin, or a mixture of both. Latin had been a living language in ancient Rome, but after the decline of the Roman empire Latin gradually morphed into an official literary language, written and spoken by the educated strata of society. It remained Latin while modern European languages gradually emerged and evolved, including the Latin languages (Italian, Spanish, Portuguese, French, & more; the Germanic languages (English, German, Northern languages, & more; and all the other European languages. In the Middle Ages, Latin was the international language used in written and oral communication by the higher strata of society. In this function it shifted from classical to Medieval Latin. Medical Latin continued on the basis of ordinary Latin with the admixture of numerous Greek and Latin medical terms. In emerging modernity, however, the national languages gradually gained ground at the expense of Latin. In some countries medical Latin survived relatively long. In Denmark for example hospital doctors wrote patients' notes in Latin until 1853. During the 20th century English became the new international lingua franca of medicine. Today most relevant medical and scientific journals are written in English, and on international conferences discussions are led in English as well. The Greek legacy in the medical language comprises until today numerous names of diseases and symptoms, such as catarrh (downflow), diarrhoea (throughflow), or dyspnoea (bad breathing).[21-23]

The classical medical descriptions, mostly symbolized in the person of Hippocrates and his writings, first in Greek and then in Latin, were quite systematic and have given the formal structure of medical descriptions up to the present day. But their background framework was a prescientific worldview. Most assumptions underlying medical texts that exerted a dominant position over one to two millennia were fundamentally flawed. Hippocrates and the classical Greek doctrine believed that the human mind was based on the balance of the four bodily fluids: blood, phlegm, yellow bile, and black bile. The heart was a warm, red space and therefore the origin of emotions, whereas the brain was cold and grey and the home of rational intellect. Predominance of one of the four types of humors or, in other words, an imbalance of the humors, corresponded to four principal types of character: blood to a sanguine personality; black bile to a melancholic personality; yellow bile to a choleric personality; and phlegm to a phlegmatic personality. Individuals with sanguine temperaments were thought to be extroverted and social; choleric people to have energy, passion, and charisma; melancholic people to be creative, kind, and considerate; and phlegmatic temperaments to be dependable, kind, and affectious.[24-26] Fever was perceived as a disease, not as a symptom that can be caused by many different diseases.[27] Epilepsy was believed to be caused by external, non-human powers that took control of the respective person.[28,29] And so on.

Galen of Pergamon, a medical doctor of Greek origin, made career in imperial Rome and managed to acquire a very prominent position during his lifetime and during a period of more than thousand years after his death. His name is known to most medical doctors and pharmacists, at least from the expression of "galenic formulation", the application form of a medicine as a pill or tablet, as a liquid, or in some other form.

Galen was well educated, highly intelligent, and extremely smart in his personal life. He started his medical career as a surgeon in a school of gladiators, an excellent opportunity to practice surgery and medicine in otherwise young healthy men who were often injured in the course of their profession. A wound not properly cared for was a death sentence. Even if only a portion of the treated gladiators survived, that was enough to establish a good name in medical care, which Galen did successfully. In a time when there was an unlimited supply of young gladiators, those that did not survive his treatment had simply been injured too badly. He was also extremely gifted in rhetoric, loved controversial debates, and was extremely prolific in his medical writing. He wrote several hundred medical texts on almost everything that existed in medicine at the time. Furthermore, he managed to get the support of the Roman emperor during his lifetime. Today in the time of the internet and the social media, somebody with his abilities might have become an "influencer". After his death, his prodigious medical written output became the official canon not only of medicine in the strict sense, but was also backed by the Catholic Church itself, as his scientific edifice was seen as consistent with Christian dogma. People who challenged his doctrine could be branded heretical by both Church and State. His books were copied and recopied before the dawn of printing. Many of his manuscripts have survived.[16-20,30,31]

The discussed systematic medical texts and descriptions go back to ancient Greece and Rome, written in the international language of the time, in Latin. But most of the framework on which these texts and descriptions were based were fundamentally flawed if looked at without current knowledge. Dissection of the human body was forbidden in ancient Rome, a ban later upheld by the Catholic Church. As a physician responsible for gladiators, Galen had had access to the human body opened by wounds received in combat. He also did anatomical studies, however, only in animals - but claimed that his descriptions applied to humans. The concept of blood circulation emerged only much later, during the Renaissance onwards, when all the traditional misconceptions in medical academic teachings were gradually corrected, initially in Latin, of course. Nevertheless, the medical terms for anatomy, diseases, their medical context, their explanation and their treatment remained based on Latin and Greek. Diagnoses und medical histories continued to be written first in Latin, later in the respective national language. However, these medical histories were not understandable to a medical lay person, as they were written in a medical slang with the described mixture of technical terms derived mostly from Latin and Greek. The concept of the humors led to the therapeutic intervention of blook letting, the standard therapy in Europe for almost two thousand years and later also in colonial North America. If the patient survived, if was a success for the doctor. If the patient died, he had been too ill.[24,26,30,31]

Midwifery, a network of oral tradition and hands-on training that had existed around the globe for thousands of years was in Europe and North America gradually supplanted by a new type of tradition based on writing and with that the exchange of ideas and thoughts between many, many players. Key elements of this new tradition were literacy, initially hand-written and copied texts from antiquity in Latin, then printed texts in Latin, with the used language gradually switching to modern European languages in the 19th century. One further key element was an increasing control by the authorities, first the church and then the secular state. The control of midwifery by the church has become famous by the witch hunts in the Middle Ages. The classical period of witch hunts in Early Modern Europe and Colonial America took place in about 1450 to 1750, spanning inter alia the upheavals of the Reformation.[32-36] The majority of women hanged and/or burned on the stake were midwifes. The hate of the Christian churches against midwifes can best be explained by the Christian church's bias against women in general,[37] and specifically those elements in humans that are most difficult to control by an authority, including personal intimate emotions, sexuality and the process of childbirth.

To this day, Latin remains the principal language of anatomical terminology, with English as the secondary language.[38-40] And until today there are some essential misunderstandings about this tradition.

First, the medical writings from antiquity until modern times were written in Latin and were regarded as reflecting a high degree of wisdom and correctness. Officially and formally these writings had a high authority and were written in a highly respected language; the disease descriptions and anatomical descriptions were systematic and superficially correct; but the ideas behind them were mostly wrong. With the exception of surgical procedures such as the amputation of an inflamed limb, simple procedures of dentistry, and other comparable hands-on surgical treatments, most therapeutic procedures performed by academically trained physicians in occidental culture were dangerous, life-threatening and by today's standards simply wrong. Most historical accounts of modern medicine and especially pediatrics begin with the ancient Greeks and Romans and claim a direct tradition of this teaching to this day, as if a collection of medical wisdom had started in classical Greece and Rome and was passed on by alleged intellectual giants like Galen.[24-26] This is an illusion. The only permanent and remaining in these texts was the medical terminology, the systematic description of the diseases and their symptoms, and their authoritative attitude. But the ideas behind these descriptions, such as the theory of the four different humors, the universal remedy of bloodletting, the belief that epilepsy was caused by demons that needed to be cast out, and so forth, all these ideas were flawed if we analyze them against the background of our current knowledge and understanding. All these flawed doctrines were completely revised from the late Renaissance on until modern times. These revisions corrected misconceptions gradually. But new misconceptions emerged in the unfolding new framework.

The second misunderstanding is that most histories of medicine describe the original guiding principles of therapeutic action by midwives as combining wisdom with experience, magic, superstition, and ritual, in opposition to modern scientific medical knowledge. But in the first centuries of modern medicine, ritual, superstition and magic were also the basis of medical belief and practice. Medical doctors' beliefs were strange and absurd by today's standard, but they were based on years of study in Latin at venerable universities, unless they had just bought their diploma for a few pounds from a university without completing a degree.[41,42]

The third misunderstanding is that histories of medicine describe the process of transition from experience, magic, superstition, and ritual as something driven by competition of old-fashioned vs. innovative ideas. Strategically this may be correct if we look back over periods of centuries. But the real-life transition was a brutal power struggle of the medical profession that established its position in modern society. When the first teaching hospitals were established, the women who gave birth to their children in these hospitals were mostly poor and defenseless. Teaching hospitals for physicians were founded from the late 18th century on. Women who were unmarried, poor, or prostitutes were forced to deliver in these hospitals or face imprisonment. The young physicians trained on these women. There was an extreme lack of hygiene and skill with the use of the obstetric forceps in these hospitals. The obstetric forceps is used to help moving the child out of the mother's body by pulling its head. In the hands of an experienced practitioner, the obstetric forceps is a wonderful instrument. But in the hands of somebody inexperienced and on top with unwashed hands and with dirty clothes, it will result in high rates of maternal and neonatal mortality. Medical doctors blamed the midwifes for this high mortality.[43] Before the 1880s mortality rates in lying-hospitals had shockingly high levels and became an area of public concern. Much of these maternal deaths were due to puerperal fever, then known as childbed fever. In the 1840s Dr. Ignaz Semmelweis noticed in Vienna that women giving birth at home had a much lower incidence of childbed fever than those giving birth by physicians in lying-hospitals. He also found that the mortality rates in two maternity clinics in Vienna differed considerably. The First Clinic, run by male physicians who also dissected cadavers to learn about anatomy, had an average maternal mortality rate of about 10% due to puerperal fever, while the Second Clinic's mortality rate was considerably lower with less than 4%. This was also known on the outside. The two clinics admitted on alternate days, but women begged to be admitted to the Second Clinic, due to the bad reputation of the First Clinic. Desperate women begged on their knees not to be admitted to the First Clinic. Some even preferred to give birth in the streets, pretending to have given sudden birth on the way to the hospital (known as street births). They would then still qualify for the child care benefits without having been admitted to the clinic. Semmelweis was puzzled that puerperal fever was rare among women giving street births. He assumed a causal relation between the unwashed hands of the medical doctors and the puerperal fever and ordered his male colleagues to wash their hands with an antiseptic solution when he had the authority to do so. He published his observations, but was stonewalled by the official medical world. He died depressed and isolated in a psychiatric hospital. Despite the publication of his findings, doctors continued not to wash their hands. It was not until the 20th century when advancements in aseptic technique and the understanding of disease would play a significant role in the decrease of maternal mortality rates. To demand that doctors should wash their hands was perceived as a bottomless accusation and furthermore as an insult against the noble profession of medicine.[41]

The arrogance of the medical world towards midwifery was not based on better understanding and better care. It was part of a power struggle that eventually the medical profession won. Strategically and long-term, the scientific exchange of ideas and opinions led to improvements. The obstetric forceps is a medical instrument used in childbirth. Advantages of the use of the forceps include reduction of delivery time, avoidance of caesarean section and its complications, provided the baby's position is with the head first towards the outside world. The forceps were used most notably in difficult childbirths. This could help to avoid some infant deaths when previous approaches such as hooks and other instruments extracted parts of the baby's stuck body. Thus an approach killed the baby and tried to save the mother's life.[44,45] Technically, the obstetric forceps was a step forward in medicine. But the teaching hospitals' first purpose was to teach medical doctors. The women who gave birth in these hospitals were utilized as training objects to train predominantly male physicians.[43] An invention that long-term and strategically was a step forward increased short-term the misery of those poor women who had the bad luck to have to give birth in a teaching hospital.

In the development of contemporary medicine pure science did not have a leading role. It was a complex event at the intersection of power, worldview, concrete observations, superstitions, taboos, and more.

The early power struggle between midwifery and academic medicine was not a struggle between experience, magic, superstition, and ritual as opposed to modern medical knowledge. The mainstream medicine replaced some old-fashioned doctrines by others. In the long term and strategically, this would advance healthcare. In the hands-on treatment, the consequences for treated women could be catastrophic.

When children were treated by medical doctors, they saw them as miniature adults. Childhood was not recognized as a unique stage of life.[46]

If we look at child healthcare with the medical and scientific knowledge of today, the first real-world improvement, which we owe to organized modern medicine was inoculation against smallpox. Such inoculations had been done in Asia and Eastern Europe for centuries. But then it was the systematic descriptions by Dr. Jenner and others, who eventually ended the smallpox epidemic in the West.

Observations comparable to those made by Dr. Ignaz Semmelweis were made from an entirely different perspective by Florence Nightingale, who managed to lead a group of English women to support the care of English wounded soldiers during the Crimean War 1954-1956. She found desolate, dirty and inadequate supplies for the soldiers. In contrast to Ignaz Semmelweis, however, she was firstly of high societal standing. She had been sent in 1854 with a staff of 38 women volunteer nurses and 15 Catholic nuns under the authorisation of Sidney Herbert, responsible for the War Office. Apart from her high social standing, she had an official task and could not simply be ignored. Secondly, she was diplomatic. She managed to improve considerably the care of the wounded soldiers.[47-49]

Long-term, the advent of science improved the survival of newborn babies. However, to put it provocatively, the transitions described above did not always improve the fate of newborn children. Mothers who gave birth to their child on the street had a higher survival chance for themselves and their child than in the male doctor-controlled clinical in Vienna and many other comparable public medical institutions.[3,9,10,50-53] Poor women that were smart enough not to trust official narratives were often better off.

To remain fair to conventional medicine, we must again see these developments in a historical perspective. These were times of social upheaval in every respect. For now, it is sufficient to emphasize that the narrative of a transition from a healthcare of childbirth based on experience, magic, superstition, and ritual in opposition to modern scientific medical knowledge is a too simple explanation and is too short-sighted. It took centuries for traditional misconceptions to weaken and finally become obsolete. However, the guiding principles that followed were not always pure science, but contained other and new misconceptions.

We also should mention that the transition from predominant midwifery towards today's predominant school medicine continues to contain serious tensions. Midwifery was historically temporarily significantly weakened by conventional medicine, behind which stood the entire international exchange of opinions first in Latin, then gradually in English. Over time, however, the midwifery has also developed an international network. Meanwhile, midwifery is also an academic degree.[54-56] But tensions with mainstream medicine persist. There is still a lot of jealousy around.[57]

Hygiene and prevention of infectious diseases

Ignaz Semmelweis failed to win over the contemporary opinion leaders in medicine with his observations on the importance of hygiene in medical treatment in general and in specifically in childbirth. At the beginning of the second half of the 19th century the official doctrine of conventional medicine regarded the medical doctor qua office as an almost supernaturally noble and unassailable person and institution. Florence Nightingale was more successful. The public belief that surgeons were more dangerous than midwives lasted until the study of bacteriology became popular in the early 20th century. The importance of hygiene in patient care was increasingly recognized in the second half of the 19th century through a variety of scientific discoveries and found finally its way also into the teachings of medicine. Hospital hygiene improved. Women began to feel safer in the setting of the hospitals with the amount of aid and the ease of birth that they experienced with doctors.[3-11]

In the mid-19th century, Soho in London, UK had a serious problem with filth due to the large influx of people and insufficient sanitary services. The London sewer system had not reached Soho. Cowsheds, slaughter houses and grease-boiling dens lined the streets and contributed animal droppings, rotting fluids and other contaminants to the primitive Soho sewer system. Physicians and scientists in London and elsewhere had two different main theories on the causes of cholera. One theory assumed that cholera was caused by particles in the air ("miasma"), the other one that germs were the cause. In 1854, a severe outbreak of cholera occurred near Broad Street in Soho within a worldwide general cholera pandemic from 1846 to 1860. The Broad Street outbreak of 1846 killed several hundreds of people. The physician John Snow did not know how precisely how cholera was transmitted, but his findings led him to believe that it was not due to breathing foul air. He argued that cholera was not a product of "miasma". He spoke with the local residents of the quarter that was mostly affected and finally was able to identify the probable source of the outbreak as a public water pump on Broad Street. He also concluded that cholera was transmitted through the digestive tract by drinking contaminated water and by using it to prepare meals without boiling it. None of the workers in a brewery nearby contracted cholera. They were given a daily allowance of beer and therefore did not drink water from the nearby well. During the brewing process, the unfermented beer is boiled in part so that hops can be added, a step that killed the cholera bacteria in the water and made it safe to drink. The germ theory was not yet firmly established, but Snow convinced the authorities of his analysis and persuaded them to interrupt the contagion by disabling the well pump he had found to be the probable cause of the outbreak. The pump's handle was removed and the cholera outbreak was stopped. Medical practices that in these days were still popular, such as bloodletting, could not help if his thoughts were correct. Snow's discovery influenced profoundly public health and the construction of improved sanitation facilities beginning in the mid-19th century. The bacterium that is responsible for cholera, Vibrio cholerae, was isolated in 1854, but this connection had not become broadly known yet. It was accepted only much later. [58-60]

We see in these days the tension between organized medicine, the hospitals dominated by know-it-all medical doctors, and the fact that many of the structures run by mainstream medicine did not prevent diseases in mothers and their children. Often these structures even facilitated diseases by improper action or made them worse. The way to successful prevention of contagious diseases was complex and included many additional factors. Florence Nightingale would not have been sent to Turkey by the ministry of war to help taking care of wounded British soldiers had not the press criticized the military's lack of interest in providing wounded soldiers with adequate medical care. The Crimean War was the first major armed conflict in which reporters reported closely from the front. Gone were the days when the military (and other institutions) could do whatever they wanted without being controlled.

Baby & infant nutrition

Breast-feeding babies and young children had been the primary way of feeding infants throughout human history. If the mother died during childbirth or was unable to produce milk for other reasons, families who could afford it hired a woman who produced enough milk: a wet nurse. In early modern times, wet nursing became a well organized profession with contracts and laws designed to regulate its practice. Despite objections during the Middle Ages and the Renaissance, wet nursing continued until the feeding bottle was introduced in the 19th century. Only when feasible alternative feeding methods became available, wet nursing as a profession began to decline, replaced by bottle feeding ("dry nursing"). From the end of the 18th to the 19th century, wet nursing shifted from well-off to laboring, lower-income families. With the onset of the Industrial Revolution, families moved from rural to more urban areas. The increased cost of living and poor wages forced many women to seek employment and contribute financially to their family, which made it difficult for many mothers to breastfeed and take care of their children. Many of these children were farmed out to peasant women. In theory, the law required peasant wet nurses to obtain a licence from local authorities and to report the death of any infant receiving their care. However, the laws were largely ignored and contributed little to change the high mortality rate of all infants.[61,62] In colonial America, wet nurse bureaus opened in all major cities. All wet nurse applicants were physically examined to receive a certificate of health. Ideal characteristics for a potential wet nurse was that she was non-menstruating, good-tempered, had small nipples, good teeth, florid gums, was sober, clean, enjoyed children, and rested. She also should eat a specific diet, be willing to take daily walks outside, be 20 to 35 years old, should not be a first-time mother, should have large breasts with bluish veins that indicate an abundant supply, be lively, sexually continent, well-formed and moderately sized. She also should not show unpleasant tendencies. It was believed that milk from an angry wet nurse could cause infant colic and even death.[63]

In the 19th century, artificial feeding became a feasible substitute for wet nursing. Advancement in the feeding bottle and the availability of animal's milk began to slowly, but steadily, affect the use of wet nurses. During the mid-19th century, great strides were made in the development of the feeding bottle and the nipple. Glass bottles were used, and the evolution of the modern bottle began. Until the end of the 19th century, animal milk was the most common source of artificial feeding. Pap and panada were used as supplements to animal milk. In the 18th century, pap, a mixture flour or breadcrumbs cooked in water or milk, had had some success as a form of artificial feeding. Panada was of more ancient origin and consisted of bread in broth or milk. Eggs were occasionally added. Boiling pap or panada sterilized these mixtures. This, and not their nutritive value made them for some time more successful than cow milk.[46] What type of animas milk was used depended on the kind of animals that were available. These could be goats, sheep, donkeys, camels, pigs, or horses. The most common and universally used milk for artificial feeding, however, was cow's milk.[61]

In the 18th century, the first chemical analyses of human mother milk and animal milk began to be made and published. In 1865, the chemist Justus von Liebig developed, patented, and marketed an infant food, first as a liquid, then as a powder for better preservation. The powder had to be mixed with water. Liebig's formula consisted of cow milk, wheat, malt flour and potassium bicarbonate and was believed to be the perfect infant food. A further scientific step forward of the 19th century was food preservation which eventually led to the invention of evaporated milk. In the 1850s, Gail Borden added sugar to the evaporated milk, canned it and sold it as Eagle Brand Condensed Milk, which became a popular infant food. There were no refrigerators yet at that time. Eagle Brand Sweetened Condensed Milk was credited with significantly lowering the infant mortality rate in North America.[64] Many further commercial products and formulas were rapidly introduced. These foods were fattening but lacked nutrients like protein, vitamins, and minerals. Over time, such nutrients were individually added. The use of artificial formula was associated with many summertime infant deaths due to the spoilage of milk left in bottles, which was not understood until the public accepted the germ theory. Between 1890 and 1910, emphasis was placed on cleanliness and the improvement in the quality of milk supplies. Improvements included providing better care for dairy cattle and forming infant milk clinics to disburse clean milk to the public. Eventually, rubber nipples became available that were easy to clean. Many homes now stored milk safely in an icebox. As formulas evolved and research supported their efficacy, manufacturers began to advertise directly to physicians. By 1929, the American Medical Association (AMA) formed the Committee on Foods to approve the safety and quality of formula composition, forcing many infant food companies to seek AMA approval or the organization's "Seal of Acceptance." Three years later, advertising became regulated so that manufacturers could not solicit information to nonmedical personnel, which facilitated a positive relationship between physicians and the formula companies. In the 1940/50s physicians and consumers regarded the use of formula as a well known, popular, and safe substitute for breastmilk. Breastfeeding declined until the 1970s, when a movement began to promote breastfeeding. In 1988, the formula industry began advertising directly to the public, which created tension between the medical profession and the formula manufacturers. By 1990, the American Academy of Pediatrics (AAP) released a statement listing reasons against advertising infant formulas to the general public. The AAP believed such advertisements created a negative effect on breastfeeding, interfered with physicians' advice on infant nutrition, led to confusion among consumers, and increased the cost of infant formula.[61]

As we see, there was a conflict of interest in physicians' and pediatricians' dealing with the question of mother milk and industrially produced formula. On one hand, it was always emphasized that mother milk was best for children. On the other hand, however, the medical profession profited from financial support by the formula producers.

During the late 19th century, commercial infant foods were often condemned by physicians. Cow's milk was acceptable for infants only if modified according to a doctor's prescription. These formulas were very complicated and required intensive training to master. Pediatrics emerged as a specialty based on the need for expertise in infant feeding. They wanted mothers to believe that they needed to visit doctors and follow their instructions, but not to have so much information that they could ignore or interfere with the doctor's advice. Certainly many physicians acted on their convictions that they truly thought they knew what was best. Others had probably more economic and political motivations in mind. An additional challenge for breastfeeding was the widespread cultural belief in the negative effects of colostrum, the first milk produced by the breasts after birth. By the 1930s more women were giving birth in hospitals.

In the 1930/40/50s, women had limited access to their babies during the first week or more after birth. Babies were brought from nurseries for a few minutes every four hours during the day. The mothers were often not allowed to see their babies at night. Of course, this interfered seriously with successful breastfeeding. By the 1950s, practitioners had moved from the belief that commercial feeding could healthfully augment or replace breastfeeding to the belief that commercial feeding was even better than breastfeeding. When educating new mothers, emphasis was placed on the ease and healthfulness of medically directed bottle-feeding. Ironically, the women's movement towards emancipation in the early part of the 20th century was symbolized by bottle-feeding. By the 1930s and 1940s, most independent women viewed breastfeeding as old-fashioned and talked about nursing babies in terms of being tied down. The breast started to be seen more in terms of female attractivity as opposed to a source of nutrition and nurturance for infants. By the 1940s, mothers were sterilizing a variety of artificial formulas at home. During World War II many women shifted roles from home to working outside. This made the use of commercial formula much more socially acceptable and spurred an increase in their use. In this sense, World War II helped to bolster what would become a general societal approval of bottle-feeding. By the 1950s, a truly modernized household included the bottle-fed baby.[65]

As often when the pendulum swings too far in one direction, it swings back eventually. Starting in the early 1970s, the low regard of breastfeeding began to change. The movement for women's rights; a strong concern about family life; advancing medical technologies; and politics supporting mothers helped to swing breastfeeding rates back toward the center. During the 1960s, a second wave of feminism took hold in America. The new feminist desire was to glory in women's ability to control their own bodies. There was a desire to overthrow many of the male and medical areas of control. Finally, in the 1970s, breastfeeding research began in earnest. The first studies focused on the benefits and limitations of human milk for full-term and preterm babies. In these works, the true composition of human milk was analyzed. These findings were followed by research that showed the short-term and long-term nutritional, immunologic, psychological, physiological, and neurocognitive benefits of mother's milk also for preterm infants.[65]

Ignorance and poverty had contributed to appalling habits of hygiene. Contaminated feeding devices such as nursing bottles and nipples caused infectious diarrheas, a leading cause of illness and death in children. Pasteur's discovery that heat destroyed bacteria contaminating and souring wine, was applied to the processing of milk. It took the tenacious efforts of several individuals, the public support they managed to create, and finally their implementation by the public administration to effectively control the epidemics associated with tainted milk. Still in the first decade of the 20th century, milk in North America was sold in the grocery counter by dipping into 5-gallon cans of unrefrigerated milk. Milk was often adulterated. The wealthy and influential philanthropist Nathan Strauss established more than certified milk stations in North America and Europe. When pasteurized milk became commonly available and it was widely established that careful cleaning and sterilization of containers and feeders were essential to eradicating microbial contamination, this led to a dramatic drop in rates of infant mortality.[41]

The improvement in child health which began in the last part of the 19th and early 20th century was largely due to improvements in hygiene and diet and the increased availability of clean, pure milk. Diarrhea had been the number one killer of children, and much of the pediatricians' efforts was devoted to its prevention. In 1897 Rochester, New York, became the first city to have municipally operated milk stations. Over a period of 20 years, the milk stations became child health stations where education on hygiene, feeding, and infant care was dispensed along with the milk. The changing social and economic climate of the 1800s allowed the government to become involved in public health and in the regulation of the dairy industry. The NY Metropolitan Board of Health was established in 1866. In 1882, spurred by the arrival of several cholera-laden ships in New York harbor, the Board established a bacteriology laboratory capable of evaluating milk for contamination. Not until 1913, however, did the Board require that all milk be pasteurized. By the beginning of the 20th century, with the cooperation of scientists, social reformers, and legislators, the age old problem of finding a safe alternative to breast-feeding was on its way to being solved.

In the first quarter of the 20th century, infant mortality continued to decline as pediatrics and social and governmental programs flourished. The major therapeutic advance of this era was the development of treatment and prophylaxis for diphtheria. Through research in physiologic chemistry, principles of fluid, electrolyte, and acid-base balance were developed and parenteral fluid replacement was initiated.

Pediatricians faced the challenge of decreasing the death rate due to prematurity, the most common cause of which was maternal infection. In order to improve infant survival, improvements in the care of pregnant women and the establishment of neonatal units in hospitals were required. The removal of deliveries from the home to the hospital also necessitated establishment of "well baby" nurseries in the hospital. By the 1920s, for the care of premature infants, incubators were developed and special nutritional protocols established.

The US national interest in child health did not wane. In 1904, four women formed the National Child Labor Committee, and the Children's Bureau of the Federal Department of Labor was established in 1912. The top priority of the Children's Bureau was to promote birth registration in order to compile accurate morbidity and mortality statistics. However, older children also received increased attention, and by 1911 nine states had laws requiring the medical examination of school children.

The climactic event of this period was the Sheppard-Towner Act (1921) which provided federal funds for states to establish programs for birth registration, maternal hygiene, infant welfare centers, and education for mothers, mothers' helpers, and midwives. The act expired in 1929 and was made part of the Social Security Act of 1935, but children did not yet have full rights protected by the law.[46]

Child advocacy

Children had until the recent past no rights on their own. They were part of the family. When they travelled, their data were entered into a family passport, together with the data and the pictures of husband and wife. It was considered as completely normal that children should help with work, which in a rural context may still have been acceptable, but triggered increasing criticism when children worked in the industry. Traditional attitudes towards children tended to consider them as mere extensions of the household and 'owned' by their parents and/or legal guardian, who exerted absolute parental control. In the 19th century, a number of laws were enacted that limited the hours children were allowed to work in a factory. Furthermore, were no longer permitted to work during the night. Children younger than nine were not allowed to work and those between 9-16 were limited to 16 hours per day.[66,67:Wiki] Parallel development included the introduction of compulsory schooling, also on the background of increasing international competition and the desire of many European states for world domination, which at the end triggered the two world wars.

The emergence of the emotionally "priceless" child from the 1870s on has created an essential condition of contemporary childhood. By the mid-nineteenth century, the middle-class parents began insuring their own life and setting up other financial arrangements such as trusts and endowments to protect their children. Working-class urban families in the late nineteenth century still depended on the wages of older children and the household assistance of younger ones. Child labor laws and compulsory education gradually eased this class lag. By the 1930s, lower-class children joined their middle-class counterparts in a new nonproductive world of children, in which the emotional value of a child made child labor no longer accetable.[68]

In the 20th century, infants and children were increasingly recognized as not simply small adults but as a group with own specific interests, including special medical needs. The infant and child welfare movement emerged. Perhaps the earliest example of this is the story of Mary Ellen in the US, an 8-year-old girl who was abused and neglected by her foster parents. Her case, requesting her removal from the home and criminal charges against the foster mother, was argued by the president of the American Society for Prevention of Cruelty to Animals (ASPCA), established in 1866, following the creation of the Royal Society for the Prevention of Cruelty to Animals (RSPCA) in the United Kingdom in 1824, which had received Royal status in 1840. Arguing that children should have at least equal protection as animals, Mary Ellen was removed from the home, her mother jailed, and the New York Society for the Prevention of Cruelty to Children was formed in 1874. In 1908, the New York City Health Department founded a Bureau of Child Hygiene, the first of its kind worldwide. Sinn in 1915, childbirth was the second leading cause of death of women, with tuberculosis being the most frequent cause of death. became law in 1921; was seriously criticized by the AMA. In 1930, the AAP was established.[69-72]

The NY Metropolitan Board of Health was established in 1866. In 1882, spurred by the arrival of several cholera-laden ships in New York harbor, the Board established a bacteriology laboratory capable of evaluating milk for contamination. Not until 1913, however, did the Board require that all milk be pasteurized. By the beginning of the 20th century, with the cooperation of scientists, social reformers, and legislators, the age old problem of finding a safe alternative to breast-feeding was on its way to being solved.

In the first quarter of the 20th century, infant mortality continued to decline as pediatrics and social and governmental programs flourished. The major therapeutic advance of this era was the development of treatment and prophylaxis for diphtheria. Through research in physiologic chemistry, principles of fluid, electrolyte, and acid-base balance were developed and parenteral fluid replacement was initiated.

Pediatricians faced the challenge of decreasing the death rate due to prematurity, the most common cause of which was maternal infection. In order to improve infant survival, improvements in the care of pregnant women and the establishment of neonatal units in hospitals were required. The removal of deliveries from the home to the hospital also necessitated establishment of "well baby" nurseries in the hospital. By the 1920s, for the care of premature infants, incubators were developed and special nutritional protocols established.

The national interest in child health did not wane. In 1904, four women formed the National Child Labor Committee, and the US Children's Bureau of the Federal Department of Labor was established in 1912. The top priority of the Children's Bureau was to promote birth registration in order to compile accurate morbidity and mortality statistics. However, older children also received increased attention, and by 1911 nine states had laws requiring the medical examination of school children. During the height of its influence, the Children's Bureau was headed, managed, and staffed almost completely by women, which was rare for a US federal agency in the early 20th century. It was most influential in bringing the methods of reform-oriented social research to bear on US federal government policy.

The climactic event of this period was the US Promotion of the Welfare and Hygiene of Maternity and Infancy Act, more commonly known as the Sheppard–Towner Act of 1921, which provided federal funds for states to establish programs for birth registration, maternal hygiene, infant welfare centers, and education for mothers, mothers' helpers, and midwives. It was the first legal step of the federal government into social security legislation and the first major law that came to exist after the full voting rights for women. It expired in 1929 and was made part of the Social Security Act of 1935, but children did not yet have full rights protected by the law.[46,73-76]

The Promotion of the Welfare and Hygiene of Maternity and Infancy Act (Sheppard–Towner Act) of 1921 was the first significant health care legislation in the US. It aimed at reducing maternal and infant mortality rates in the US by providing centers for prenatal and child health care. The American Medical Association (AMA), however, did not support it. In 1922 the AMA House of Delegates condemned it for an alleged radical and socialist approach to medicine, in contrast to the pediatric section of the AMA. With intense lobbying by the AMA, the law was eventually repealed in 1929. In 1930 the AMA pediatric section broke away because of the underlying ideological differences, and the American Academy of Pediatric (AAP) was established. The involved pediatricians were no longer prepared to tolerate the fundamental philosophical differences that existed between them and the other AMA members.[41,69,77]

The American Academy of Pediatrics (AAP) and conflicts of interest

In 1988, the formula industry began advertising directly to the public, which created tension between the medical profession and the formula manufacturers. By 1990, the American Academy of Pediatrics (AAP) released a statement listing reasons for the organization's opposition to advertising infant formulas to the general public. The AAP believed the advertisements created a negative effect on breastfeeding, interfered with physicians' advice on infant nutrition, led to confusion among consumers, and increased the cost of infant formula.[61]

The US Promotion of the Welfare and Hygiene of Maternity and Infancy Act (Sheppard–Towner Act) of 1921 had been the first significant US health care legislation. It aimed at reducing maternal and infant mortality rates by providing centers for prenatal and child health care. Since the publication of the book "Children's Health the Nation's Wealth" in 2004 the value of children to society has steadily risen, since the rights of the child were enshrined in the United Nations convention.[78,79]

The American Academy of Pediatrics (AAP) is the largest US national professional association of pediatricians and worldwide.[80-83] It has grown to include 67,000 members who operate in AAP chapters spread across the United States. It publishes over a dozen pediatric care journals and shares information with pediatricians around the country regarding medical best practices and standards in pediatric care.[84] As it is the largest national pediatric association worldwide, it has also considerable influence in pediatric issues and policies worldwide. The AAP also engages in political advocacy campaigns.

When pediatrician Harry Shirkey formulated the concept of children as therapeutic orphans, he was the first chairman of the AAP committee on drugs.[85] We will explore this concept in more detail in a later chapter. Suffice it to say here that this concept claimed concern for the health care of children, who had been issued separate drug labels by the FDA since the aftermath of the thalidomide disaster with the 1962 Kefauver-Harris Amendment to the Food, Drugs and Cosmetics Act (FDCA). The FDCA demanded proof of safety and efficacy of drugs to be proven in order to get a label. As now the "pediatric population" was defined by an age limit, which is an administrative age limit, a period of time began when advocates for separate pediatric studies criticized and branded any use of drugs by minors as unsafe. Ward et al. claim that without children's participation in clinical trials, no pediatric prescribing information was generated for inclusion in the label for the new medication and claim on this basis, that pediatric prescribing often occurred with nothing more than anecdotal experience, that prescribers had no formal guidance in the use of medications for pediatric patients and had to rely on the familiar text in many approved labels. This claim was based on the pediatric warnings which many drug manufacturers had included into the drug labels that safety and effectiveness of the respected drug had not been established in pediatric patients.[86]

The catch in this argumentation is that the definition of children by an age limit is not based on science, but on an administrative definition. Children are not another species. Of all professions, specifically pediatricians know that minors have an adult body well before their 17th or 18th birthday. Furthermore, the age of puberty which ends the physiological status of a minor's body from pediatric to adult has accelerated considerable during the 20th century.[87-89]

The reason for not applying the learnings of developmental physiology and developmental pharmacology to the drug treatment of minors is rather banal.[90-92] The US pediatric legislation has resulted in thousands of clinical studies in minors. Most of these studies did not advance child healthcare. The only tangible results were pediatric labels. You do not have to have studied medicine or pharmacology to know that the human body does not change on the 17th or 18th birthday. What changes is the young person's legal and administrative status. There is no doubt that a preterm infant's physiology and its medical needs are different from an adolescent. However, the AAP and its justifications of "pediatric drug development" have since the emergence of this concept constantly blurred the difference between the legal meaning of the term "child", and its physiological meaning.[28,29,93-96] Behind this blur that appears at semantic only at first sight lie fundamental conflicts of interest, elegantly justified and hidden by referring to the alleged well-being of "children".

Children's rights and their alleged right to have properly tested medicines

In the history of modern medicine we see that government recognition of this profession is an integral part of the framework of its work. Most of the political activities and demands of the AAP have certainly contributed to improving the healthcare of minors. But the seemingly logical justification of clinical studies on "children" who are often physically no longer children made no medical sense. Using the blur in the different meanings of the term "child", the really existing physiological differences between preterm newborns and adults were used to justify clinical trials in "children", as if children and adults were two different species.[28,29] Demands for separate clinical drug studies in children are justified scientifically for young babies and specifically for preterm newborns, but not for all legally and/or administratively defined minors. Children are not another species.[97] The only ones who benefited were the researchers who conducted these studies and who had guaranteed research contracts on minors through these laws for decades.

There are several reasons why we have examined the history of medicine and pediatrics in such depth. The first is that the usual narrative that pediatrics consists in replacing superstition and mysticism with science is incorrect in this form. The inadequate care of expectant mothers in the maternity clinics of the 19th century was based on an established position of conventional medicine, more concerned with the spheres of self-aggrandizement than critical examination of its own actions and/or analyzing data. Semmelweis and others foundered on the concrete wall of this self-aggrandizement, which had its roots in antiquity, in the writings of Galen, in the Christian churches' claim to divine knowledge, and more. Government enforcement of separate "pediatric" studies is the numerically largest abuse of humans in medical research (or should we say "research"?) since the Tuskegee study.

The dynamics of this process at the intersection of politics, science, state authority and institutional self-interest gained further strength through the internationalization of scientific and "scientific" discussion of terms such as "pediatric drug development",[86] "better medicines for children,"[98] and similar descriptions. Both the FDA and the European Medicines Agency (EMA) justify "pediatric" studies by repeating the claim that children are not small adults.[99,100] The US FDA has moved from an originally rigid dogma to a rather flexible approach to "pediatric" studies in several clinical areas.[28,29] However, both FDA and EMA emphasize in joint statements the fundamental correctness of the underlying concept.[101,102] The EMA has in this development become a stronghold of dogmatism that terrorizes the pharmaceutical industry with blindly demanded "pediatric" studies. This will continue as long as (1) the public opinion does not care about it; (2) as long as relevant parts of academic research and teaching continue to cover the concept of "pediatric drug development"; (3) as long as international high level scientific journals continue to publish banal results such as that insulin and other drugs work before and after the 16th or 17th birthday;[103] and as long as plain flawed statements about allegedly pediatric diseases such as nasopharyngeal carcinoma are accepted and not challenged by the editors of scientific journals. The reason for their acceptance may be that there are FDA pediatric written requests or EMA pediatric investigation plans (PIPs) that reward or demand such "pediatric" studies. Regulatory "pediatric" requests or demands should not be accepted uncritically as being based on science. A simply screening of the literature shows that nasopharyngeal carcinoma exists in children, but is not a "pediatric" disease. Instead, it occurs in all age groups.[104-106]

The first paragraphs of the preamble of the EU pediatric regulation contain the justification of "pediatric" studies in a condensed form. They argue that before a medicinal product for human use is placed on the market, it undergoes extensive studies, including preclinical tests and clinical trials, to ensure that it is safe, of high quality and effective for use in the target population. [107] Such studies may not have been undertaken in the "pediatric population" and many of the drugs used to treat the pediatric population have not been studied or authorised for such use. Market forces alone have proven insufficient to stimulate adequate research into, and the development and authorisation of, drugs for the pediatric population.[107] Potential problems resulting from the absence of suitably adapted drugs for the "pediatric population" include inadequate dosage information which leads to increased risks of adverse reactions including death, ineffective treatment through under-dosage, non-availability to the pediatric population of therapeutic advances, suitable formulations and routes of administration, as well as use of magistral or officinal formulations to treat the pediatric population which may be of poor quality.[107] Any concerns about conducting trials in the "pediatric population" should be balanced by the ethical concerns about giving medicinal products to a population in which they have not been appropriately tested. Public health threats from the use of untested medicinal products in the pediatric population can be safely addressed through the study of medicinal products for the pediatric population[107]

The really important point is not that studies are conducted in the "pediatric population". First, the "pediatric population" would need to be defined scientifically, not legally. Second, it is medically and scientifically crucial that studies make sense. Clinical trials are not an end in themselves. If there are justified doubts that a given drug might not work in minors, this can be clarified in medically and scientifically meaningful studies. But not in regulatory-based studies that are ordered blindly because a given dogma claims that everything is different in - legally defined - "children". Children are not another species.[97] Replacing market forces with bureaucratic decisions by public administration involves the risk that the administration will order things that are formally justified, but in reality can be pointless and dangerous because they are not based on the investigation of the matter at hand, but on unworldly formal criteria.

Conclusions

The framework of medical research and drug development has changed fundamentally with the establishment of the regulatory authorities and the processing of the thalidomide disaster first by US lawmakers and eventually by all states worldwide.[108] Next key fundamental events were step were the exposure of the Tuskegee study in the lay press and somewhat later the unveiling of overt abuse of humans in US academic medical research by Beecher.[109,110] The current framework of clinical research in humans reflects the challenges international research faced in the decades immediately following the end of World War II. A concept has crept into this framework that is supposed to advance pediatric healthcare, but demands and even enforces often pointless, banal and/or exaggerated studies that in several cases even have harmed or continue to harm young patients. These studies have to be paid for by the pharmaceutical industry as a condition for the submission of the data of newly developed drugs to be looked at all by the authorities. The EMA refuses to even process an application for the approval of a new drug unless there is a "pediatric investigation plan" (PIP) accepted by the EMA. This would not have been possible without the concept of children as "therapeutic orphans" presented for the first time at a conference in 1963 by Shirkey and eventually published in 1968.[85] Furthermore, the solidification and implementation of this concept would not have been possible without the massive support of the AAP,[111] its collaboration with other scientific organizations, its collaboration with the FDA, and eventually the support of this concept also from the pharmaceutical industry.[86,98,99,111-115] The framework that has kept us safe from further catastrophes comparable to the thalidomide disaster for more than half a century has been infiltrated by new types of conflicts of interest that are wrapped in the invocation of the need to take care of child healthcare even more, expressed with elegant rhetoric and repetition.[86,91,116] In the following chapters, we list concrete examples of allegedly pediatric studies that were completely pointless; how other studies have harmed and continue to harm young patients, how schools of "pediatric" research have emerged that benefit from the described successful camouflage. Furthermore, we show how the existing mechanisms of protection that are intended to prevent and interfere with such conflicts of interest have so far failed to work. Until today, the facade of alleged promotion of child healthcare has not yet been scratched in the public discussion. A fundamental new challenge for the discussion of medical ethics in human research.

References

1. Donzelot J. Policing of Families. Welfare Versus the State. HarperCollins, New York, NY, USA, 1981
2. Shortland M. The Policing of Families by Jacques Donzelot (Book Review). History of Political Thought 1982,3(2),359-362 URL: https://www.jstor.org/stable/26212246
3. Roush RE. The development of midwifery--male and female, yesterday and today. J Nurse Midwifery. 1979 May-Jun;24(3):27-37. doi: 10.1016/0091-2182(79)90078-8.
4. Lops VR. Midwifery: past to present. J Prof Nurs. 1988 Nov-Dec;4(6):402-7. doi: 10.1016/s8755-7223(88)80090-5.
5. Likis FE. Revisiting the hallmarks of midwifery. J Midwifery Womens Health. 2010 Jan-Feb;55(1):1.
6. Barnaw N, Richter S, Habib F. Midwifery and Midwives: A Historical Analysis. J Res Nursing Midwifery (JRNM) 2013 Dec,2(8):114-121. https://www.interesjournals.org/articles/midwifery-and-midwives-a-historical-analysis.pdf
7. Sherrat DR. A history of midwifery. 2011 http://www.bnemid.byethost14.com/HISTORY%20OF%20MIDWIFERY%201.pdf?i=2
8. Wikipedia, Midwifery. https://en.wikipedia.org/wiki/Midwifery
9. O'Sullivan JF. Two hundred years of midwifery 1806-2006. 2006 Sep;75(3):213-22. https://www.ncbi.nlm.nih.gov/pmc/articles/PMC1891762/pdf/umj7503-213.pdf
10. Thomas BG. A History of Midwifery in the Western World. 2016. https://memoriesofnursing.uk/wp-content/uploads/History-of-midwifery-BGT.pdf
11. The origins of midwifery. 2022. https://www.internationalmidwives.org/icm-news/the-origins-of-midwifery.html

12. Nriagu JO. Saturnine gout among Roman aristocrats. Did lead poisoning contribute to the fall of the Empire? N Engl J Med. 1983 Mar 17;308(11):660-3.

13. Nriagu JO. Occupational exposure to lead in ancient times. Sci Total Environ. 1983 Nov;31(2):105-16.

14. Nriagu JO. Lead and Lead Poisoning in Antiquity. John Wiley & Sons, Hoboken NJ, USA, 1983.
https://dl.tufts.edu/pdfviewer/db78tq04h/6395wk23b

15. Cilliers L, Retief FP. Medical practice in Graeco-Roman antiquity. Curationis. 2006 May;29(2):34-40.

16. Moog FP. [Physicians of Gladiators in the Ancient Rome]. Dtsch Med Wochenschr 2018 Dec;143(25):1842-1846

17. Scott WA. The practice of medicine in ancient Rome. Canad Anaes Soc J 1955,2 Jul (8)
https://link.springer.com/content/pdf/10.1007/BF03016172.pdf

18. Wikipedia, Medicine in Ancient Rome
https://en.wikipedia.org/wiki/Medicine_in_ancient_Rome

19. Kotb Allam MR. The Roman Physicians in The Light of Some Private Funerary Inscriptions. 2007.
https://bcps.journals.ekb.eg/article_26726_30d446488bf3df336cef644e452ddfac.pdf

20. Bujalkova M. Sklaven in der antiken Medizin. Graeco-Latina Brunensia 2013,18(2),67-76.
https://www.researchgate.net/publication/289745566_Slaves_in_ancient_medicine/link/5845609908aeda69681a04ed/download

21. Wulff HR. The Language of Medicine. J R Soc Med 2004 Apr;97(4): 187-8.
https://www.ncbi.nlm.nih.gov/pmc/articles/PMC1079361/pdf/0970187.pdf

22. Dzuganova B. A brief outline of the development of medical English. Bratisl Lek Listy 2002; 103 (6): 223.227
http://bmj.fmed.uniba.sk/2002/10306-07.PDF

23. Connor H. The language of medicine. J R Soc Med 2004 Jun;97(6):310-1. https://www.ncbi.nlm.nih.gov/pmc/articles/PMC1079514/pdf/0970310B.pdf

24. West JB. Galen and the beginnings of Western physiology. Am J Physiol Lung Cell Mol Physiol. 2014 Jul 15;307(2):L121-8. https://journals.physiology.org/doi/epdf/10.1152/ajplung.00123.2014

25. Apuzzo ML. The legacy of Galen of Pergamon. Neurosurgery. 2000 Sep;47(3):545.

26. Nutton V. Galen: A Thinking Doctor in Imperial Rome. Routledge, London, UK, 2020

27. Gensini GF, Conti AA. The evolution of the concept of 'fever' in the history of medicine: from pathological picture per se to clinical epiphenomenon (and vice versa). J Infect. 2004 Aug;49(2):85-7.

28. Rose K. Considering the Patient in Pediatric Drug Development. How good intentions turned into harm. Elsevier, London, UK, 2020

29. Rose K. Blind Trust - How parents with a sick child can escape the labyrinth of lies, hypocrisy and false promises of researchers and regulatory authorities. Hammersmith, London, UK, 2022.

30. Youngson R, Schott I (Authors). Medical Blunders. Amazing True Stories of Mad, Bad and Dangerous Doctors. Robinson, London, UK, 1996

31. Wikipedia, Galen https://en.wikipedia.org/wiki/Galen

32. Espina-Jerez B, Romera-Álvarez L, Cott-Andino M, et al. Midwives in Health Sciences as a Sociocultural Phenomenon: Legislation, Training and Health (XV-XVIII Centuries). Medicina (Kaunas) 2022 Sep 19;58(9):1309. https://www.ncbi.nlm.nih.gov/pmc/articles/PMC9502592/pdf/medicina-58-01309.pdf

33. Witch Trials in Early Modern Europe and New England. Berkeley Law, 2023. https://www.law.berkeley.edu/research/the-robbins-collection/exhibitions/witch-trials-in-early-modern-europe-and-new-england/

34. Behringer W. Witches and Witch-Hunts: A Global History. Polity (Wiley), Cambridge, UK, 2004

35. Thurston R. The Witch Hunts: A History of the Witch Persecutions in Europe and North America. Routledge, London, UK, 2006

36. Wikipedia, Witch-hunt. https://en.wikipedia.org/wiki/Witch-hunt

37. Haskins, CY. Gender Bias in the Roman Catholic Church: Why Can't Women be Priests? 3 U. Md. L.J. Race Relig. Gender & Class 2003,99:1,Article 4 https://digitalcommons.law.umaryland.edu/cgi/viewcontent.cgi?article=1037&context=rrgc

38. Sakai T. Historical evolution of anatomical terminology from ancient to modern. Anat Sci Int. 2007 Jun;82(2):65-81. doi: 10.1111/j.1447-073X.2007.00180.x.

39. Wikipedia, Terminologia Anatomica https://en.wikipedia.org/wiki/Terminologia_Anatomica

40. Wikipedia, International Federation of Associations of Anatomists https://en.wikipedia.org/wiki/International_Federation_of_Associations_of_Anatomists

41. Colón AR, Colón PA. Nurturing children: a history of pediatrics. Greenwood Press, Westport, CT, USA 1999

42. Loudon I. Why are (male) surgeons still addressed as Mr? BMJ 2000 Dec 23; 321(7276): 1589–1591. https://www.ncbi.nlm.nih.gov/pmc/articles/PMC1119265/pdf/1589.pdf

43. Scheuermann K. Midwifery in Germany. Its past and present. J Nurse Midwifery 1995 Sep-Oct;40(5):438-47

44. Wikipedia, Obstetrics https://en.wikipedia.org/wiki/Obstetrics

45. Wikipedia, Obstetrical forceps https://en.wikipedia.org/wiki/Obstetrical_forceps

46. Mayefsky JH. The development of pediatrics in the United States. Henry Ford Hosp Med J. 1988;36(4):178-82. https://scholarlycommons.henryford.com/hfhmedjournal/vol36/iss4/3/

47. McEnroe N. Celebrating Florence Nightingale's bicentenary. Lancet. 2020 May 9;395(10235):1475-1478 https://www.ncbi.nlm.nih.gov/pmc/articles/PMC7252134/pdf/main.pdf

48. Olans RD, Olans RN, DeMaria A Jr. Florence Nightingale and Antimicrobial Stewardship. Florence Nightingale J Nurs. 2022 Feb;30(1):106-108. https://www.ncbi.nlm.nih.gov/pmc/articles/PMC8958231/pdf/fnjn-30-1-106.pdf

49. Wikipedia, Florence Nightingale https://en.wikipedia.org/wiki/Florence_Nightingale

50. Schlumbohm J. The practice of practical education: male students and female apprentices in the Lying-in Hospital of Göttingen University, 1792-1815. Med Hist. 2007 Jan;51(1):3-36. https://www.ncbi.nlm.nih.gov/pmc/articles/PMC1712359/pdf/medhis5101-003.pdf

51. Stang A, Standl F, Poole C. A twenty-first century perspective on concepts of modern epidemiology in Ignaz Philipp Semmelweis' work on puerperal sepsis. Eur J Epidemiol. 2022 May;37(5):437-445. https://www.ncbi.nlm.nih.gov/pmc/articles/PMC9209376/pdf/10654_2022_Article_871.pdf

52. Gupta VK, Saini C, Oberoi M, et al. Semmelweis Reflex: An Age-Old Prejudice. World Neurosurg. 2020 Apr;136:e119-e125.

53. Wikipedia, Ignaz Semmelweis https://en.wikipedia.org/wiki/Ignaz_Semmelweis

54. Bachelor in Midwifery https://www.zhaw.ch/en/health/a-course-of-study-in-health-care/bachelors-programmes-in-the-health-professions/bachelor-in-midwifery-1/

55. International Confederation of Midwifes (ICM) https://www.internationalmidwives.org/

56. Midwifery. An Executive Summary for The Lancet's Series. The Lancet, 2014

https://www.thelancet.com/pb/assets/raw/Lancet/stories/series/midwifery/midwifery_exec_summ-1407728206867.pdf

57. Wagner M. A global witch-hunt. Lancet. 1995 Oct 14;346(8981):1020-2

58. Wikipedia, 1854 Broad Street cholera outbreak https://en.wikipedia.org/wiki/1854_Broad_Street_cholera_outbreak

59. Wikipedia, History of water supply and sanitation https://en.wikipedia.org/wiki/History_of_water_supply_and_sanitation

60. Fine P, Victora CG, Rothman KJ, et al. John Snow's legacy: epidemiology without borders. Lancet 2013 Apr 13;381(9874):1302-11. https://www.ncbi.nlm.nih.gov/pmc/articles/PMC3730273/pdf/nihms493871.pdf

61. Stevens EE, Patrick TE, Pickler R. A history of infant feeding. J Perinat Educ. 2009 Spring;18(2):32-9. https://www.ncbi.nlm.nih.gov/pmc/articles/PMC2684040/pdf/jpe-18-032.pdf

62. Schuman AJ. A concise history of infant formula (twists and turns included). Contemporary Pediatrics, February 1, 2003. https://www.contemporarypediatrics.com/view/concise-history-infant-formula-twists-and-turns-included

63. Baumgartel KL, Sneeringer L, Cohen SM. From royal wet nurses to Facebook: The evolution of breastmilk sharing. Breastfeed Rev. 2016 Nov;24(3):25-32. https://www.ncbi.nlm.nih.gov/pmc/articles/PMC5603296/pdf/nihms860019.pdf

64. Eagle Brand History. https://www.eaglebrand.com/eagle-brand-history/

65. Thulier D. Breastfeeding in America: a history of influencing factors. J Hum Lact. 2009 Feb;25(1):85-94.

66. Wikipedia, Child Advocacy https://en.wikipedia.org/wiki/Child_advocacy

67. Wikipedia, Children's rights movement https://en.wikipedia.org/wiki/Children%27s_rights_movement

68. Zelizer VA. Pricing the Priceless Child: The Changing Social Value of Children. Princeton University Press, Princeton, NJ, USA, 1994

69. Mahnke CB. The growth and development of a specialty: the history of pediatrics. Clin Pediatr (Phila). 2000 Dec;39(12):705-14.

70. Wikipedia, American Society for the Prevention of Cruelty to Animals (ASPCA) https://en.wikipedia.org/wiki/American_Society_for_the_Prevention_of_Cruelty_to_Animals

71. Wikipedia, New York Society for the Prevention of Cruelty to Children https://en.wikipedia.org/wiki/New_York_Society_for_the_Prevention_of_Cruelty_to_Children

72. Wikipedia, Royal Society for the Prevention of Cruelty to Animals (RSPCA) https://en.wikipedia.org/wiki/Royal_Society_for_the_Prevention_of_Cruelty_to_Animals

73. Wikipedia, National Child Labor Committee (NCLC) https://en.wikipedia.org/wiki/National_Child_Labor_Committee

74. Wikipedia, United States Children's Bureau https://en.wikipedia.org/wiki/United_States_Children's_Bureau

75. Wikipedia, Sheppard-Towner Act https://en.wikipedia.org/wiki/Sheppard-Towner_Act

76. Wikipedia, Social Security Act https://en.wikipedia.org/wiki/Social_Security_Act

77. Oberg CN. Pediatric advocacy: yesterday, today, and tomorrow. Pediatrics. 2003 Aug;112(2):406-9.

78. Bearer CF, Roland D, Molloy EJ. Value of children in our world. Pediatr Res. 2022 Nov;92(5):1202-1203. https://www.nature.com/articles/s41390-021-01609-0

79. National Research Council (US), Institute of Medicine (US). Children's Health, The Nation's Wealth: Assessing and Improving Child Health, 29 (National Academies Press, 2004). https://www.ncbi.nlm.nih.gov/books/NBK92206/pdf/Bookshelf_NBK92206.pdf

80. American Academy of Pediatrics (AAP) https://www.aap.org

81. American Academy of Pediatrics (AAP) History https://www.aap.org/en/about-the-aap/gartner-pediatric-history-center/aap-history/

82. American Academy of Pediatrics (AAP) Membership https://www.aap.org/en/membership-application/join-aap/

83. Wikipedia, American Academy of Pediatrics (AAP) https://en.wikipedia.org/wiki/American_Academy_of_Pediatrics

84. Influence Watch: American Academy of Pediatrics. InfluenceWatch2023. https://www.influencewatch.org/non-profit/american-academy-of-pediatrics/

85. Shirkey H. Therapeutic Orphans. J Pediatr 1968 Jan; 72 (1), 119-120. https://pdfs.semanticscholar.org/f1cb/acdbac19fa56236b919fb7799eaacaa10c77.pdf

86. Ward RM, Benjamin DK Jr, Davis JM, Gorman RL, Kauffman R, Kearns GL, et al. The Need for Pediatric Drug Development. J Pediatr. 2018 Jan;192:13-21.

87. Cone TE Jr. Secular acceleration of height. J Pediatr 1961 Nov;59:736-40.

88. Komlos J, Lauderdale BE. The mysterious trend in American heights. Ann Hum Biol Mar-Apr 2007;34(2):206-15.

89. Beunen GP, Rogol AD, Malina RM. Indicators of biological maturation and secular changes in biological maturation. Food Nutr Bull. 2006;27(4 Suppl Growth Standard):S244–S256. https://journals.sagepub.com/doi/pdf/10.1177/15648265060274S508.

90. Burggren W. Developmental Physiology: Grand Challenges. Front Physiol. 2021 Jun 10;12:706061. https://www.ncbi.nlm.nih.gov/pmc/articles/PMC8225327/pdf/fphys-12-706061.pdf

91. Wilson G. Developmental Pharmacology. Anaesthesia & Intensive Care Medicine 2021;22(9),587-593

92. Kearns GL, Abdel-Rahman SM, Alander SW, Blowey DL, Leeder JS, Kauffman RE, et al. Developmental pharmacology--drug disposition,

action, and therapy in infants and children. N Engl J Med. 2003 Sep 18;349(12):1157-67.

93. Rose K, Neubauer D, Grant-Kels JM. Ethical Issues in Pediatric Regulatory Studies Involving Placebo Treatment. J Pediatr Epilepsy 2020; 9(03): 073-079 DOI: 10.1055/s-0040-1712147

94. Rose K, Neubauer D, Grant-Kels JM. Rational Use of Medicine in Children – The Conflict of Interests Story. A Review. Rambam Maimonides Med J. 2019 Jul 18; 10(3): e0018. Review. doi:10.5041/RMMJ.10371. https://www.rmmj.org.il/userimages/928/2/PublishFiles/953Article.pdf

95. Rose K. The Challenges of Pediatric Drug Development. Curr Ther Res Clin Exp. 2019, https://www.sciencedirect.com/science/article/pii/S0011393X18300353

96. Rose K, Grant-Kels JM. Pediatric Melanoma – The Whole (Conflicts Of Interest) Story. Int J Womens Dermatol 2018,Nov 19;5(2):110-115. doi: 10.1016/j.ijwd.2018.10.020 https://www.ncbi.nlm.nih.gov/pmc/articles/PMC6451736/pdf/main.pdf

97. Gillis J, Loughlan P. Not just small adults: the metaphors of paediatrics. Arch Dis Child. 2007 Nov;92(11):946-7 https://www.ncbi.nlm.nih.gov/pmc/articles/PMC2083631/pdf/946.pdf

98. European Medicines Agency (EMA): Better Medicines for Children. EMA 2015 https://www.ema.europa.eu/en/documents/leaflet/better-medicines-children_en.pdf

99. FDA 2016. Drug Research and Children. https://www.fda.gov/drugs/information-consumers-and-patients-drugs/drug-research-and-children

100. Ethical considerations for clinical trials on medicinal products conducted with minors. Recommendations of the expert group on clinical trials for the implementation of Regulation (EU) No 536/2014 on clinical trials on medicinal products for human use. Revision 1, 18th September 2017

https://health.ec.europa.eu/system/files/2018-02/2017_09_18_ethical_consid_ct_with_minors_0.pdf

101. FDA/EMA 2020: FDA / EMA Common Commentary on Submitting an initial Pediatric Study Plan (iPSP) and Pediatric Investigation Plan (PIP) for the Prevention and Treatment of COVID-19. https://www.fda.gov/media/138489/download and https://www.ema.europa.eu/en/documents/other/fda/ema-common-commentary-submitting-initial-pediatric-study-plan-ipsp-pediatric-investigation-plan-pip_en.pdf

102. Rose K. The COVID-19 Pandemic: A Global High-Tech Challenge at the Interface of Science, Politics, and Illusions. Elsevier, London, UK, 2022 https://www.elsevier.com/books/the-covid-19-pandemic/rose/978-0-323-99149-0

103. Thalange N, Deeb L, Iotova V, et al. Insulin degludec in combination with bolus insulin aspart is safe and effective in children and adolescents with type 1 diabetes. Pediatr Diabetes 2015 May; 16(3):164-76. https://www.ncbi.nlm.nih.gov/pmc/articles/PMC4413367/pdf/pedi0016-0164.pdf

104. Casanova M, Enis Özyar E, Patte C, et al. International randomized phase 2 study on the addition of docetaxel to the combination of cisplatin and 5- fluorouracil in the induction treatment for nasopharyngeal carcinoma in children and adolescents. Cancer Chemother Pharmacol 2016 Feb;77(2):289-98.

105. Brennan B. Nasopharyngeal carcinoma. Orphanet J Rare Dis 2006;1:23.

106. Kamran SC, Riaz N, Lee N. Nasopharyngeal carcinoma. Surg Oncol Clin N Am 2015;24:547–61.

107. Regulation (EC) No. 1901/2006 Of The European Parliament and of the Council of 12 December 2006 on medicinal products for paediatric use and amending Regulation (EEC) No 1768/92, Directive 2001/20/EC, Directive 2001/83/EC and Regulation (EC) No 726/2004. https://eur-lex.europa.eu/legal-content/EN/TXT/PDF/?uri=CELEX:32006R1901&from=EN

108. Rägo L, Santo B: Drug Regulation: History, Present and Future. In: Drug Benefits and Risks: International Textbook of Clinical Pharmacology, revised 2nd edition, van Boxtel CJ, Santo B & Edwards IR (editors). IOS Press & Uppsala Monitoring Centre, Uppsala, Sweden, 2008, chapter 6, pp. 65-77 https://www.who.int/medicines/technical_briefing/tbs/Drug_Regulation_History_Present_Future.pdf

109. Brandt AM. Racism and research: The case of the Tuskegee Syphilis study. The Hastings Center Report 1978;8(6): 21-29. https://dash.harvard.edu/handle/1/3372911

110. Beecher HK. Ethics and clinical research. N Engl J Med. 1966 Jun 16;274(24):1354-60. https://www.observatoriobioetica.org/wp-content/uploads/2016/09/Beecher_Ethics_and_Clinical_Research_1966.pdf

111. American Academy of Pediatrics (AAP): Guidelines for the Ethical Conduct of Studies to Evaluate Drugs in Pediatric Populations, Committee on Drugs. American Academy of Pediatrics. Pediatrics, 1995 Feb;95(2):286-94

112. Pharmaceutical Research and Manufacturers of America (PhRMA) https://www.phrma.org

113. Pharmaceutical Research and Manufacturers of America (PhRMA) Research & Development: Pediatrics/ Industry Commitment to Pediatric Research. PhRMA 2023. https://www.phrma.org/Pediatrics

114. European Federation of Pharmaceutical Industries and Associations (EFPIA). https://www.efpia.eu

115. European Federation of Pharmaceutical Industries and Associations (EFPIA). Stimulating the development of new medicines for children. EFPIA 2023. https://www.efpia.eu/about-medicines/development-of-medicines/regulations-safety-supply/stimulating-the-development-of-new-medicines-for-children/

116. Van den Anker JN. Developmental Pharmacology. Dev Disabil Res Rev 2010;16(3):233-238

Chapter 3
What is a Child?

You can ask anyone on this planet if she or he knows what a child is, and you will get a positive reply. And yet one of the key questions in this book is what a child is. Archaic humans, including Neanderthals, Denosivans and others; ancient Romans & Greeks; people in the European Middle Ages; they all had an idea what children were. Since the existence of written testimonies a lot has been written about children, their care, their health, their illnesses, & more. On the one hand these testimonies were more or less precise direct observations, on the other hand they were written against the background of a worldview that was quite different from ours today. In those times the material world and its spirits, its gods, and the supernatural forces which men believed regularly intervened in their affairs were not as sharply divided from each other as they are today. We have to interpret all these historical testimonies in the light of our today's understandings. But all our thoughts have not yet answered the questions what the term "child" and "pediatric population" mean. A lost has changed since the Neanderthals and the ancient Greeks and Romans.

The US National Research Council within the Institute of Medicine explains in depth how it uses the term "children": a group of individuals from birth to their 18th birthday. Furthermore, the authors emphasize that from a developmental perspective, there is no exact age at which childhood definitively ends; numerous factors affect the timing of one's transition from adolescence to adulthood and, as a result, individuals transition from child to adult roles at different rates; for some, adult roles are assumed during adolescence, while for others this does not occur until the middle of the third decade of life. The authors chose age 18 as the minimum age for ending childhood. They also recommend to collect data for those older than 18. Although the terms "youth" or "adolescents" often refer to older children and the terms "infants" and "toddlers" to very young children, the authors use the term "children" to encompass all these groups.[1]

The most recent policy statement of the American Academy of Pediatrics (AAP) about the age limit of pediatrics explains that the former upper age limit of 21 years is no longer regarded as adequate. It characterizes the age of 21 years as an arbitrary demarcation line for adolescence because there is increasing evidence that brain development has not reliably reached adult levels of functioning until well into the third decade of life. For young adults with disabilities often pediatricians are the only ones with specific training, background understanding and experience to take care of them. Establishing arbitrary age limits on pediatric care by health care providers should be discouraged. Health care insurers and other payers should not place limits that affect a patient's choice of care provider solely on the basis of age.[2]

Both the positions of the US National Research Council as well as of the AAP are correct within the framework of their purpose. The AAP defines which persons should be seen by a pediatrician as opposed by a physician who treats adult patients. The US National Research Council outlines about which persons it wants data to be collected. Nothing can be said against these approaches. However, the AAP definition must not be construed as giving a guide at which age the physiological characteristics of the child's body terminate and at which age the person becomes bodily mature. It is not a guide to make clinical decisions. It simply sets an administrative, hands-on, practical framework.

Also, the regulatory authorities and the International Council for Harmonisation of Technical Requirements for Pharmaceuticals for

Human Use (ICH) use fixed age limits. A first ICH E11 Guideline on Clinical Investigation of Medicinal Products in the Pediatric Population was issued in 2000. It has in the last years been complemented by the addendum E11(R1), and by the document E11A on pediatric extrapolation. ICHE11 and ICH E 11(R1) differentiate the age groups of preterm newborn infants; term newborn infants (0 to 27 days); infants and toddlers (28 days to 23 months); children (2 to 11 years); and adolescents [12 to 16-18 years (dependent on region)].[3]

There will never be a universal definition of a good time limit to define the transition from childhood over adolescence to adulthood.[4]

On the one hand, children today are the same as children a hundred, a thousand or a million years ago. They have the same genetic pool, have two arms, one head, can be healthy or sick, and so on. On the other hand, they are also very different. Never in history have young people reached puberty as early as they do today. This is a measurable physiological difference. There are certainly many reasons for this, and they can be debated endlessly. One is good and balanced nutrition; but so are improved hygiene; better clothes; vaccinations, which now prevent the vast majority of formerly fatal, disfiguring, or crippling infectious diseases; the changed intellectual environment, in which the young brain is challenged more than in the distant past; and much more.[5-8] In short, the measurable external circumstances have changed, but so have the spiritual circumstances that are much more difficult to measure. The basic challenge for medicine is that on the one hand it looks at, examines and treats the body of the patient, but on the other hand patient and doctor are part of a society. This also includes the hopes and expectations that we project into children, into the medical doctor, and into the healthcare system in general, as well as the social experiences of the recent and more distant past and the parents' gut feelings.

Not only the beginning and end of puberty has changed. Compulsory schooling was introduced in the middle of the 19th century. Only since then a systematic look at children's learning abilities and disabilities emerged. It took more than a century from then on until mankind has developed a reasonably clear idea of mentally handicapped children and has learned to distinguish between mysticism and unbiased inquiry. Challenges such as being blind or deaf were not systematically addressed before modern times, although high tech is not needed to develop and use a sign language for deaf people or a writing system for those who cannot see, such as the braille tactile writing system. There was simply not enough systematic interest in such questions; there was not enough communication about such special issues; the communication technology did not yet reach in real time across entire countries and continents; and there was no tradition to take care of special people. Even if a family could have afforded a specialized teacher, there were neither institutions nor a tradition that would have been able to train such teachers.[9]

The social, emotional and economic position and importance of children has changed fundamentally since the middle of the 19th century. Not always in the context of pleasant movements. States competed for dominance of the world and needed usable human supplies for their economic and military conflicts, culminating finally in the two world wars.

Between the 1870s and the 1930s, a profound transformation in the economic and sentimental value of children took place both in Europe and North America. It was reflected in the emergence of many new books about children and the emergence of a new juvenile literature. The period between the late 19th and early 20th centuries is known as the "Golden Age of Children's Literature" because many classic children's books were published then.[10] The heightened emotional status of children resulted also, inter alia, in the legal justification of children's life insurance policies and in large damages awarded by courts to their parents in the event of death.[11] Pediatric hospitals emerged in Europe and North America during the 19th century.[12,13]

Medicine works in the social space of society. In this book we discuss a specific aspect the interplay between medicine and law: clinical studies with minors, i.e., their experimental medical treatment. Historically, experimental medical treatment emerged as a two-sided sword. Discussions about experimental medical treatment still resonate with the Nazi crimes and attempts after World War II to prevent criminal and criminal research through a broadly based scientific and ethical framework. In this debate, the accusation has often been made that clinical research uses humans as guinea pigs.[14-17] But clinical research during the 20th century has improved the quality of life and saved the lives of millions of adults and children. Modern research-based medicine has become part of our society and has also established a firm place in today's economy. Diseases that were lethal in the past have become conditions that may be unpleasant, but which today allow a normal life, including diabetes, HIV, cystic fibrosis and many others. Vaccines prevent today many diseases that used to kill mercilessly. Newly developed drugs and vaccines are continuously changing the composition of mankind.

In the justification and the demand for clinical studies for the approval of drugs in minors (the authorities use the term "pediatric population"), different dimensions of being a child are mixed up. Modern society cannot exist without setting different formal age limits for different activities: from when one may have a tattoo done, from when one may vote, be elected, drink alcohol or go hunting. But here an administrative/legal age limit is given an apparently physiological quality, thus blurring various dimensions of childhood.

You do not have to have studied medicine to see that it makes no sense for a drug to be approved for and considered safe in someone over the age of 18, but not one day before the 18th birthday, and thus be officially considered unsafe and untested for a 17-year-old minor. This in itself is still rather banal. However, it is not banal that for all new drugs for all minors the authorities require a repetition of the proof of efficacy, as if minors were a different species. To understand this, it is necessary to consider a few things that have changed in society's relationship to minors over the past century or two.

Reviews of developmental pharmacology emphasize that understanding the pharmacokinetics and pharmacodynamics of drugs used in treating patients across the pediatric age spectrum from infants to adolescents represents a major challenge for clinicians;[18] that effective drug therapy to optimally influence disease requires an understanding of a drug's pharmacokinetic, pharmacodynamic, and pharmacogenomic interrelationships. In pediatrics, age is a continuum that can and does add variability in drug disposition and effect.[19] There are countless reviews and overviews over developmental pharmacology. A recent publication, written by a "multidisciplinary group of experts", summarizes current knowledge, and provides suggestions to pharmaceutical companies, regulatory agencies and academicians on how to incorporate the latest knowledge regarding developmental pharmacology and innovative techniques into "neonatal and pediatric drug development." On one side, it mentions that due to rapid physiological changes (e.g., maturation of liver and kidney function, organ-specific growth), developmental impact on pharmacokinetics (PK) and pharmacodynamics (PD) is most remarkable in the neonatal period and first year of life. But the authors also emphasize that PK and/or PD may also differ from adults during childhood and adolescence.[20]

The key physiological changes take place in neonates and to a lesser degree during the first year of life. During the first year of life, extreme caution is necessary indeed in dosing drugs for young patients. Thereafter, however, the body has acquired already a certain level of maturity. One year old babies are still smaller than school age children, and so are their internal organs. But they are no longer as vulnerable as newborns.[21]

When we look at reviews or overviews of developmental pharmacology we need to differentiate those that justify as many clinical pharmacology studies in minor patients as possible,[18-20] as opposed to a balanced discussion where clinical studies to establish correct treatment doses and avoid toxicities are necessary, and where not. FDA officers investigated the outcomes of dose recommendations that resulted from clinical studies in adolescents and found that in 94.5% of all drugs the resulting doses in adolescents and adults were identical.[22] Figure 1 in a paper from 2003 which has been shown in hundreds of conferences to illustrate developmental pharmacology shows five organ systems: (A) metabolic capacity (the liver); (B) developmental changes in distribution sites (total body water/ extracellular water(; (C) changes in gastrointestinal function; (D) integumentary development (the skin); and (E) acquisition of renal function.[21] The mentioned paper shows the maturation of the liver function (A) from birth to 10 years; the maturation of distribution sites from birth to 40 years (B); the maturation of the gastrointestinal function from birth to 10 years followed by adults (C); the maturation of the skin from pre-term neonates to adults, and the renal function from birth to 12 years (E). The skin ages over the years. From a certain age on, women invest vast sums of money to reverse this process. Men have meanwhile joined this movement. Anti-aging medicine has become a budding and rapidly growing medical specialty. Organizations such as the American Academy of Anti-Aging Medicine (A4M) offer training and certification. As of 2011, approximately 26,000 practitioners had been given A4M certificates.[23-25] Also the liver, kidneys, joints, and most other organs age over time. The physiological border between an adult and a child body is the end of puberty. But as we see in figure 1 of Kearns 2003, even the physiological transitions are fluid. Maturation of the mind and brain is even more complicated. Adolescents can be intellectually mature early, and adults can behave childishly. But this is another story.

The key changes in developmental pharmacology occur in the neonatal population. In general, weight based dosing often results in the underdosing of infants and children, while overdosing neonates; dosing using body surface area often overestimates the dose for infants.[26] But also this publication concludes that ideal dosing regimens are based on pharmacokinetic and pharmacodynamic variables from studies in neonates, toddlers, children and adolescents. Also here we have the sudden jump from justifiable added caution and need for studies to a generalization into "children," now no longer defined physiologically.

To put it provocatively, one can formulate a far-fetched justification for almost any clinical trial in order to be "perfectly certain" in the interest of the patient. Often extremely obese or extremely thin adolescents are listed as examples that simple dose recommendations are often insufficient. But these limitations have nothing to do with a fixed age limit. Somebody can be obese or underweight before and after the 18th birthday.

Are all the justifications for pediatric clinical studies done in the interest of the patient, or in the interest of those who follow a dogma, and those who have based their career on the justification of such studies? The question of whether such studies make medical sense is not answered in many papers. Sometimes it is worth not only to focus on what a paper says, but also to focus on what it does not say. Smits et al. shows how a coalition of scientists has emerged that justifies clinical studies in administratively/ legally defined minors.[20] The "pediatric population" for which "pediatric drug development" is justified in this publication is not a group based on a scientific definition, but departs from an administratively/ legally defined group of humans for which it finds grounds for clinical trials after accepting the existence of this group.

A parallel observation is possible from yet another perspective. The European Medicines Agency (EMA) emphasizes that in the EU, "fifty per cent or more of medicines used in children have never actually been studied in this population, but only in adults, and not necessarily in the same indication (or the same disease)".[27] A paper by Italian regulators and clinicians describes the "lack of availability of appropriate medicines for children as an extensive and well known problem."[28] Wilson reports that up to 90% of drugs administered to children are unstudied, with infants accounting for the highest percentage of off-label drug administration.[29] Departing from legitimate concerns about drug treatment in preterm and term newborns, we suddenly find ourselves in the extrapolation from newborns to all "children," i.e. all members of the "pediatric population," – i.e. suddenly term that is no longer defined scientifically and physiologically, but administratively and/or legally.

A hundred years ago, effective drugs were almost non-existing. People believed that medicines that were sold in pharmacies helped, but most did not. If drugs did or did not work in minors would therefore have been a rather irrelevant question. Before World War I, the precise date of birth of a minor played a much minor role than today. Somebody whose body appeared to be mature was considered mature for physical issues. A young man who wanted to enlist in the armed forces could give a fake date of birth. If he was strong and healthy on physical examination, he was enlisted. A young woman who wanted to work in a factory was accepted as an adult worker without being asked to show an identity document

(ID). Back then, appearance was the most important differentiator used by common sense. It was certainly different when it came to the question of when a young person could become king or queen. The date of birth of kings and queens and of their children has been handed down in writing. But this is not a book about royal children.

The conceptual distinction between children and adults in medicine emerged during the course of the 19th century. Until then, children had largely been seen as small adults in medical treatment.[30] But only with the observation in the 1940s/50s that antibiotics given to preterm newborns could be toxic,[31] and the warnings on drug labels from 1962 that these drugs had not been tested in children,[32] led to the emphasis of newly emerged scientific disciplines, including developmental physiology and developmental pharmacology, and the formation of advocacy groups, specifically the AAP Committee on Drugs, which emphasized the difference between children and adults in the discussion of pediatric drug treatment. From this point of view, if we look at early and modern documents dealing with this question, we see that the legal and the medical definitions of childhood have been mixed up from the very beginnings. The AAP used the age of giving legally accepted informed consent to study participation as the key differentiator between adults and children.[31] The European Union's definition of children is from birth to the 18th birthday.[33] This is a *legal* definition. But it justifies physical clinical studies, i.e., a definitely *medical* intervention. When we read overviews of developmental pharmacology, we see tendencies. One correctly describes the need for exactly measuring absorption, distribution, metabolism and excretion of drugs in neonatology.[26] The other one does not define physiologically what children are but pretends to assume that everybody knows anyway what this term means.[18,19,29] The boundaries between these two tendencies or schools are not precise. Even Crane extrapolates the need for dose assessment into all "children". The existing and important bodily difference between newborns and more so preterm newborns and adults is blurred by the use of the term "child" by justifying clinical trials in minors of all ages, whether these trials make sense or not.

All of this may still seem banal to the unbiased reader. But the funding of pointless, massively overblown, or often even harmful "pediatric" studies has become a multi-billion Dollar or Euro global business. A report of the European Commission of 2017 estimates the costs for pediatric investigation plans (PIPs) as € 2,1 billion per year.[34,35] If we multiply the € 2,1 billion with the 17 years since the EU pediatric regulation is in force, i.e. from 2007 to 2023, this is a sum of more than € 35 billion. Definitely not peanuts.

In its justification of "better medicines for children," also the European Medicines Agency (EMA) uses continuously the term "children" without addressing the difference between the physiological and the legal/ administrative meanings of the term "child."[36]

In several medical areas, pediatric and adult medicine use completely different names for the identical disease in adults and "children," for example in pediatric vs. adult rheumatology.[37] This is well known by specialists, but the confusion continues and results in wrong treatment of young patients with various rheumatoid diseases once they reach adulthood and are treated by an adult rheumatologist.[38] This challenge of medicine in modern society would not require high tech approaches to be resolved. The obstacle to its solution is conflicts of interest of those professional groups that take care of adult vs. adolescent and pediatric patients, adolescents mostly being counted as "pediatric" patients although bodily they are no longer children. Some conflicts of interest are open, some are hidden. Some are maintained by persons who are aware of the conundrums. Others are maintained by traditions that are hard to crack. Of course, all professional groups emphasize that they want only the best for all their patients.

Conclusion

Everybody has an idea what a child is. But the use of this term in a medical and legal context, and particularly at the intersection of medicine, law, clinical research and drug development uses the instinctive association of the term with small, immature children and vulnerable babies and young children to obscure the administrative side of the concept of children and childhood. The need for special caution in newborns is extended in regulations requiring separate repetition of drug trials in all minors, whether or not it is genuinely medically necessary. The mantra that children are not small adults and that in children everything is different is used shamelessly to convey to the medical layman and to lawmakers that the entire current machinery that drains billions of dollars, pounds or euros every year is based on solid science. An entire scientific discipline uses this impression to justify the pharmaceutical industry's continued funding of clinical trials with minors ("children"). The "pediatric population" is a modern term that reflects the changed position of children in our society during the last one to two centuries. This term has so far also helped to prevent a distinction between clinical research with young people that is really necessary and pseudo-scientifically justified "research" that exclusively or predominantly benefits careers that are not motivated by the desire for expansion of knowledge and insight, but by the desire for economic security in a framework in which "research" is perceived as something noble. This closes the loop on previous abuses in medical research. Those involved in the Tuskegee Study,[39,40] and in the academic experiments and clinical studies criticized by Beecher,[41] could do so with ease as long as official society accepted their activities unquestioningly as noble research.[42-44] It was only when these research activities were brought into the public eye that consequences were drawn.

References

1. National Research Council (US), Institute of Medicine (US). Children's Health, The Nation's Wealth: Assessing and Improving Child Health, 29 (National Academies Press, 2004). https://www.ncbi.nlm.nih.gov/books/NBK92206/pdf/Bookshelf_NBK92206.pdf

2. Hardin AP, Hackell JM. Committee on Practice and Ambulatory Medicine. Age limit of pediatrics. Pediatrics 2017;140(3):e20172151. https://pediatrics.aappublications.org/content/pediatrics/140/3/e20172151.full.pdf

3. International Council for Harmonisation of Technical Requirements for Pharmaceuticals for Human Use (ICH) Harmonised Guideline E11(R1). Clinical Investigations of Medicinal Products in the Pediatric Population. Final version, ICH 2017. https://database.ich.org/sites/default/files/E11_R1_Addendum.pdf

4. Canêo LF, Neirotti R. The Importance of the Proper Definition of Adulthood: What is and What is Not Included in a Scientific Publication. Braz J Cardiovasc Surg 2017;32(1):60-1. https://www.ncbi.nlm.nih.gov/pmc/articles/PMC5382900/pdf/rbccv-32-01-0060.pdf

5. Cone TE Jr. Secular acceleration of height. J Pediatr 1961 Nov;59: 736-40.

6. Komlos J, Lauderdale BE. The mysterious trend in American heights. Ann Hum Biol Mar-Apr 2007;34(2):206-15.

7. Beunen GP, Rogol AD, Malina RM. Indicators of biological maturation and secular changes in biological maturation. Food Nutr Bull. 2006;27(4 Suppl Growth Standard):S244–S256. https://journals.sagepub.com/doi/pdf/10.1177/15648265060274S508.

8. Ohlsson C, Bygdell M, Celind J, et al. Secular Trends in Pubertal Growth Acceleration in Swedish Boys Born From 1947 to 1996. JAMA Pediatr. 2019;173(9):860-865. https://jamanetwork.com/journals/jamapediatrics/fullarticle/2738259

9. Rose K. Intellectually Impaired People: The Ongoing Battle. Elsevier, London, UK, 2023

10. Wikipedia, Children’s literature https://en.wikipedia.org/wiki/Children’s_literature

11. Zelizer VA. Pricing the Priceless Child: The Changing Social Value of Children. Princeton University Press, Princeton, NJ, USA, 1994

12. Radbill SX. A History of Children's Hospitals. AMA Am J Dis Child. 1955;90(4):411-416

13. Colón AR, Colón PA. Nurturing children: a history of pediatrics. Greenwood Press, Westport, CT, USA 1999

14. Pappworth M. Human Guinea Pigs: Experimentation on Man. Routledge, London, UK, 1967

15. Mwale S. Healthy Volunteers in Commercial Clinical Drug Trials: When Human Beings Become Guinea Pigs. Palgrave Macmillan, Basingstoke, Hampshire, England, 2017

16. Rasmussen RM (Ed.) Human Guinea Pigs, by Kenneth Mellanby: A Reprint with Commentaries. Springer Nature Switzerland, Cham, Switzerland, 2020

17. Maxeiner S, Gebhardt S, Schweizer F, et al. Of mice and men - and guinea pigs? Ann Anat. 2021 Nov;238:151765

18. Van den Anker JN. Developmental Pharmacology. Dev Disabil Res Rev 2010;16(3):233-238

19. Van den Anker JN, Reed MD, Allegaert K, et al. Developmental Changes in Pharmacokinetics and Pharmacodynamics. J Clin Pharmacolog 2018 Oct;58(Suppl 10) S10–S25 https://accp1.onlinelibrary.wiley.com/doi/epdf/10.1002/jcph.1284

20. Smits A, Annaert P, Cavallaro G, et al. Current knowledge, challenges and innovations in developmental pharmacology: A combined conect4children Expert Group and European Society for Developmental, Perinatal and Paediatric Pharmacology White Paper. Br J Clin Pharmacol. 2022 Dec;88(12):4965-4984. https://www.ncbi.nlm.nih.gov/pmc/articles/PMC9787161/pdf/BCP-88-4965.pdf

21. Kearns GL, Abdel-Rahman SM, Alander SW, Blowey DL, Leeder JS, Kauffman RE, et al. Developmental pharmacology--drug disposition, action, and therapy in infants and children. N Engl J Med. 2003 Sep 18;349(12):1157-67.

22. Momper JD, Mulugeta Y, Green DJ, et al. Adolescent dosing and labeling since the Food and Drug Administration Amendments Act of 2007. JAMA Pediatr. 2013 Oct;167(10):926-32. https://jamanetwork.com/journals/jamapediatrics/fullarticle/1723817

23. Wikipedia, Anti-aging movement https://en.wikipedia.org/wiki/Anti-aging_movement

24. Wikipedia, American Academy of Anti-Aging Medicine https://en.wikipedia.org/wiki/American_Academy_of_Anti-Aging_Medicine

25. American Academy of Anti-Aging Medicine https://www.a4m.com/

26. Crane E, Tutag Lehr E, Mathew M, et al. Developmental Pharmacology and Therapeutics. In: Buonocore G, Bracci R, Weindling M (eds.). Neonatology. A Practical Approach to Neonatal Diseases. Springer Italy, Milano, Italy, 2012, Chapter 52

27. Evidence of harm from off-label or unlicensed medicines in children. EMA 2004. https://www.ema.europa.eu/en/documents/other/evidence-harm-label-unlicensed-medicines-children_en.pdf

28. Rocchi F, Paolucci P, Ceci A, et al. The European paediatric legislation: benefits and perspectives. Ital J Pediatr 2010 Aug 17;36:56. https://www.ncbi.nlm.nih.gov/pmc/articles/PMC2933611/pdf/1824-7288-36-56.pdf

29. Wilson G. Developmental Pharmacology. Anaesthesia & Intensive Care Medicine 2021;22(9),587-593

30. Schaller JG. The history of pediatric rheumatology. Pediatr Res. 2005 Nov;58(5):997-1007.

31. American Academy of Pediatrics (AAP): Guidelines for the Ethical Conduct of Studies to Evaluate Drugs in Pediatric Populations,

Committee on Drugs. American Academy of Pediatrics. Pediatrics, 1995 Feb;95(2):286-94

32. Shirkey H. Therapeutic Orphans. J Pediatr 1968 Jan; 72 (1), 119-120. https://pdfs.semanticscholar.org/f1cb/acdbac19fa56236b919fb7799eaacaa10c77.pdf

33. Regulation (EC) No. 1901/2006 Of The European Parliament and of the Council of 12 December 2006 on medicinal products for paediatric use and amending Regulation (EEC) No 1768/92, Directive 2001/20/EC, Directive 2001/83/EC and Regulation (EC) No 726/2004. https://eur-lex.europa.eu/legal-content/EN/TXT/PDF/?uri=CELEX:32006R1901&from=EN

34. EU Commission 2017: Report From The Commission To The European Parliament And The Council. State of Paediatric Medicines in the EU - 10 years of the EU Paediatric Regulation. https://ec.europa.eu/transparency/regdoc/rep/1/2017/EN/COM-2017-626-F1-EN-MAIN-PART-1.PDF

35. Flyer of the EU Commission 2017: State of Paediatric Medicines in the EU. 10 years of the EU Paediatric Regulation. Report from the Commission to the European Parliament and the Council. COM (2017) 626. https://ec.europa.eu/health/sites/health/files/files/paediatrics/docs/2017_childrensmedicines_report_en.pdf

36. European Medicines Agency (EMA): Better Medicines for Children. EMA 2015 https://www.ema.europa.eu/en/documents/leaflet/better-medicines-children_en.pdf

37. Nigrovic PA, Colbert RA, Holers VM, et al. Biological classification of childhood arthritis: roadmap to a molecular nomenclature. Nat Rev Rheumatol. 2021 May;17(5):257-269

38. Nigrovic PA, Raychaudhuri S, Thompson SD. Review: Genetics and the Classification of Arthritis in Adults and Children. Arthritis Rheumatol. 2018 Jan;70(1):7-17. https://onlinelibrary.wiley.com/doi/epdf/10.1002/art.40350

39. Adashi EY, Walters LB, Menikoff JA. The Belmont Report at 40: Reckoning With Time. Am J Public Health. 2018 Oct;108(10):1345-1348. https://www.ncbi.nlm.nih.gov/pmc/articles/PMC6137767/pdf/AJPH.2018.304580.pdf

40. Washington HA. Medical Apartheid: The Dark History of Medical Experimentation on Black Americans from Colonial Times to the Present. 2006, Doubleday Publishing Group, New York, NY, USA

41. Beecher HK. Ethics and clinical research. N Engl J Med. 1966 Jun 16;274(24):1354-60. https://www.observatoriobioetica.org/wp-content/uploads/2016/09/Beecher_Ethics_and_Clinical_Research_1966.pdf

42. Rose K. Blind Trust - How parents with a sick child can escape the labyrinth of lies, hypocrisy and false promises of researchers and regulatory authorities. Hammersmith, London, UK, 2022.

43. Rose K. Considering the Patient in Pediatric Drug Development. How good intentions turned into harm. Elsevier, London, UK, 2020.

44. Rose K, Grant-Kels JM, Striano P, Ettienne EB, Oishi T, Neubauer D. "Pediatric" Drug Studies Might Be the Largest Abuse in Medical Research in History. It Is Time for Lawyers to Step In. J Law Med 2023,30(1), in press

Chapter 4

Emergence of Pediatric Medicine in the 20th Century

The discovery of the importance of antisepsis in the late 19th century was one of the first major milestones in the development of modern medicine with hands-on practical consequences. It affected fundamentally the healthcare of both adults and children. There are numerous overview publications on the development of pediatrics as a whole, which we do not want to compete with. We focus on the contribution of modern drugs to the development of pediatrics. And since our special focus is the interface between drug development, drug approval and the role of modern drugs in daily therapeutic treatment, we discuss in the following some key areas in which pediatric medicine has made astronomical progress in the 20th century.

Surgery

Surgery plays a major role in many areas in pediatric medical care, including emergency surgery, organ transplantation, orthopedics, plastic & reconstructive surgery, and many more. In the following, we discuss just two key example areas: surgical treatment of trauma and accidents, and the treatment of congenital heart disease.

In the first decades of the 20th century, most cities had a convalescent home for children with rheumatic fever. They were treated by general pediatricians. Specialty clinics emerged, and children with heart sounds (that required a stethoscope to detect) were mostly followed up in a rheumatic fever clinic. Pediatricians with an interest in cardiology but little training saw children with rheumatic heart disease, unproblematic heart sounds, and some with congenital heart disease. Although it had been recognized that inflammation of the throat (pharyngitis) often preceded acute rheumatic fever, only in the middle of the 20th century the crucial role of the bacterium streptococcus in its pathogenesis was confirmed. Overcrowding and generally bad conditions had allowed streptococcal infections to flourish. Better hygiene, nutrition, and living conditions helped reduce the number of infections including the incidence of rheumatic fever. Then first the discovery and then the industrial production and broad availability of sulfonamide, penicillin, and further antibiotics allowed streptococcal infections to be treated effectively. With this prophylaxis, recurrent episodes of rheumatic fever could now be prevented. With the triumph over rheumatic fever, congenital heart disease became the predominant form of heart disease in children.[1]

As long as the baby lives in the womb, the mother takes care of the oxygen supply to her child. The baby's heart beats very early and pumps blood throughout the child's body. But the lungs are not yet connected to the outside world. The child is not breathing yet. The mother does that for the child. The mother's blood is enriched with oxygen in her lungs. It flows through the placenta into the child, where it is distributed throughout the body. The worn out, now oxygen-poor blood then flows back to the mother via the placenta, back into her lungs, where it is again enriched with oxygen. As long as the baby lives in the womb, there is also an extra vessel linking the two main vessels that go from the heart to the lungs and into the main body. This extra vessel allows most of the blood from the main pumping chamber to bypass the lungs that are not yet engaged in the oxygen enriching business. Usually, this vessel, called the arterial duct, closes at birth. As long as the child lives in the womb, also children with malformations of the heart and/or the large central blood vessels live comfortably. But that changes abruptly the moment the child is born.

If the valve that controls the blood flow from the heart's main pumping chamber, the left ventricle, to the main artery, the aorta, is narrowed, this may result in the left ventricle muscle thickening because it has to work harder. This is called aortic valve stenosis. If the aorta itself is narrowed, this can also impede the blood flow. Also, the valve that controls the blood flow from the right ventricle to the lungs can be narrowed. Then the right ventricle has to pump harder. There can be a hole between the two collecting chambers of the heart (atrial defect), or the two main pumping chambers (ventricular septal defect). In these cases, normal blood flow is disrupted, and the heart has to work much harder than if everything were normal. Also, if the arterial duct does not close, it can cause similar problems, comparable to those where there is a hole between the two collecting chambers or the two main pumping chambers. There are many other forms of congenital heart malformations. Altogether they are rather rare. They can have genetic causes. Children with trisomy 21 have relatively often congenital heart malformations, and there are many more genetic causes. Other causes can be viral infections of the mother during pregnancy; if the mother smokes or drinks alcohol during pregnancy; if the mother has diabetes mellitus; and more. Many cases of congenital heart disease are today diagnosed before birth by ultrasound. But in the beginning of the 20th century ultrasound diagnostic did not yet exist.

If congenital heart defects are mild, such as small holes between the heart's two normally separated pumping chambers or collecting chambers, they often do not have to be treated, as they may improve on their own. On the other side, surgery and/ or other interventional procedures are needed if the defect is significant, causes problems immediately after birth, and there is no hope that the situation will improve on its own. Modern surgical techniques can often restore most or all of the heart's normal function.[2-4]

The first attempts to operatively correct congenital heart disease began in the early 20th century. As with all complex challenges, it required courage from the performing surgeon, and the willingness not to give up after initial failures. Today corrective surgery can be performed at a very young age with considerable good long-term results.[5] Without the invention of the heart-lung machine, the availability of antibiotics, of effective anaesthetic agents, of modern biologics such as erythropoietin, and a number of further innovations today's routine correcture of many congenital heart malformations would not have been possible. Guidelines for pediatric cardiology training were rapidly developed, and in 1961, pediatric cardiology became the first sub-board of pediatrics to be formed.[1] Progress in pediatric anaesthesia and microsurgical techniques allowed in the 20th century increasingly the treatment of challenges of congenital heart malformations that would have been unthinkable decades earlier.[6] By the way, it was a woman, Helen Taussig, who established pediatric cardiology. In her career, she had to overcome many hurdles. In 1921, she was denied admission to the Harvard Medical School because she was a woman. She took then classes at Boston University, where she had to sit apart from her male colleagues at the back of the lecture theaters and was not supposed to speak to them. Eventually, she completed her MD at the John Hopkins university. She had wanted to specialize in internal medicine, but the one position available for a woman was already taken. So she opted for pediatrics, ended up in pediatric cardiology, a field that was still in its infancy, and eventually wrote the first textbook on pediatric cardiology that incorporated hemodynamic principles.[7-10]

While surgical treatment of congenital heart malformations represents an early success story of pediatric healthcare and is on this basis of high historical interest, our other area of interest is surgery in accidents & emergency. To this day, the most common cause of death among young people after the age of one year is accidents, (and not cancer and other malignancies).[11,12] Without good accident care, patient transport and availability of surgical intervention, the number of deaths by accidents would be much higher.

The initial experimental surgical interventions and the first use of the drugs without which they would not have been possible were not based on a pediatric approval of the drugs used. It was the other way around. The first major advances in pediatric surgery came from pioneers using the surgical techniques, machines, and drugs then available without making much of a difference as to whether the patient was operated on was older or younger than 18 years of age. Towards the end of the 20th century, the death rate from several major congenital malformation syndromes has gone down to almost zero.

Cancer and other malignancies

With the increasing prevention of infectious diseases, a number of specific childhood diseases came into the focus of medical research which in the years, decades, centuries and millennia before had not been given much attention in the sea of many infant deaths. One of these disease groups were malignant diseases, i.e., cancer, leukemia and others. Malignancies had previously been known to occur in adults, but with improved communication, mobility, advances in diagnostics, technology, & more it was gradually recognized that malignancies also exist in young people. But when the first wards for children with cancer opened in the mid-20th century, there was no effective treatment. There was not much more that could be done than giving the little patients painkillers including acetylsalicylic acid (aspirin), opiates, consoling the parents and distracting the children.

First successes in treating pediatric malignancies did not come with the development of new drugs. On the contrary. Adult cancer treatment had advanced with the use of surgery, chemotherapy and radiation. Initial successes in young patients were achieved with the use of chemotherapeutic drugs in leukemia. The chemotherapeutic treatment was refined until the most common malignant disease in childhood, acute lymphoblastic leukemia (ALL), could be successfully treated with an eventual survival rate of 90%. This track record has brought tremendous prestige to pediatric oncology. But what is crucial from our particular point of view is that the drugs used to treat it had already been approved for treating adult cancer for decades. The pioneers of pediatric oncology used what was available to them.[13-16] Pediatric oncology emerged as an own discipline of pediatric medicine unnoticed by the regulatory authorities. To put it pointedly, pediatric oncology evolved "off-label" decades before the term off-label even existed. This term first appeared in the literature in 1988.[17]

Vaccines and vaccination

Vaccines protect against viral infections. Their introduction has revolutionized the prevention of viral infectious diseases and has made a massive contribution to reducing child mortality. The COVID-19 pandemic has recently shown us once again how much modern society depends on the prevention of viral infections and the importance of combining cutting-edge science with industrial production of vaccines. The small German company BioNTech originally worked on the development of therapeutic messenger RNA (mRNA) vaccines against various types of malignant diseases. With the COVID-19 pandemic, the company re-focused, partnered with the giant company Pfizer, and successfully developed the first truly effective mRNA vaccine against the corona virus. Russia and China developed their own vaccines, hoping for global diplomatic successes by promoting them worldwide, and then failed miserably because their effectiveness was significantly worse than the mRNA vaccines, because they could not produce enough vaccines fast enough, and because their clinical trials did not meet modern standards.

In the early months of the pandemic, it was thought that C-19 would not affect young people. That assessment quickly changed. The FDA quickly cleared a number of drugs to treat C-19. As in all other areas of medicine, the EMA required pediatric investigation plans (PIPs) for all C-19 drugs and vaccines as if young people under the age of 18 were a different species. BioNTech/Pfizer conducted the pivotal studies of their vaccine in people 16 years and older, most other companies in those 18 years and older. Younger patients were denied vaccination until separate vaccine trials had been conducted in "children," which medically and scientifically did not make sense, but was in line with prevailing regulatory requirements. While the FDA published dosing recommendations for many drugs also for very young patients, the EMA insisted on separate "pediatric" studies in numerous PIPs.[18,19] Hopefully, as the pandemic subsided, most parents will have refused to let their children participate in these questionable studies.

Vaccines are being developed since more than hundred years. Most modern vaccines have been developed in the 20th century, many of them in children. The additional requirement for "pediatric investigation plans" (PIPs) is nothing is nothing but an extra bureaucratic burden on vaccine developers, without any additional benefit for young people. It may increase the feeling of self-importance for the involved employees of the EMA. Clinically and scientifically, these PIPs are pointless.

Rheumatology

When a joint is inflamed, this is called arthritis. The joint and its surroundings hurt, the joint is swollen and becomes stiffer. There are more than hundred different types of arthritis: just one joint with a local inflammation; a few joints; or many joints with an underlying systemic inflammatory disease that can also affect other organs.[20] Rheumatic arthritis which affects adults begins mostly when the patient is 30 to 50 years old, but it can also begin earlier or later. With improvements in hygiene, nutrition, clothing, housing, vaccinations, more infectious diseases being prevented, a range of diseases started to be looked at more closely. These diseases had not previously been systematically observed because too many children had died of contracted infectious diseases. One of the newly investigated disease groups were a group of inflammations of joints and tissue which started in young people, in contrast to the common rheumatoid arthritis. These specific diseases were initially observed only in young people, and researchers assumed they were pediatric diseases. The North American Pediatric Rheumatology Collaborative Study Group (PRCSG) was established in 1973, and became a clinical trials network that performed clinical trials of new therapies for young people with rheumatic diseases.[21,22] For several decades, treatment of pain and inflammation had relied predominantly on acetylsalicylic acid (aspirin), which had been manufactured since the turn of the century,[23] and was widely prescribed for chronic inflammations of all sorts, including those in young patients.[24] Eventually, new types of non-steroidal anti-inflammatory drugs (NSAIDS) were developed beyond aspirin. Now dedicated investigators started to collaborate in North America in the early 1970s to examine their efficacy and safety also in young patients. The PRCSG performed the first study that compared the NSAID tolmetin with aspirin in young patients.

At the beginning, the terms "juvenile rheumatoid arthritis" and "juvenile chronic arthritis" were used to describe chronic painful inflammations in young patients. The term "juvenile idiopathic arthritis" (JIA) was established in 1995 by the International League of Associations for Rheumatology (ILAR) to provide a framework to describe the different types of chronic arthritis that begins in childhood. Today, JIA is an umbrella term referring to a heterogeneous group of diseases characterised by arthritis of unknown origin with onset before age of 16 years. Clinically, the diagnosis JIA is made if a person that is up to 15 years old suffers from arthritis, defined as swelling or limitation of motion of the joint accompanied by heat, pain, or tenderness for at least 6 weeks, after other identifiable causes of arthritis have been excluded. JIA is at present divided into six subtypes (it used to be seven until a few years ago). Its main characteristic is joint inflammation with tissue destruction. It is not completely understood how environmental triggers and genetic susceptibility interplay, disrupting the balance in the body's immune system.

Disease-modifying antirheumatic drugs (DMARDs) are a group of chemically unrelated disease-modifying drugs used in rheumatoid arthritis to slow down disease progression. The term is often used in contrast to nonsteroidal anti-inflammatory drugs (NSAIDs), agents that treat the inflammation, but not the underlying cause, and steroids, which suppress the immune response but cannot slow down the progression of the disease.[25] DMARDs include synthetic DMARDs such as methotrexate and many more, and biologic DMARDs, including T-cell inhibitors, anti-Tumor Necrosis Factor (TNF)α agents, Interleukin (IL)1 and IL6 blockers, tyrosin kinase inhibitors such as Janus Kinase (JAK) inhibitors, and more. DMARDs have significantly improved the clinical management of JIA. [26-32]

Adult and pediatric rheumatology have developed different disease classifications that, however, in several diseases describe the identical disease under different names, depending on its diagnoses before and after the 16th birthday. This is well known in the world of clinical specialists,[31-34] but to change international classifications of diseases once they have been established takes years.[15,16] In the US, the Center for Adults with Pediatric Rheumatic Illness (CAPRI) offers advice and treatment for patients that were diagnosed in childhood with JIA, have in the meantime grown up, and are often misdiagnosed and treated not correctly by adult rheumatologists.[35-37]

Unlike pediatric oncology, for pediatric rheumatology there were no drugs already developed and approved when types of arthritis were recognized that can begin already in young people. Aspirin and early synthetic types of DMARDs could slow down the inflammatory process and relieve pain and other symptoms to a certain extent, but they could not significantly influence the course of the disease. A generation ago, many young people with a chronic arthritis had to expect a lifetime of pain and disability. When the joints of the face were affected, is could also lead to external disfigurement. Today, the outlook for young patients has massively improved thanks to modern biologic DMARDs.[38,39]

Modern biologics were not specifically developed for pediatric disease. They were developed in the process of increasing understanding of inflammatory processes and the resulting developments of modern biological medicines. The monoclonal antibody canacinumab against interleukin 1 beta (IL-1β) was for example initially developed in the hope to develop a further drug that would help in rheumatoid arthritis. But the clinical response was not sufficient. Then the team searched for further indications in which its antibody might be of use. They were successful and identified a number of rare diseases caused by an overproduction of IL-β that previously had been known only to clinical specialists, including crypoyrin associated periodic syndrome (CAPS); systemic JIA (sJIA) and its adult form, Adult Onset Still's Disease; mevalonate kinase deficiency (MKD), TNF Receptor Associates Periodic Syndrome (TRAPS), and Familial Mediterranean Fever (FMF). Canakinumab is highly effective in disorders triggered by an overproduction of IL-1β, and is now development for further diseases.[40]

Depression

Depression is a common and serious medical illness that negatively affects how you feel, the way you think and how you act. Fortunately, it is also treatable. Depression causes feelings of sadness and/or a loss of interest in activities you once enjoyed. It can lead to a variety of emotional and physical problems and can decrease your ability to function at work and at home. Symptoms include feeling sad , loss of interest or pleasure in activities once enjoyed, changes in appetite, sleeping too much or too little, loss of energy or fatigue, increase in purposeless physical activity, feeling worthless or guilty, difficulty thinking, concentrating or making decisions, and thoughts of death or suicide.[41]

It is completely normal to be sad for a specific reason, such as having lost a job, a friend, a husband, wife or child, & more. The difference between being sad and being depressed is that being sad reflects a specific reason or a bunch of reasons, while in depression sadness has taken on a life of its own and is an expression of an illness.

Depression is a fascinating area of illness that still in the early 20th century was characterized more by myths and superstition than by scientific analysis and understanding. Depression was then called "melancholy". The term "melancholy" combines two roots from classical Greek: mélas (μέλας) for black, and cholé (χολή) for bile. The mainstream scholarly belief was based on the theories of psychoanalysis. It regarded melancholy as the manifestation of internal conflicts that had their roots in the childhood of the respective patient. Psychoanalytic therapy tries to make the underlying unconscious tensions accessible to the patient's and the therapist's consciousness, assuming that this will help to reduce and finally solve the internal tensions. There is a myriad of different psychoanalytic theories around, of which none can be scientifically proven and therefore can also not be disproved. Either you believe in it, or not. That is not science. Furthermore, as a psychoanalysis takes several years, the costs of treatment were for most people an unsurmountable obstacle.

Babies cry often, but they are not depressed. They cannot yet speak, but they can communicate. In order to become depressed, the brain needs a certain maturity. Forty years ago, academic science was deeply convinced that depression did not exist in minors.[42] This is one of the many myths about childhood that medicine and science had to overcome. Today we know that depression can also occur before the 18th birthday.[43,44]

In the 1950s a revolution occurred with the development of drugs that could treat depression. Several groups of effective antidepressants emerged.[45] One of the many prerequisites for this was that the symptoms of depression were made measurable so that an improvement in the symptoms could be documented. This, in turn, was the prerequisite for conducting clinical trials involving many patients cared for by different doctors in different centers. This made it possible to systematically investigate the effectiveness of medication in depression.

Depression is a horrible and very complex disease. It is a combination of a misperception of the environment, an erroneous negative self-esteem, and many other factors. An imbalance of neurotransmitters in the brain is involved. But the existing antidepressants do not allow for a miracle cure. The more grounded a young person is through upbringing and attachment to parents, solid education, and having received the fundaments for a healthy self-confidence, the greater the chance that gradual improvement can occur over time. There are many different therapeutic tools in this healing process, including antidepressants; oral therapies in various forms; meaningful activities, group therapy, friends, sports, and much more.

Depression and other diseases do not change their characteristics with the 18th birthday.

Conclusion

Today's well-established pediatric sub-disciplines emerged during the 20th century. In all of them the increasing availability of modern effective drugs played a key role, as did other aspects of technical innovation, beginning from the availability of baby warmers, stethoscope, X-rays, ultrasound, modern imaging methods, measuring brain waves, electrocardiography, and many more, as well as improved communication, transport, & more. All pioneering physicians who advanced pediatric healthcare did so with a hands-on practical approach. The regulatory authorities and the separate approval of drugs in minors did not play a major role in the emergence of pediatric healthcare during the 20th century. If approved drugs were already around, they were used by pioneers also for young patients, as this was the case in pediatric oncology. If no effective medicines were yet around, as this was the case in the early days of pediatric rheumatology, all the clinicians and researchers could do was to prescribe those drugs that were of limited use, such as aspirin and later other NSAIDs and DMARDs. Most of the historical overviews over specific aspects of the history of pediatric subdisciplines do not even mention the need for separate pediatric approval of drugs.[1,6,13,46-55] They all assume correctly that the respective treating physicians and pediatricians knew what they were doing.

There is one academic discipline whose proponents have been praised by the regulatory authorities on numerous occasions: pediatric rheumatology.[56,57] There is probably no other clinical area of academic research where the organisations that focused on clinical studies in "children" have profited as much from "pediatric drug development" as did the organisation focusing on "juvenile idiopathic arthritis" (JIA).[22,58] We discuss the reasons for this more in depth in chapter 7 (questionable pediatric studies) and in chapter 13 (new types of conflict of interest).

During the 20th century, there was never a crisis in pediatric medicine that would have needed a systematic intervention by the state. Such interventions occurred for medical reasons with the thalidomide disaster, and for ethical reasons with Beecher's revelations of many unethical academic clinical trials in the US in 1966,[59] and finally with the exposure of the Tuskegee study, which was then quickly terminated.[60-62]

The state intervention in the interface of drug development, drug approval, and pediatric healthcare was enacted in the US as FDAMA in 1997, followed in the ensuing years by several more pediatric pharmaceutical legislation, and was then taken up, copied and expanded by the European Union (EU) with the EU pediatric regulation, which came into force in 2007. These laws were not triggered by actual catastrophes, but by the alleged threat of impending and potential catastrophes pronounced by a group of scientists and researchers that eventually managed to get the support of the regulatory authorities and later of the law makers. Just like you can paint the devil on the wall even if the devil does not exist.

References

1. Noonan JA. A history of pediatric specialties: the development of pediatric cardiology. Pediatr Res 2004 Aug;56(2):298-306.
2. National Health System (NHS). Congenital heart disease. https://www.nhs.uk/conditions/congenital-heart-disease/
3. National Health System (NHS). Types of congenital heart disease. https://www.nhs.uk/conditions/congenital-heart-disease/types/
4. Centers for Disease control and prevention (CDC). Congenital heart defects. https://www.cdc.gov/ncbddd/heartdefects
5. Castañeda A. Congenital heart disease: a surgical-historical perspective. Ann Thorac Surg 2005 Jun;79(6):S2217-20. 10.1016/j.athoracsur.2005.03.031
6. Colón AR, Colón PA. Nurturing children: a history of pediatrics. Greenwood Press, Westport, CT, USA 1999
7. Taegtmeyer H. Helen Taussig. Tex Heart Inst J. 2010; 37(2): 254. https://www.ncbi.nlm.nih.gov/pmc/articles/PMC2851418/pdf/20100400s00032p254.pdf
8. Wikipedia, Helen B Taussig https://en.wikipedia.org/wiki/Helen_B._Taussig
9. Karl TR, Martin GR, Jacobs JP, et al. Key events in the history of cardiac surgery and paediatric cardiology. Cardiol Young. 2017 Dec;27(10):2029-2062.
10. Chang JH. Timelines in the history of pediatric surgery. J Pediatr Surg. 1986 Dec;21(12):1068-72.
11. US Centers for Disease control and prevention (CDC). Leading causes of death and injury. https://www.cdc.gov/injury/wisqars/LeadingCauses.html
12. US Centers for Disease control and prevention (CDC). Ten leading causes of death by age group, United States – 2018 https://www.cdc.gov/injury/wisqars/pdf/leading_causes_of_death_by_age_group_2018-508.pdf

13. Adamson PC. Improving the outcome for children with cancer: Development of targeted new agents. CA Cancer J Cli 2015 May-Jun; 65(3), 212-20

14. DeVita VT Jr, Chu E. A history of cancer chemotherapy. Cancer Res. 2008 Nov 1;68(21):8643-53. http://cancerres.aacrjournals.org/content/68/21/8643.full-text.pdf

15. Rose K. Blind Trust - How parents with a sick child can escape the labyrinth of lies, hypocrisy and false promises of researchers and regulatory authorities. Hammersmith, London, UK, 2022.

16. Rose K. Considering the Patient in Pediatric Drug Development. How good intentions turned into harm. Elsevier, London, UK, 2020.

17. Plate V. The Impact of Off-Label, Compassionate and Unlicensed Use on Health Care Laws in preselected Countries. https://bonndoc.ulb.uni-bonn.de/xmlui/bitstream/handle/20.500.11811/4152/1936.pdf

18. Rose K, Grant-Kels JM, Ettienne E, Tanjinatus E, Striano P, Neubauer D. COVID-19 and Treatment and Immunization of Children – The Time to Redefine Pediatric Age Groups is Here. Rambam Maimonides Med J. 2021. Online first, https://www.rmmj.org.il/userimages/1187/1/PublishFiles/1209OnlineFirst.pdf

19. Rose K. The COVID-19 Pandemic: A Global High-Tech Challenge at the Interface of Science, Politics, and Illusions. Elsevier, London, UK, 2022 https://www.elsevier.com/books/the-covid-19-pandemic/rose/978-0-323-99149-0

20. US Centers for Disease control and prevention (CDC). Arthritis types. 2022. https://www.cdc.gov/arthritis/types/index.html

21. Brunner HI, Rider LG, Kingsbury DJ, Co D, Schneider R, Goldmuntz E, et al. Pediatric Rheumatology Collaborative Study Group - over four decades of pivotal clinical drug research in pediatric rheumatology. Pediatr Rheumatol Online J. 2018 Jul 11;16(1):45.

22. Pediatric Rheumatology Study Group (PRCSG) https://web.prcsg.org/

23. Desborough MJR, Keeling DM. The aspirin story – from willow to wonder drug. Br J Haematol 2017 Jun;177(5):674-683. https://onlinelibrary.wiley.com/doi/epdf/10.1111/bjh.14520

24. Levinson LE, Baum J, Brewer E Jr., et al. Comparison of tolmetin sodium and aspirin in the treatment of juvenile rheumatoid arthritis. J Pediatr 1977 Nov;91(5):799-804

25. Wikipedia, Disease modifying antirheumatic drug https://en.wikipedia.org/wiki/Disease-modifying_antirheumatic_drug

26. Weiss JE, Ilowite NT. Juvenile idiopathic arthritis. Pediatr Clin North Am. 2005 Apr;52(2):413-42,

27. Prakken B, Albani S, Martini A. Juvenile idiopathic arthritis. Lancet. 2011 Jun 18;377(9783):2138-49.

28. Ravelli A, Martini A. Juvenile idiopathic arthritis. Lancet. 2007 Mar 3;369(9563):767-778.

29. Zaripova LN, Midgley A, Christmas SE, et al. Juvenile idiopathic arthritis: from aetiopathogenesis to therapeutic approaches. Pediatr Rheumatol Online J. 2021 Aug 23;19(1):135. https://www.ncbi.nlm.nih.gov/pmc/articles/PMC8383464/pdf/12969_2021_Article_629.pdf

30. Arthritis Foundation: Juvenile Idiopathic Arthritis https://www.arthritis.org/diseases/juvenile-idiopathic-arthritis

31. Martini A, Ravelli A, Avcin T, et al. Toward New Classification Criteria for Juvenile Idiopathic Arthritis: First Steps, Pediatric Rheumatology International Trials Organization International Consensus. J Rheumatol. 2019 Feb;46(2):190-197. https://www.jrheum.org/content/jrheum/46/2/190.full.pdf

32. Martini A, Lovell DJ, Albani S et al. Juvenile idiopathic arthritis. Nat Rev Dis Primers. 2022 Jan 27;8(1):5

33. Nigrovic PA, Raychaudhuri S, Thompson SD. Review: Genetics and the Classification of Arthritis in Adults and Children. Arthritis Rheumatol. 2018 Jan;70(1):7-17. https://onlinelibrary.wiley.com/doi/epdf/10.1002/art.40350

34. Nigrovic PA, Colbert RA, Holers VM, et al. Biological classification of childhood arthritis: roadmap to a molecular nomenclature. Nat Rev Rheumatol. 2021 May;17(5):257-269.

35. Center for Adults with Pediatric Rheumatic Illness (CAPRI) https://www.brighamandwomens.org/medicine/rheumatology-inflammation-immunity/services/pediatric-rheumatology-for-adults

36. Nigrovic PA 2013 What Adult Rheumatologists Need to Know about Juvenile Arthritis. https://www.the-rheumatologist.org/article/what-adult-rheumatologists-need-to-know-about-juvenile-arthritis/

37. Nigrovic PA, White PH. Care of the adult with juvenile rheumatoid arthritis. Arthritis Rheum. 2006 Apr 15;55(2):208-16. https://onlinelibrary.wiley.com/doi/pdf/10.1002/art.21857

38. Stoll ML, Cron RQ. Treatment of juvenile idiopathic arthritis: a revolution in care. Pediatr Rheumatol Online J. 2014 Apr 23;12:13. https://www.ncbi.nlm.nih.gov/pmc/articles/PMC4003520/pdf/1546-0096-12-13.pdf

39. Schaller JG. The history of pediatric rheumatology. Pediatr Res. 2005 Nov;58(5):997-1007.

40. Gram H. The long and winding road in pharmaceutical development of canakinumab from rare genetic autoinflammatory syndromes to myocardial infarction and cancer. Pharmacol Res. 2019 Jan 14. pii: S1043-6618(18)31983-2. https://www.sciencedirect.com/science/article/pii/S1043661818319832

41. American Psychiatric Association (APA). What is depression? https://www.psychiatry.org/patients-families/depression/what-is-depression

42. Varley CK. Treating depression in children and adolescents: what options now? CNS Drugs 2006;20(1):1_13.

43. Ogundele MO. Behavioural and emotional disorders in childhood: A brief overview for paediatricians. World J Clin Pediatr 2018 Feb 8;7(1):9-26 https://www.ncbi.nlm.nih.gov/pmc/articles/PMC5803568/pdf/WJCP-7-9.pdf

44. Brent DA, Maalouf FT. Pediatric depression: is there evidence to improve evidence-based treatments? J Child Psychol Psychiatry. 2009 Jan;50(1-2):143-52.
https://www.ncbi.nlm.nih.gov/pmc/articles/PMC4071452/pdf/nihms-601246.pdf

45. López-Muñoz F, Alamo C. Monoaminergic Neurotransmission: The History of the Discovery of Antidepressants from 1950s Until Today. Curr Pharm Des. 2009;15(14):1563-86.
https://www.researchgate.net/publication/24427266_Monoaminergic_Neurotransmission_The_History_of_the_Discovery_of_Antidepressants_from_1950s_Until_Today

46. Mai CL, Coté CJ. A history of pediatric anaesthesia: a tale of pioneers and equipment. Paediatr Anaesth 2012 Jun;22(6):511-20.

47. McGrath PJ. Science is not enough: the modern history of pediatric pain. Pain. 2011 Nov;152(11):2457-2459.

48. Hillhouse TM, Porter JH. A brief history of the development of antidepressant drugs: From monoamines to glutamate. Exp Clin Psychopharmacol. 2015 Feb;23(1):1-21.
https://www.ncbi.nlm.nih.gov/pmc/articles/PMC4428540/pdf/nihms667554.pdf

49. Philip AG. The evolution of neonatology. Pediatr Res. 2005 Oct;58(4):799-815.
https://www.nature.com/articles/pr2005743.pdf?origin=ppub

50. Rees GJ. Paediatric anaesthesia--past, present and future. Z Kinderchir. 1987 Apr;42(2):67-80.

51. Chesney RW. The development of pediatric nephrology. Pediatr Res. 2002 Nov;52(5):770-8

52. Hertz S. 2016. Analgesic developments for pediatric patients. Available from:
https://www.fda.gov/downloads/AdvisoryCommittees/CommitteesMeetingMaterials/PediatricAdvisoryCommittee/UCM495096.pdf

53. Rees GJ. Paediatric anaesthesia--past, present and future. Z Kinderchir. 1987 Apr;42(2):67-80.

54. Brown TC. The child in hospital--changes in the last 50 years Paediatr Anaesth. 2013 Jun;23(6):565-6. doi: 10.1111/pan.12150.

55. Baker JP, Katz SL. Childhood vaccine development: an overview. Pediatr Res 2004 Feb;55(2):347-56. doi: 10.1203/01.PDR.0000106317.36875.6A. https://www.nature.com/articles/pr200452

56. Ruperto N, Eichler I, Herold R, et al. A European Network of Paediatric Research at the European Medicines Agency (Enpr-EMA). Arch Dis Child. 2012 Mar;97(3):185-8.

57. Ruperto N, Vesely R, Saint-Raymond A, Martini A, for the Paediatric Rheumatology International Trials Organisation (PRINTO). Impact of the European paediatric legislation in paediatric rheumatology: past, present and future. Ann Rheum Dis 2013;72:1893–1896.

58. PRINTO - Paediatric Rheumatology International Trials Organisation www.printo.it

59. Beecher HK. Ethics and clinical research. N Engl J Med. 1966 Jun 16; 274(24):1354-60. https://www.observatoriobioetica.org/wp-content/uploads/2016/09/Beecher_Ethics_and_Clinical_Research_1966.pdf

60. Washington HA. Medical Apartheid. The Dark History of Medical Experimentation on Black Americans from Colonial Times to the Presen. Anchor Books (Random House), New York, NY, USA 2006

61. Jones JH. Bad Blood. The Tuskegee Syphilis Experiment. The modern classic of race and medicine update with an additional chapter on the Tuskegee Experiment's legacy in the age of AIDS. The Free Press (Simon & Schuster), New York, NY, USA, 1981

62. US Centers for Disease control and prevention (CDC). The U.S. Public Health Service Syphilis Study at Tuskegee. CDC 2023. https://www.cdc.gov/tuskegee/index.html

Chapter 5

The Thalidomide Disaster Triggers Modern Drug Development

Effective medicines do not fall from heaven like manna did in the Old Testament.[1] Drug development today is no longer the research for and production of hopefully helpful substances by individual research pioneers in simple laboratories. The idea to synthesize a specific substance or to develop a monoclonal antibody or receptor blocker for a specific receptor or any other biological structure may come from an individual, but drug development has become a process at the interface of science, commerce, approval, clinical trials and other, earlier, "pre-clinical" investigations. In this book we focus on children in the framework of drug development, and in this context specifically on clinical studies in minors.

Drug development could only arise on the basis of evolving science and industrialization, coupled with improved communications, improved transportation, and better medical understanding of ever more profound disease contexts. But the most important new element was the control of a government institution over the efficacy and safety of newly developed therapeutic substances. This need contradicted the classic liberal understanding of economics, which grants the individual the competence to make purchasing decisions for whatever. However, the medical layperson is overburdened by assessing medical risks of medicinal products that reflect a complex development process. Nobody can see with the naked eye which side effects a single drug might have and which side effects it has already shown in the past. The assessment of the danger of a given newly developed substance is beyond the horizon of a single scientist or observer. Comparatively common side effects of a new drug can be observed and classified early and easily, but side effects that affect, say, one in a thousand people can easily slip through the net of observation in clinical trials. In addition, the therapeutic context is important. Cytotoxic substances are used in cancer and other malignancies *because* they are toxic. For every drug, a cost-benefit analysis is required that massively exceeds the horizon of the individual.

Two disasters played key roles in the development of this government oversight. The first was with Sulfanilamide Elixir, a liquid formulation of sulfanilamide, an early type of antibiotic. It led in the US to the death of a more than 100 people in 1937 who died of diethylene glycol poisoning after having consumed Sulfanilamide Elixir, for which diethylene glycol had been used as a solvent. There had not been any safety testing. Diethylene glycol is a widely used solvent, but it is rather toxic and it may be contained in food only in very low concentrations. It does not kill everybody exposed to it, but many, specifically those that are very young or are not very healthy. Many of those that died in the Sulfanilamide Elixir catastrophe were children. This disaster was still "local" as it occurred "only" in the US. It led to the introduction of the US Federal Food, Drug and Cosmetic Act (FDCA) of 1938, which brought cosmetics and medical devices under the control of the FDA. It required that drugs be labeled with adequate directions for safe use. Moreover, it mandated pre-market approval of all new drugs. Manufacturers had now to prove to FDA that a drug were safe before it could be sold. It also prohibited false therapeutic claims for drugs.[2-5]

The second disaster was already international and affected people in almost every country in the world.

Thalidomide had been developed by the German company Grünenthal as a tranquillizer, was believed to be very safe and was marketed as such. From 1957 to 1961 it was promoted for anxiety, insomnia, nervousness, and morning sickness, which often occurs in pregnancy. In these days, nobody could imagine that an apparently harmless tablet could do serious harm. In these days, drugs were tested for toxicity only on rodents, but not for teratogenic effects. Despite early observations of potential dangers it took almost four years until the connection between the increased number of birth defects and thalidomide was made. The German pediatrician Widukind Lenz interviewed in 1961 twenty mothers of children who had been born with deformed limbs. He inquired about the history and circumstances of their pregnancies, inspected together with the mothers their medicine chest, and interviewed the doctors who had looked after them during their pregnancy. He concluded that thalidomide was the cause of the malformations and presented his findings at a medical conference. A week later, the German newspaper "Welt am Sonntag" informed its readers. The next day the drug was taken from the market - in Germany. In several other countries the sales of thalidomide continued for a while. Thalidomide had in Germany been sold over the counter (OTC), which led to much higher sales and affected many more babies than in the other countries where a prescription by a physician was required. Apart from causing externally visible deformities, thalidomide affects during pregnancy also internal organ development, including tissues that later form eyes, ears, face, cardiovascular system, gastrointestinal system, reproductive system, urinary system, and the spine. Due to internal malformations of internal organs, probably 40% of those babies that survived thalidomide intake by their mothers at all died in their first year of life. All in all, the thalidomide epidemic affected at least 10,000 and possibly up to 100,000 persons, not even counting those that were affected so strongly in an early stage of pregnancy that the child did not develop further and was spontaneously aborted.[6-8]

In the 1950s, drug development was in a very early stage. Few laws or no laws at all governed drug development and marketing. Grünenthal was a subsidiary of a soap and cosmetics manufacturer.

Synthetic drugs were something new and were perceived as an opportunity for significant financial reward. The 1950s were also the years of the sleeping pill, with one in eight prescriptions being against insomnia. Most countries did not have an independent assessment of safety and efficacy. In the years preceding the release of thalidomide, many other compounds in early stages of development had been shown to affect the fetus in the womb, either killing many or inducing malformations. The concept of drug induced harm to the fetus existed already. However, animal testing was not mandated, and it was left to the rigor and discipline of individual companies to perform suitable testing. Grünenthal had chosen not to do so. When warning signals emerged, Grünenthal and other companies that in the meantime sold thalidomide worldwide under 51 different tradenames were reluctant to admit its dangers and blocked attempts to take it from the market. When finally it was removed from the market in Germany, the international withdrawal was not coordinated. Many malformations still occurred in Japan. Sales in Italy continued for ten months after removal from Germany. Swedish manufacturers continued to market it in Argentina even after it had been withdrawn in Sweden. In Sweden, mothers were not aware of the national withdrawal and continued to receive the drug from local pharmacies.[9,10]

Few children in the US were affected by thalidomide. Sales representatives were in these days allowed to distribute pills to medical doctors who passed them on to patients they thought might benefit, which in the US occurred with roughly a dozen pregnant women. Such distribution of not yet approved drugs was in these days legitimate and not controlled. When the dangerousness of thalidomide became known, there was no documentation to whom the pills had been given. Although every single case of a malformation was a human tragedy, altogether the situation in the US was comparatively benign compared to the worldwide epidemic. Compared to the rest of the world, US lawmakers acted most decisively. They modified the US Federal Food, Drug and Cosmetic Act (FDCA) in a way that new drugs now needed to have developed sufficient safety and efficacy data before the company could submit an application for approval. This testing of safety and effectiveness, which met with determined resistance from both the organized medical profession and the organized chemical industry, was the beginning of the unprecedented development of an entire branch of industry, which gave rise to the pharmaceutical industry from the original chemical industry, the research-intensive spearhead of which is today the life science industry.[11] Alongside this, an entire branch of industry developed eventually that produces and sells drugs whose patents have already expired: generics. Once a drug has reached a point in development where there is already some proof of its efficacy, efficacy and safety must be confirmed in one to two pivotal clinical studies. Pivotal because they are the crucial basis for approval, provided they have a positive result.

The US Food and Drug Administration (FDA) is a federal agency of the Department of Health and Human Services (DHHS), responsible today for protecting and promoting public health by controlling and supervising food safety, tobacco products, caffeine products, dietary supplements, prescription and OTC drugs, vaccines, biopharmaceuticals, blood transfusions, medical devices, electromagnetic radiation emitting devices, cosmetics, animal foods & feed, and veterinary products[12,13] When the US modified its Food, Drug and Cosmetic Act (FDCA) in 1962, it was the first country worldwide to introduce such strict regulations for the approval of medicines. Meanwhile, the rest of the world has by and large followed suit, particularly those countries and regions that are leaders in drug development and approval, i.e., the EU, the UK, Switzerland, and Japan. The days of isolated national drug development are over. All major companies now develop their medicines on an international level, and the registration studies are carried out worldwide. On the other hand, the approval of the respective drug has remained a national task, so that the international companies have to apply for the approval country by country, in the EU meanwhile at the central European Medicines Agency (EMA).[14,15]

The power of the regulatory authorities that decide about the approval of new drugs has increased considerably over time. Companies that want to approve new drugs have to meet the demands of the authorities, in our case the demands for additional studies in minors, even if the company in question knows that these studies lack medical and scientific sense or are massively exaggerated.

With its economic success, the chemical industry, which has developed via the pharmaceutical industry into today's life sciences industry provided an excellent projection surface onto which the hopes and disappointments of modern life could be projected. There is an army of writers who claim that the pharmaceutical industry is driven solely by greed, is untrustworthy, and is no better overall than organized crime.[16-20] Furthermore, proud academics boast that, unlike industry, they are free of conflicts of interest and have nothing but pure science and truth in mind. [21-23]

On the other hand, drug development has undeniably improved medical care, lengthened life, and improved the quality of life. Pharmaceutical and life science companies operate within the rules of the market. Competition in the market is ruthless. Not the biggest dinosaurs survived, but the fastest and most flexible ones. Birds are direct descendants of dinosaurs. Their closest relatives in the non-bird animal kingdom are crocodiles.[24] Not the biggest companies survive and thrive. This applies to all areas of the economy, be it pharmaceutical companies, banks, or real estate companies. In March 2023, the second largest Swiss bank "Credit Suisse" collapsed within a few days and had to be bought by its main competitor with the help of the Swiss government. The development of the first highly effective vaccine against the COVID-19 infection occurred by the collaboration of the young, tiny, but extremely innovative German company BioNTech and the dinosaur-like huge pharmaceutical company Pfizer.[25,26] This collaboration resulted in a win-win situation during the COVID-19 pandemic.[27]

The demand to let children participate from medical progress and the advancement of drug development reflects various dimensions that flow into the perception of drug development and healthcare.

There is the carefully cultivated self-image of doctors and health workers in the western world that they do their work on the basis of charity, not self-interest. If we look closely, however, we see that people who work in the health sector do not earn badly and, moreover, enjoy a high reputation. In contrast to this is the rather low reputation of the pharmaceutical industry, which is accused of greed and contempt for human beings.

All these ideas have evolved over more than half a century and in many respects have come to a standstill. They often hide the fact that the world has progressed in the meantime. In "pediatric drug development," its proponents mercilessly exploit the high academic standing of research, medicine, the medical community, and government agencies to justify scientifically questionable studies.

Thalidomide has meanwhile experienced a medical and therapeutic renaissance. It is now used in the treatment of cancer, in the treatment of pain in leprosy, and a number of other indications. It is approved for this in numerous countries. Of course, it must be prescribed and administered with extreme caution, but it has this in common with many other drugs, such as chemotherapeutic substances used in cancer treatment.[28,29]

Just as humanity had to go through World War II and its horrors to facilitate the industrial production of penicillin, radar, atomic fission, and malaria research programs, supported by the US Office of Scientific Research and Development (OSRD),[30] the intellectual and organizational processing of the thalidomide disaster has contributed to providing a framework buildup in which drug development has so far been possible without further major catastrophes. The time has come to separate the "side effects" of this framework, in which many careers in pseudo-research have been established, from the main foundations that have advanced drug development, healthcare, and science.

References

1. Wikipedia, Manna https://en.wikipedia.org/wiki/Manna
2. Changes in Science, Law and Regulatory Authorities. Part II: 1938, Food, Drug, Cosmetic Act. FDA 2018. https://www.fda.gov/about-fda/changes-science-law-and-regulatory-authorities/part-ii-1938-food-drug-cosmetic-act
3. Wax PM. Elixirs, Diluents, and the Passage of the 1938 Federal Food, Drug and Cosmetic Act. Ann Intern Med 1995 Mar 15;122(6):456-61
4. Rägo L, Santo B: Drug Regulation: History, Present and Future. In: Drug Benefits and Risks: International Textbook of Clinical Pharmacology, revised 2nd edition, van Boxtel CJ, Santo B & Edwards IR (editors). IOS Press & Uppsala Monitoring Centre, Uppsala, Sweden, 2008, chapter 6, pp. 65-77
5. Wikipedia, Diethylene glycol https://en.wikipedia.org/wiki/Diethylene_glycol
6. Vargesson N. Thalidomide-induced teratogenesis: History and mechanisms. Birth Defects Res C Embryo Today. 2015 Jun; 105(2): 140–156. https://www.ncbi.nlm.nih.gov/pmc/articles/PMC4737249/pdf/BDRC-105-140.pdf
7. Thomann KD. Die Contergan-Katastrophe. Die trügerische Sicherheit der "harten" Daten. Dtsch Arztebl 2007;104(41): A 2078-2082. https://www.aerzteblatt.de/pdf.asp?id=57224
8. Wikipedia, Widukind Lenz. https://de.wikipedia.org/wiki/Widukind_Lenz
9. Ridings JE. The thalidomide disaster, lessons from the past. Methods Mol Biol 2013;947:575-86.
10. Lachmann PJ. The penumbra of thalidomide, the litigation culture and the licensing of pharmaceuticals. QJM. 2012 Dec;105(12):1179-89. https://www.ncbi.nlm.nih.gov/pmc/articles/PMC3516063/pdf/hcs148.pdf

11. Hilts PJ. Protecting America's Health: The FDA, Business, and One Hundred Years of Regulation . Alfred A Knopf Publishers, New York, NY, USA 2003

12. FDA: What we do. FDA 2018. https://www.fda.gov/about-fda/what-we-do

13. Wikipedia, Food and Drug Administration (FDA) https://en.wikipedia.org/wiki/Food_and_Drug_Administration

14. European Medicines Agency (EMA) www.ema.europa.eu

15. Wikipedia, European Medicines Agency (EMA) https://en.wikipedia.org/wiki/European_Medicines_Agency

16. Angell M. The Truth about the Drug Companies: How They Deceive Us and What to Do about It. Random House Publishers, New York, USA, 2004

17. Rosenthal, Elisabeth (2017). An American Sickness: How Healthcare Became Big Business and How You Can Take it Back. Penguin Press. ISBN 9780698407183

18. Gøtzsche PC. Deadly Medicines and Organised Crime: How Big Pharma Has Corrupted Healthcare. Routledge, London, UK, 2013

19. Goldacre B. Bad Pharma: How drug companies mislead doctors and harm patients. HarperCollins Publishers, London, UK, 2012

20. Goldacre B. Bad Science: Quacks, Hacks, and Big Pharma Flacks. Farrar, Straus and Giroux (FSG) Adult, NY, USA, reprint 2010

21. Angell M. Industry-sponsored clinical research: a broken system. JAMA. 2008 Sep 3;300(9):1069-71.

22. Steinbrook R, Kassirer JP, Angell M. Justifying conflicts of interest in medical journals: a very bad idea. BMJ. 2015 Jun 2;350:h2942

23. Angell M. Conflicts in serving both non-profit and for-profit medical centres. BMJ. 2015 Oct 21; 351: h5491. doi: 10.1136/bmj.h5491.

24. Tixier-Boichard M, Bed'hom B, Rognon X. Chicken domestication: From archeology to genomics. C R Biol 2011 Mar;334(3):197-204. https://www.sciencedirect.com/science/article/pii/S163106911000301X

25. BioNTech https://www.biontech.com/de/de/home.html

26. Pfizer https://www.pfizer.com/

27. Rose K. The COVID-19 Pandemic: A Global High-Tech Challenge at the Interface of Science, Politics, and Illusions. Elsevier, London, UK, 2022 https://www.elsevier.com/books/the-covid-19-pandemic/rose/978-0-323-99149-0

28. Ribatti D, Vacca A. Therapeutic renaissance of thalidomide in the treatment of haematological malignancies. Leukemia 2005 Sep;19(9):1525-31.

29. Vargesson N, Stephens T. Thalidomide: history, withdrawal, renaissance, and safety concerns. Expert Opin Drug Saf. 2021 Dec;20(12):1455-1457. https://www.tandfonline.com/doi/epdf/10.1080/14740338.2021.1991307

30. Gross DP, Sampat BN. Organizing Crisis Innovation: Lessons From World War II. National Bureau Of Economic Research (NBER) Working Paper Series, Working Paper # 27909, 2020. https://www.nber.org/system/files/working_papers/w27909/revisions/w27909.rev0.pdf

Chapter 6

Children as "Therapeutic Orphans" and Developmental Pharmacology

The concept that infants and children are "therapeutic orphans" was presented a first time in 1963 at a conference of professional and scientific societies in Chicago by the pediatrician Harry Shirkey.[1,2] Dr. Shirkey was the first chairman of the American Academy of Pediatrics (AAP) committee on drugs. In 1968 he published it.[3,4] His publications have from then on been quoted uncountable times and became over the years and decades the fundamental basis of today's pediatric legislation in the US, the EU, UK and Switzerland. Shirkey's position paper lists several examples of the pediatric warnings that drug manufacturers had inserted into their drug labels since 1962, when the Kefauver-Harris Amendment of 1962 to the US federal pharmaceutical law, The Food Drug and Cosmetic Act (FDCA) had been enacted: "Not to be used in children; ... not recommended for use in infants and young children, since few studies have been carried out in this age group; ... clinical studies have been insufficient to establish any recommendations for use in infants and children; ... should not be given to children." Shirkey then complains that despite such clear warnings, many physicians ignored the warnings and prescribed the restricted drugs. He then asks the rhetorical question what a jury of laymen would decide after a defending physician admitted in court to the use of a drug despite such a clear warning. In the following, he argues that the FDCA amendments were introduced to make drugs safer, but that children are now deprived of the use of safe drugs. He brings examples of drugs that that previously had been considered as harmless but may be associated with side effects in the newborn, including the gas oxygen. He demands separate clinical trials to proof safety and efficacy also in children.[4]

The FDCA amendments of 1962 required companies to prove their products to be safe and effective using "adequate and well-controlled studies" and established informed consent in clinical drug studies. The reason why many drug manufacturers had inserted "pediatric warnings" into their labels was predominantly *legal*: to avoid damage lawsuits in the litigious US legal environment.[5-7]

At first glance Shirkey's concept seems logical and coherent. But let us start with a few critical questions: should medical doctors really have followed the pediatric warnings and not have prescribed life-saving drugs to young patients? Shirkey uses two main arguments. He argues *medically* that drugs previously considered harmless later showed negative side effects in newborns. Oxygen had been given in the early years of neonatology to preterm newborns in the hope to improve their survival. Many developed retinopathy of prematurity, in the beginning called retrolental fibroplasia, which was for a while the largest single cause of infant blindness. exceeding all other causes of blindness in childhood. The suspicion that oxygen played a major role in this led in the early 1950s led to reducing oxygen administration to premature infants. In consequence, the incidence of retinopathy of prematurity decreased dramatically throughout the world.[8,9] But retinopathy of prematurity was a specific challenge to children born prematurely and is a good example of the conundrum of pioneering medicine in general: should physicians have preterm newborns let die because antibiotics, oxygen, and other substances used in their care were not yet examined in depth? It is the same question as with the use of antibiotics in preterm newborns where toxicities had been reported in the 1940/50s.[10-12] Shirkey's medical argumentation used the extreme examples of really observed toxicities in a small sub-group of patients, preterm newborns, but then switches to the use of the term "children" in its *legal* sense: minors, persons under age. Also, his rhetorical question about a medical doctor in a court is misleading. In this hypothetical case, the prosecution argues that he prescribed a drug with a warning of pediatric use. But in the 1960s, physicians, pediatricians and family doctors used mechanical formulas and dosing tables to adjust drug doses to the smaller body of minors.[13] These formulas and tables did by and large their job. However, they were not sufficient in premature newborns. Shirkey's argumentation uses as a threat the nightmare of every physician that he might be accused of medical malpractice. But what might be dangerous in a preterm newborn is not dangerous in a minor of school age or in an adolescent.

Furthermore, his argumentation is *legal* and *formal*, but neither *medical* nor *scientific*. No jury of laymen would convict a doctor for administering a life-saving drug to a 15-year-old. The terms "neonatology" and "neonatologist" were introduced in 1960. Incubators were already routinely in use in 1968. The Apgar score to assess the health of all newborns at 1 and 5 minutes after birth was already in use since more than ten years. The dangers of antibiotics in preterm newborns had been reported more than ten years earlier and were well known.[14-16] In 1968, no general practitioner or family doctor would have dared to take care of a preterm newborn, except maybe in an emergency situation. And in an emergency, no court would expect that doctor to have exactly the same level of knowledge and the same array of tools, drugs and machines as a specialist who attends to premature babies and newborns routinely in a neonate intensive care unit (NICU).

The concept of infants and children as "therapeutic orphans" uses medical terminology, moral pressure, threat with litigation, and the different meanings of the term "child" to give the impression that minors ("children", defined *legally*) are fundamentally different *physiologically* from adults. This blur at the interface of medicine, law, and drug approval used the profound changes the meaning of the terms infancy and children had undergone over the previous half-century.[5]

The concept of children as "therapeutic orphans" was taken up by the AAP. In several policy statements, the AAP described the following alleged ethical dilemma: "The physician must frequently either not treat children with potentially beneficial medications or treat them with medications based on adult studies or anecdotal empirical experience in children. Nonvalidated drug treatment may not provide optimal benefit to the individual child. ... such nonvalidated administration of medications may place more children at risk than if the drugs were administered as part of well-designed, controlled clinical trials."[12] Comparable statements were published already in 1977 and were repeated in 2010. The 1977 statement declared that the Committee believed it to be unethical "to adhere to a system which forces physicians to use therapeutic agents in an uncontrolled experimental situation virtually every time they prescribe for children." [17] Also the 2010 statement declares the performance of research studies to evaluate drugs in children as critical for determining their safety and efficacy in children, and that without such research, medication use in children will be limited to extrapolation from adult studies or off-label use for indications that have not been studied in children, putting children at increased risk of adverse effects. "Growth and maturation can alter the kinetics, end-organ responses, and toxicities of drugs used in infants, children, and adolescents compared with adults." [18]

Was there ever a system that forced physicians to use therapeutic agents in an uncontrolled experimental situation virtually every time they prescribe for children? Formally yes. But only if we accept that all minors are fundamentally different from adults. Common sense says no. A system that forced physicians to use drugs in an uncontrolled experimental situation whenever they prescribe for children has never existed. This formal argumentation that twists different meanings of one word to create a fundamentally flawed impression is one of the reasons medical doctors (and anybody else) are scared of legal disputes in which smart and unscrupulous lawyers twist the meaning of words in a way that in the end they get a guilty verdict.

In the AAP statement of 1995, children are defined as persons who have not attained the legal age for independent consent to treatments or procedures involved in research, under the applicable law of the jurisdictions in which the research is conducted.[12] This definition is neither medical nor physiological, but purely legal. Nevertheless, the AAP claimed together with Harry Shirkey during several decades that prescribing medicines to a person that is legally under age puts this person in danger. But the human body changes slowly from a child's body to an adult body during the relatively slow process of puberty, and not in the night of a birthday.

It was a deception of the public opinion in which the AAP threw its scientific authority into play. The question of whether this was a cunning deception done on purpose or whether it was simply the spirit of the time being expressed is not relevant here. Furthermore, we can no longer question the contemporary witnesses.

No major disasters in pediatric medicine

Unlike the Sulphinalmide Elixir disaster of 1936 and the thalidomide disaster of 1957-1961, there were no major disasters in pediatric drug use. When antibiotics had been administered to newborns, toxicities, some of them fatal, had occurred and were published in the medical press in order to warn other doctors about the careless administration of antibiotics to premature babies and to prevent new poisoning.[10-12] The reason for pharmaceutical manufacturers to insert pediatric warnings had been a *legal* reason. Shirkey interpreted these warnings *medically* and claimed now that by "an odd and unfortunate twist of fate, infants and children are becoming 'therapeutic or pharmaceutical orphans.'"[1,4] There was no odd and unfortunate twist of fate. And there were no major pediatric disasters. But what was there was the will of a group of influential pharmacologists and pediatricians to conjure such an alleged crisis. A subheading in a lecture from 1999 was "CONTINUED PEDIATRIC THERAPEUTIC DISASTERS" (sic!). The paper listed real problems encountered in neonatology, including acute toxicity of chloramphenicol caused by immature glucoronidation in the neonate, described in the 1950s; mortality and an increased incidence of kernicterus among premature neonates receiving a sulfonamide antibiotic, also described in the 1950s; serious problems and death among low birth weight infants exposed to E-Ferol; the well known toxicity of oral ingestion of propylene glycol; toxicity of benzyl alcohol often used to flush intravenous catheters. Immaturity of detoxification of its benzoic acid metabolite in premature neonates appears responsible for the toxicity.[19] All listed examples were in preterm neonates.

From a public relations (PR) point of view we have to admit that the campaign that the AAP was running in coordination with the FDA and development pharmacology colleagues worldwide was a resounding success.

What we furthermore see from the AAP statements is the emphasis on performing clinical studies in children. Superficially, these are justified by different body characteristics of minors. By oscillating between the medical and the legal meaning of the term "child", this conveys the impression that the legal age limit of childhood corresponds to a physiological change. Which is not the case.

The disciplines of paediatrics in general and specifically that of neonatology have experienced an unprecedented growth over the last century. A newborn that in 1960 was born with a body weight of one kg had a risk of death of 95%. In 2000, it had a 95% probability of survival.[14,15] A hundred years ago, congenital malformations of the cardiovascular system, of the face, or of the internal organs were either untreatable or meant that the child in question was disfigured for the rest of its life. The same was true for young people who contracted autoimmune inflammatory diseases at a young age; who had a congenital defect like cystic fibrosis, which a hundred years ago did not even survive their first birthday; or one of the myriad diseases that today we can treat. This path of development was not an easy one. Mistakes were made and setbacks occurred. To describe this period of time as a continued pediatric therapeutic disaster is a crude distortion of actual history. However, from a PR point of view this representation has worked rather well.

Developmental physiology and pharmacology

Physiology as a sub-discipline of biology is the science of how living organisms and their organ systems, individual organs, cells, and biomolecules run their chemical and physical functions. Human physiology seeks to understand the mechanisms that work to keep the human body alive and functioning. Medical physiology studies the body functions both in the normal state and under non-normal conditions, including diseases.[20] The human body changes over time. It develops after conception in the womb, continues to develop after birth, remains stable for a relatively long period of time, and changes slowly with age. Developmental physiology looks at these changes over time.[21]

Pharmacology is a branch of medicine, biology, and pharmaceutical sciences concerned with drugs and medicines. Clinical pharmacology is the discipline that teaches, does research, frames policy, gives information and advice about the actions and proper uses of medicines in humans and implements that knowledge in clinical practice".[22] It measures the key parameters of how the body processes the respective drug, and what the respective drug does to the body. In technical terms, these dimensions are measured in absorption, distribution, metabolism and excretion (ADME) of drugs.[23] Developmental clinical pharmacology adds the additional factor that the human body is not static, but changes throughout the entire life. Developmental clinical pharmacology investigates how ADME develops and changes over time.[24] There are not two human species, one called "adults" – those after the 18th birthday – and the other one called "children" – those before the 18th birthday.[6,7,25] However, the regulatory framework today still reflects such a static view of the human body, with the additional assumption of a fundamental change of the human body at its 18th birth. But the 18th birthday is an administrative and/or legal time limit, not a physiological one. Interestingly, most publications about developmental pharmacology discuss only the transition from childhood to adulthood.[26-32]

A key review from 2003 gives a more complete overview. Its often-quoted figure 1 shows, inter alia, the distribution of fat, water, and fat, total body water and extracellular water in the human body up to 40 years of age. The percentage of total body water decreases steadily and slowly with age; the percentage of fat first goes down and then goes a bit up again between 20 and 40 years of age. The skin's perfusion (blood flow) and hydration (ability to absorb and store water and fluids) goes down with age until we become adults.[24] From adolescence on, women are beginning to spend vast amounts of money to regain the skin tone and appearance of a younger age, or at least to slow down the aging process. And men are catching up in this movement. The whole movement is called anti-aging.[33] There is now an American Academy of anti-aging medicine, which as of 2013 claimed 26,000 members from 120 countries.[34,35] The study of the processes that occur during human aging has become an entire science in its own right.[36]

It was the discipline of developmental pharmacology and the representatives of its main organisations that were most involved in the intellectually justifying the "therapeutic orphans" concept.

The mentioned presentation from 1999 that complains the alleged continued pediatric therapeutic disasters was given at a meeting of representatives from European Society for Developmental Pharmacology (today the European Society for Perinatal and Pediatric Pharmacology),[37] the Japanese Society for Pediatric Clinical Pharmacology),[38] and the US Pediatric Pharmacology Research Unit [PPRU] Network.[39] These representatives had convened to discuss the solution to the therapeutic orphan problem.[40,41]

An almost uncountable number of publications claims that in "children" everything is different, and that on this basis both the discipline of developmental pharmacology and pediatric drug development in general represent major steps forward in the development of modern pediatric health care.[28,29,32] Some of these publications are differentiated. Others make crude claims that even the medical layperson would identify as nonsense at first glance: "The lack of availability of appropriate medicines for children is an extensive and well-known problem. Pediatricians and physicians who take care of the pediatric population are primarily exposed to cope with this negative situation very often as more than half of the children are prescribed off-label or unlicensed medicines."[42] "The lack of availability of appropriate medicines for children is an extensive and well known problem. As a consequence off label or unlicensed administration of medicinal products in every day pediatric practice is frequent."[43] These are just two examples for exaggerated and crude misrepresentations.

Children: a neglected population?

There is a common accusation that children are a neglected group. In 2021, Wilson refers to estimates that suggest that up to 90% of drugs administered to children are unstudied, with infants accounting for the highest percentage of off-label drug administration, and concludes that neonates, infants and children can be considered a neglected population in drug research.[27] The European Medicines Agency (EMA) uses the same argumentation in a statement from 2007 that complains that the use of unlicensed and off-label medicines in children is widespread and has been an increasing concern over the last years. It adds that in the EU, 50% or more of medicines used in children have never actually been studied in this population, but only in adults, and not necessarily in the same indication (or the same disease). It warns that this general lack of information and appropriate pharmaceutical formulations of many medicines in children may expose them to unwanted side effects or underdosing without the expected efficacy and concludes from this that the need for more studies to obtain pediatric information for medicines used in children is now a matter of consensus on a global basis.[44]

If we accept the outlined tongue-twisting argumentation, then indeed children are a neglected population. However, if we look deeper and acknowledge that the term "pediatric population" is an is an artificially created administrative construct that does not represent a medically defined human group, than we see through the myth of children as therapeutic orphans and all further myths connected to this flawed concept. We need to use our common sense, to look at statistics, and to accept the discrepancy between a risk of death of 95% for a newborn born in 1960 with a body weight of one kg as opposed to a 95% probability of survival of a newborn with the same body weight born in 2005.[14] The story of children as an allegedly neglected population is a carefully prepared tall tale without any scientific basis. It is pseudo-science.

On-label/ off-label use of drugs in children

A label is in everyday life the name and description of the product on the package of in a package insert. For drugs, it is the description approved by the regulatory authority. In the US, every prescription drug marketed has an individual, FDA-approved label, a written report with detailed instructions on the drug's approved uses and doses, based on the results of clinical studies that the manufacturers submitted to the FDA to get approval. There are three sub-terms in this context: off-label use; off-label prescription, and off-label promotion. The FDA does not regulate off-label use (by patients) or off-label prescription (by medical doctors). But it regulates the marketing of drugs. If a company registers a new drug in a rather rare disease and then promotes it in a frequent disease, this would be off-label promotion which is heavily sanctioned by the FDA, which has issued fines of billions of $ US to pharmaceutical companies.[45]

The claim that children represent a neglected population is repeatedly made, justified by emphasizing that up to 90% of drugs administered to children are unstudied.[27,44]

Will a given drug work better in a 17 year old patient once it has a pediatric label? No. The label does not have a magic power.

The discussion about on-label/ off-label prescription, treatment and marketing of medicines is ongoing since decades, keeps US lawyers and courts busy and is the subject of many publications in scientific journals and books.[45-51]

Regarding off-label prescription, the AAP argues on two levels. On the one hand, it supports clinical studies in "children" with the aim to get "pediatric" labels. On the other hand, it emphasizes that therapeutic decision-making should always be guided by the best available evidence and the importance of the benefit for the individual patient; practitioners must often rely on less definitive information than gold standard clinical trials. Off-label use is neither incorrect nor investigational if based on sound scientific evidence, expert medical judgment, or published literature. Reimbursement institutions and payers should not use the labeling status as the only criterion to determine reimbursement of drugs prescribed in in children.[52] Thus, the AAP defends reasonable decision making by pediatric practitioners, but continues to demand "pediatric" research, irrespectively if the researched minors are physiologically still children, or physiologically already mature.[5-7]

The argument that children are a neglected group because of the high percentage of drugs prescribed and used off-label in their medical care would be correct if we had regular major disasters in the history of pediatrics. But if we take a sober look at the success story of pediatrics, we have to state that the off-label use of drugs in minors does not represent the major medical problem that advocates of "pediatric drug development" keep repeating like a mantra.

While on a general level the debate about on-label/off-label prescription will probably never end, we should state here that the wild claims about children as a neglected group in medical treatment are simply wrong.

Extrapolation from adults to "children"

For drugs to treat epilepsy, the FDA now accepts "extrapolation" of effects in adults down to two years of age. The term "extrapolation" itself is still misleading, but at least it is now accepted that antiepileptic drugs work in minors. After much hesitation, the EMA has followed this example to a certain extent. The EMA accepts now "extrapolation" from adults to children down to the age of four. For the topical skin drug crisaborole for neurodermatitis, the FDA accepted patients aged 2 to 79 years in the pivotal studies.

The key advances in pediatrics did not occur through the active involvement of regulatory authorities, but rather through clinicians and researchers using what was available to treat their young patients as best they could. This has been the case with the development of the iron lung for children with polio, the development of the incubator for preterm and newborn babies, the antibiotic treatment of preterm infants to prevent or treat streptococcal infections, and much more.[14,15] Disciplines such as pediatric oncology or neonatology developed independently from interventions by the regulatory authorities.[5-7]

Pediatric exclusivity

When the first US pediatric legislation was introduced in 1997, the key issue was an alleged compromise between the developers of innovative drugs, the pharmaceutical companies, the pediatric researchers, and the FDA. For patented drugs, companies could propose "pediatric" studies. If the FDA accepted the proposal, it issued a "pediatric request", which the company had to accept in written. When the company had fulfilled the requirements of the pediatric request, it got 6 months prolongation of the drug's patent life, called "pediatric exclusivity". The FDA maintains a list of the pediatric exclusivities it has granted.[53] The texts of many, but not of all written requests for the respective individual drugs are published online.[5-7]

Six months patent extension at peak sales can be rather rewarding for a drug that sells with several billions $ US per year. These rewards have been discussed in depth in the literature.[54-56] However, there is another side: the fact that pediatric researchers profited massively from 1997 from pediatric clinical trials. Before 1997, manufacturers of drugs intended predominantly for adult use had little interest to consult pediatricians. This changed fundamentally from 1997 on when companies now had to consider clinical trials in minors for their drugs.[5-7]

The dimensions of the costs of pediatric drug development are considerable. The costs of "pediatric" studies of 54 drugs were estimated at $ US 49 billion in 2017.[56] A report by the EU Commission estimates the costs of pediatric investigation plans (PIPs) as € 2,1 billion per year, including overhead costs. If we multiply 2.1 with the number of years the EU pediatric regulation is already in force (since 2007), it is 17 years until 2023. Seventeen times 2.1 is roughly € 3 billion.[57,58] Definitely not peanuts, and worse if we consider that most of these studies are medically pointless, many even harm young patients, and that these studies have become an obstacle to do truly innovative research in pediatric healthcare.

Reality is slowly kicking in, but this is not yet officially recognized

Over the past years, the FDA has in several key clinical areas stepped back from the children-are-not-small-adults mantra.

For drugs to treat epilepsy, the FDA now accepts "extrapolation" of effects in adults down to two years of age. The term "extrapolation" itself is still misleading, but at least it is now accepted that antiepileptic drugs work in minors. After much hesitation, the EMA has followed this example to a certain extent and now accepts "extrapolation" from adults to children down to the age of four. For the topical skin drug crisaborole for neurodermatitis, the FDA accepted patients aged 2 to 79 years in the pivotal studies.

In malignant diseases in adolescents, the FDA now recommends inclusion of patients into promising adult studies. Malignancies in adolescents are very rare. In most cases, the malignancies are the same as in adults. Such a malignancy can also affect somebody before the 18th birthday.

In the next chapter we will go more in depth, analyzing studies in a number of clinical areas that have been performed with minors, studies that are demanded by the EMA and are recruiting, studies that are demanded by the EMA but cannot recruit enough patients, and many more bizarre "pediatric" studies.

References

1. Burckart GJ, Kim C. The Revolution in Pediatric Drug Development and Drug Use: Therapeutic Orphans No More. J Pediatr Pharmacol Ther. 2020; 25(7): 565–573. https://www.ncbi.nlm.nih.gov/pmc/articles/PMC7541025/pdf/i1551-6776-25-7-565.pdf
2. Shirkey HC: Conference on Professional and Scientific Societies, Commission on Drug Safety, June 27-28, 1963, Chicago.
3. Shirkey HC. Therapeutic Orphans—Everybody's Business. Drug Intelligence. 1968;2(12):323-323. https://journals.sagepub.com/doi/epdf/10.1177/106002806800201201
4. Shirkey H. Editorial Comment: Therapeutic Orphans. J Pediatr 1968 Jan; 72 (1), 119-120
5. Rose K, Grant-Kels JM, Striano P, Ettienne EB, Oishi T, Neubauer D. "Pediatric" Drug Studies Might Be the Largest Abuse in Medical Research in History. It Is Time for Lawyers to Step In. J Law Med 2023,30(1), in press
6. Rose K. Considering the Patient in Pediatric Drug Development. How good intentions turned into harm. Elsevier, London, UK, 2020
7. Rose K. Blind Trust - How parents with a sick child can escape the labyrinth of lies, hypocrisy and false promises of researchers and regulatory authorities. Hammersmith, London, UK, 2022.
8. Patz A. The role of oxygen in retrolental fibroplasia. Trans Am Ophthalmol Soc. 1968;66:940-85. https://www.ncbi.nlm.nih.gov/pmc/articles/PMC1310320/pdf/taos00033-0953.pdf
9. Tasman W, Patz A, McNamara JA, et al. Retinopathy of prematurity: the life of a lifetime disease. Am J Ophthalmol. 2006 Jan;141(1):167-74.
10. Burns LE, Hodgman JE, Cass AB. Fatal circulatory collapse in premature infants receiving chloramphenicol. *N EngI 1 Med.* 1959;261:1318-1321

11. Silverman WA, Andersen DH, Blanc WA, et al. A difference in mortality rate and incidence of kernicterus among premature infants allotted to two prophylactic antibacterial regimens. Pediatrics 1956;18:6

12. American Academy of Pediatrics (AAP) 1995 | Committee on Drugs |Guidelines for the Ethical Conduct of Studies to Evaluate Drugs in Pediatric Populations Pediatrics 1995 Feb,95(2),286–294.

13. Blumer JL. Developmental Pharmacology: Past, present and future. Acta Paediatr Jpn 1996 Dec;38(6):555-61

14. Philip AG. The evolution of neonatology. Pediatr Res 2005;58(4):799_815
https://www.nature.com/articles/pr2005743.pdf?origin5ppub

15. Jorgensen AM. Born in the USA _ The history of neonatology in the United States: A century of caring.
https://static.abbottnutrition.com/cms-prod/anhi.org/img/Nurse%20 Currents%20NICU%20History%20June%202010.pdf

16. Vidyasagar D. Half a century of evolution of neonatology: A witness's story" Dr. K. C. Chaudhuri Lifetime Achievement Award Oration Delivered at AIIMS, New Delhi on 7th September 2014 Indian J Pediatr 2015;82(12):1117_25.
https://doi.org/10.1007/s12098-015-1838-8

17. American Academy of Pediatrics. Committee on Drugs. Guidelines for the ethical conduct of studies to evaluate drugs in pediatric populations. Pediatrics. 1977 Jul;60(1):91-101.

18. Shaddy RE, Denne SC, The Committee on Drugs and Committee on Pediatric Research. Guidelines for the Ethical Conduct of Studies to Evaluate Drugs in Pediatric Populations. Pediatrics 2010;125(4):850–860.
https://publications.aap.org/pediatrics/article/125/4/850/73133/Guidelines-for-the-Ethical-Conduct-of-Studies-to?autologincheck=redirected

19. Christensen ML, Helms RA, Chesney RW. Is pediatric labeling really necessary? Pediatrics. 1999 Sep;104(3 Pt 2):593-7.

20. Wikipedia, Physiology
https://en.wikipedia.org/wiki/Physiology

21. Burggren W. Developmental Physiology: Grand Challenges. Front Physiol. 2021 Jun 10;12:706061. https://www.ncbi.nlm.nih.gov/pmc/articles/PMC8225327/pdf/fphys-12-706061.pdf

22. Wikipedia, Clinical pharmacology https://en.wikipedia.org/wiki/Clinical_pharmacology

23. Wikipedia, Pharmacology https://en.wikipedia.org/wiki/Pharmacology

24. Kearns GL, Abdel-Rahman SM, Alander SW, Blowey DL, Leeder JS, Kauffman RE, et al. Developmental pharmacology--drug disposition, action, and therapy in infants and children. N Engl J Med. 2003 Sep 18;349(12):1157-67.

25. Gillis J, Loughlan P. Not just small adults: the metaphors of paediatrics. Arch Dis Child. 2007 Nov;92(11):946-7 https://www.ncbi.nlm.nih.gov/pmc/articles/PMC2083631/pdf/946.pdf

26. Wilson JT: An Update on the Therapeutic Orphan. Pediatrics 1999, 104 (3) Suppl. September, 585-590, http://pediatrics.aappublications.org/cgi/content/full/104/3/S1/585

27. Wilson G. Developmental Pharmacology. Anaesthesia & Intensive Care Medicine 2021;22(9),587-593

28. Van den Anker JN. Developmental Pharmacology. Dev Disabil Res Rev 2010;16(3):233-238

29. Van den Anker JN, Reed MD, Allegaert K, et al. Developmental Changes in Pharmacokinetics and Pharmacodynamics. J Clin Pharmacolog 2018 Oct;58(Suppl 10) S10–S25 https://accp1.onlinelibrary.wiley.com/doi/epdf/10.1002/jcph.1284

30. Smits A, Annaert P, Cavallaro G, et al. Current knowledge, challenges and innovations in developmental pharmacology: A combined conect4children Expert Group and European Society for Developmental, Perinatal and Paediatric Pharmacology White Paper. Br J Clin Pharmacol. 2022 Dec;88(12):4965-4984. https://www.ncbi.nlm.nih.gov/pmc/articles/PMC9787161/pdf/BCP-88-4965.pdf

31. Aranda JV, Soyka LF. Developmental Pharmacology and Therapeutics - Who Needs It? Dev Pharmacol Ther 1980;1:1–5

32. Ward RM, Benjamin DK Jr, Davis JM, et al. The Need for Pediatric Drug Development. J Pediatr 2018 Jan;192:13-21. https://www.ncbi.nlm.nih.gov/pmc/articles/PMC7942021/pdf/nihms-1601167.pdf

33. Wikipedia, Anti-aging movement https://en.wikipedia.org/wiki/Anti-aging_movement

34. Wikipedia, American Academy of Anti-Aging Medicine https://en.wikipedia.org/wiki/American_Academy_of_Anti-Aging_Medicine

35. American Academy of Anti-Aging Medicine https://www.a4m.com/

36. da Costa JP, Vitorino R, Silva GM, et al. A synopsis on aging - Theories, mechanisms and future prospects. Ageing Res Rev 2016 Aug;29:90-112. https://www.ncbi.nlm.nih.gov/pmc/articles/PMC5991498/pdf/nihms858344.pdf

37. European Society for Developmental, Perinatal and Paediatric Pharmacology (ESDPPP)

38. https://www.esdppp.org/

39. Japanese Society for Pediatric Clinical Pharmacology https://www.jscpt.jp/eng/

40. US Department of Health and Human Services (DHHS). Pediatric Pharmacology Research Units (PPRU) Network (Historical/For Reference Only). DHHS 2021. https://www.nichd.nih.gov/research/supported/ppru

41. Yaffee S. Foreword. Pediatrics 1999 Sep;104(3 Pt 2):581.

42. Blumer JL. Introduction. Pediatrics. 1999 Sep;104(3 Pt 2):582

43. Rocchi F, Paolucci P, Ceci A, et al. The European paediatric legislation: benefits and perspectives. Ital J Pediatr 2010 Aug 17;36:56. https://www.ncbi.nlm.nih.gov/pmc/articles/PMC2933611/pdf/1824-7288-36-56.pdf

44. Rocchi R, Tomasi P. The development of medicines for children. Part of a series on Pediatric Pharmacology, guest edited by Gianvincenzo Zuccotti, Emilio Clementi, and Massimo Molteni. Pharmacol Res 2011 Sep;64(3):169-175

45. European Medicines Agency (EMA). History of the Paediatric Regulation. EMA 2007. https://www.ema.europa.eu/en/documents/other/european-paediatric-initiative-history-paediatric-regulation_en.pdf

46. Janssen WM. A Historical Perspective on Off-Label Medicine: From Regulation, Promotion, and the First Amendment to the Next Frontiers. Food and Drug Law Institute, Levy MC (Editor). First Washington, D.C., USA, 2008

47. Razzaque Nohri A. Off-Label Use of Medicines: A Door For Research. Independently published, 2021

48. Parziale A. The Law of Off-label Uses of Medicines: Regulation and Litigation in the EU, UK and USA. Routledge, London, UK, 2022

49. Cavalla D. Off-label Prescribing: Justifying Unapproved Medicine. Wiley-Blackwell, Hoboken, NJ, USA 2014

50. Plate V. The Impact of Off-Label, Compassionate and Unlicensed Use on Health Care Laws in preselected Countries. https://bonndoc.ulb.uni-bonn.de/xmlui/bitstream/handle/20.500.11811/4152/1936.pdf

51. Janssen WF. The Story of the Laws Behind the Labels. FDA Consumer magazine (June 1981). https://www.fda.gov/media/116890/download

52. Syed SA, Dixson BA, Constantino E, et al. The Law and Practice of Off-Label Prescribing and Physician Promotion. J American Acad Psychiatry & Law 2020 Nov, JAAPL.200049-20; https://jaapl.org/content/jaapl/early/2020/11/24/JAAPL.200049-20.full.pdf

53. Frattarelli DA, Galinkin JL, Green TP, et al. Off-label use of drugs in children. Pediatrics 2014 Mar;133(3):563-7.

54. FDA. Pediatric exclusivity granted. FDA 2023. https://www.fda.gov/drugs/development-resources/pediatric-exclusivity-granted

55. Li JS, Eisenstein EL, Grabowski HG, et al. Economic Return of Clinical Trials Performed Under the Pediatric Exclusivity Program. JAMA 2007 Feb 7;297(5):480-8. https://www.ncbi.nlm.nih.gov/pmc/articles/PMC2773665/pdf/nihms155305.pdf

56. Varnai P, Farla K, Simmonds P, et al. Study on the economic impact of the Paediatric Regulation, including its rewards and incentives. December 2016. https://health.ec.europa.eu/system/files/2017-10/paediatrics_10_years_economic_study_0.pdf

57. Sinha MS, Najafzadeh M, Rajasingh EK, et al. Labeling Changes and Costs for Clinical Trials Performed Under the US Food and Drug Administration Pediatric Exclusivity Extension, 2007 to 2012. JAMA Intern Med 2018 Nov 1;178(11):1458-1466 https://www.ncbi.nlm.nih.gov/pmc/articles/PMC6248195/

58. EU Commission. Report from The Commission To The European Parliament And The Council. State of Paediatric Medicines in the EU – 10 years of the EU Paediatric Regulation. 2017. https://eur-lex.europa.eu/legal-content/EN/TXT/PDF/?uri=CELEX:52017DC0626&from=en

59. EU Commission. State of Paediatric Medicines in the EU. 10 years of the EU Paediatric Regulation. Report from the Commission to the European Parliament and the Council. COM (2017) 626.2017. https://ec.europa.eu/health/sites/health/files/files/paediatrics/docs/2017_childrensmedicines_report_en.pdf

Chapter 7

Questionable Pediatric Studies

When the US enacted its first pediatric legislation in 1997, the lawmakers' overall belief was that in minors medically everything is different from adults, and that therefore all medicines need separate testing in minors. With a few exceptions, lawmakers are neither pharmacologists, scientists, nor medical doctors. Their belief had been successfully created by alarmist narratives of disastrous gaps in pediatric medical care that needed to be closed by separate pediatric approval of drugs based on clinical studies in minors of all ages. The narrative had been created by developmental pharmacologists in a close working relationship with the American Academy of Pediatrics (AAP). The US legislation of 1997 was still a "local" US matter. It became international by close collaboration of developmental pharmacologists from North America, Europe, and Japan. The mood in which the alleged need for separate drug testing in minors of all ages is well captured in the publications that arose from the contributions made at a key conference in 1997. All of these papers are contained in a supplement in the journal Pediatrics in 1999.[1] The introduction proudly outlines that for the last three decades a small group of dedicated and highly motivated pediatricians and pediatric clinical pharmacologists had worked tirelessly to ensure that sick and injured children were able to benefit from the therapeutic advances of the last half of the 20th century, resulting not only in a general level of comfort with pediatric clinical trials but also the passage of legislation designed to ensure that infants and children would benefit from modern medicine's progress. This conference examined the status of the "therapeutic orphan" problem [2] The foreword gave a bit more background information. The drivers were the European Society for Developmental Pharmacolog (today European Society for Perinatal,

Developmental and Paediatric Pharmacology),[3] the Japanese Society for Pediatric Clinical Pharmacology (today the Japanese Society of Clinical Pharmacology and Therapeutics),[4,5] and the US Pediatric Pharmacology Research Unit (PPRU) Network,[6] to eliminate the therapeutic orphan situation. The foreword also mentions a preceding workshop at the US Institute of Medicine of the National Academy of Sciences in 1990.[6] As an editorial comment Shirkey's paper from 1968 was reproduced.[7,8] One presentation lamented the "CONTINUED PEDIATRIC THERAPEUTIC DISASTERS", listing in an entire sub-chapter with this alarmistic title examples of toxicities in premature newborn babies.[9] But the listed challenges had meanwhile, in 1997, already been resolved by the now well-developed medical discipline of neonatology.[10,11] All the contributions in the supplement use the term "children" as if the administrative/legal time limit of 18 years would correspond to a physiological change. Not a single contribution puts the rapid physical development of premature and newborn babies into perspective in relation to the maturing of the young body until it is physically mature, which does not correspond to reaching the legal age of adulthood.[1] The participants of the 1997 conference were not fanatics. They were clinicians or clinical pharmacologists specializing in the drug treatment of children, measuring the serum concentration of drugs in humans of all ages, and investigating the development of absorption, distribution, metabolism and excretion (ADME) of drugs and the interaction between drugs and the body over time. Here at last they could express their desire for a better appreciation and use of their special knowledge, and, of course, for more funds. They were united in the feeling that they were making a vital contribution to the advancement of science and pediatric healthcare. They could not foresee how their good wishes and their desire for recognition would become a monster, unleashing unethical studies on young people on a scale unprecedented in history, based on the narrative of a fundamental difference between people before and after the age of 18.[12-15] In the following, we discuss how this oversimplified and mechanistic view of physiological development resulted in regulatory rewards and demands for studies in minors, how the considerable cash flow triggered by FDA and EMA decisions led to conflicts of interest among clinicians and researchers, and finally resulted in unethical studies in minors that have barely been addressed in the literature to date.

Cancer and malignancies before the 18th birthday

When cells become malignant, their behavior in relation to other cells gradually changes. Normal cells emerge, grow, cooperate with other cells and the rest of the body, die, and are eliminated and/or removed. Malignant cells coordinate no longer well with the body. They grow, invade neighboring tissues, can enter the bloodstream and form new colonies in other parts of the body, called metastases. When they block the esophagus, no more food gets into the stomach. If they injure an artery, internal bleeding occurs. If they damage nerves, this causes abnormal sensations and/or paralysis. And so forth. On the one hand, they almost develop a life of their own. But they are, on the other hand, still nourished and oxygenated by the blood stream. The immune system does not recognize them as hostile agents and tolerates them. There are many reasons for cells to become malignant. Broadly speaking, these reasons are related to irritations and harmful external influences over time. Long-term smoking puts you at risk of lung cancer and many more cancer types. Processed food typical of industrialized society brings with it the risk of contracting colonic and rectal cancer. If you have fair skin and expose yourself to a lot of ultraviolet light, you risk skin cancer, especially malignant melanoma.

The one element that malignancies in adults and children do not have in common is that in children the long-standing harmful influence of external circumstances does not contribute to the extent to which they become malignant. By definition, minors are young humans. Cancer can originate from solid tissue and form solid tumors; from mobile cells and become leukemia (Greek for "white blood"); cells of the lymphatic system that extends throughout the body can degenerate into lymphoma. There are many more malignancies that can derive from other cell types. The risk for cancer and other malignancies increases with age. But malignancies and cancer in children do occur as well, although much less frequently. When infectious diseases killed so many children, the relatively few young people who contracted malignant diseases went unnoticed. Too many children died in these days. The death of a child was a common event. Only when infectious diseases were pushed back did research begin to focus on very specific diseases in children such as malignancies, rheumatic diseases beginning in childhood, neurodegenerative diseases beginning in childhood, and more. The first wards for childhood cancer were established in the late first half of the 20th century. At that time there was little or nothing that could be done to help, apart from administering strong painkillers and sedatives to the young patients, consoling the parents and siblings, empathetic care, and having trained staff take over the caregiving activities of the parents. Pediatric cancer was perceived as the last disease that continued to kill children, left treating doctors helpless, and defied society and science.[16] But the challenge was now known, and work started on it. After many failed initial attempts, chemotherapy became stepwise successful first in the treatment of pediatric leukemias and then of solid tumors. Chemotherapy was often combined with surgery and radiation. Early successes in overall cancer treatment resulted in the US National Cancer Act of 1971 that declared "war on cancer". In the 1960s, not even oncology was a clinical specialty. The overall attitude towards chemotherapy was rather hostile. But children coped with doses that surprised the oncological pioneers. Young patients have more reserves, provided they are given the chance to show them.[13-15,17]

Pediatric oncology became a highly respected discipline. But regarding the drugs it used it had a very special starting point. Unlike many other disease areas the eventually life-saving medicines, the chemotherapeutic agents, were well known and had already existed for decades. Originating in chemical warfare research, chemotherapeutics were gradually used in the therapy of various types of adult cancers, including cancer of the colon, the rectum, the lungs, the skin, & more. Until roughly the 1990s pediatric oncology had reached a plateau. Survival in the most frequent malignancy in childhood, acute lymphoblastic leukemia (ALL), had reached about 90%. In general, roughly four out of five young patients with cancer could be expected to be healed.[18,19] These successes were achieved by fine-tuning chemotherapy with a variety of different cytostatic agents ("cocktails"), combined with surgery, radiation, and additional innovations including preventing infections by antibiotics, treatment of anemia by recombinant erythropoietin, advances in intensive care, and many more. However, this success came at a price. Chemotherapy is not very specific. It subjects all of the body's cells to poison in the hope of killing off enough malignant cells so that the body can eventually finish off the rest of the malignant cells. It destroys the fast-growing cancer cells but will also damage fast-growing healthy cells. Side effects include fatigue, flu-like symptoms, nausea & vomiting, weight loss or weight gain, hair loss, anaemia, bleeding, increased risk of infection, and more. Some side effects will show up right away, while others may develop over time. Some children only have a few side effects, while others may have many. Furthermore, long-term side effects can include damage to the heart, lungs, brain, nerves, kidneys, thyroid gland, or reproductive organs.[20]There is also the danger of new malignancies many years later.[14,15,21]

Pediatric oncology was from the very beginning a clinical, not a regulatory challenge. It did not emerge with the development of new drugs,[22] but by using existing drugs in young patients. The pioneers in pediatric oncology used whatever was available to help the young patients. That is the logic of medicine. But this logic now collided with the logic of the regulatory authorities, as the drugs used in pediatric oncology were not specifically approved in children. Furthermore, there was now the concept of children as "therapeutic orphans".[7] In 2003, over hundred drugs were FDA-approved for the treatment of malignancies. FDA authors complained that only 15 had also a pediatric label, and that less than half of the drugs commonly used in pediatric oncology had specific pediatric use information in their label.[23] From 1997 on, the FDA rewarded additional studies with individual chemotherapeutic agents in young patients after the respective malignancy, treated with established cocktails, had relapsed (the cancer or other malignancy had come back) or did not respond to treatment (was refractory). The FDA issued 16 written requests until 2012 for individual cytotoxic agents, including pemetrexed, clofarabine, and anastrozole.[24] The patients that were recruited into these studies were already extensively pre-treated. Most of these "pediatric" oncology studies were performed in terminally ill young patients in whom previous rounds of chemotherapy had failed.[13-15] The FDA justified the study participation by emphasizing that in pediatric oncology participation in a clinical trial had become state-of-the-art.[25] But the FDA-rewarded studies had a different aim compared to the studies organized by the pediatric oncology collaborative groups. They aimed at pediatric labels, not at clinical improvement. In the late 1990s and early 2000s, these studies triggered wrong hope in patients and parents. These patients had no better chance of survival with the offered additional treatment. They abused young patients and their parents to get pediatric labels. They were fundamentally unethical and were a blatant breach of the principles of the Declaration of Helsinki, see also chapter 8.

While most FDA-triggered pediatric oncology studies were done with individual cytotoxins, a study in nasopharyngeal carcinoma (cancer of the nose and throat) recruited patients up to 21 years of age into a comparison of docetaxel alone vs. docetaxel plus cisplatin and 5-fluouracil in patients. The study report claimed boldly that nasopharyngeal carcinoma is a pediatric disease,[26] which is definitely untrue. Nasopharyngeal carcinoma occurs in humans of all ages.[27,28] The reason for the manufacturer to finance this study was the written request the FDA had issued for docetaxel.[29] A fulfilled written request results in a patent extension of six months.

Meanwhile, cancer treatment has progressed from chemotherapy to drugs that target specific molecules, cellular structures, or other mechanism of cellular interactions to block the growth and spread of cancer cells. Many molecular targeted therapies have been approved by the FDA, the EMA, and other regulatory authorities, and have demonstrated remarkable clinical success in the treatment of many cancer types including breast, leukemia, colorectal, lung, and ovarian cancer. This has been made possible in large part by technological advances in our understanding of the mutational landscape of human cancer and the genetic drivers present in individual tumors, and by the conversion of these learning into new drugs and biologics by the life science industry. We are rapidly discovering a growing number of mutations that occur in targetable pathways. Tumor genetic testing has become an important component in cancer development and in the choice of appropriate therapies.[30,31]

The mechanistic concept of children as "therapeutic orphans" was expanded by the European Union (EU) and its European Medicines Agency (EMA). Since 2007, the EMA demands for all new drugs a "pediatric investigation plan" (PIP), in which the company must commit to "pediatric" studies. If the EMA regards the proposed studies as not sufficient, it rejects the PIP and the company cannot submit a marketing authorisation application unless it has gone through another round of PIP negotiation in which the EMA has finally accepted the PIP. There is a myriad of PIPs that demand "pediatric" cancer studies in patients up to 17 years of age for targeted therapy drugs. But the DNA mutations that drive malignancies do not change their characteristics in the night of the 18th birthday. None of the EMA-demanded studies have resulted in an improvement of pediatric cancer care.[13-15] However, the official EMA reports emphasize the contrary. They claim that now many more drugs are "available" to children and have a pediatric label.[32] But drugs in minors do not help or heal because they have a pediatric label. They are also available without a pediatric label. They help or heal because they act effectively in the human body. The on-label/ off-label challenge in children adds a further dimension to the general on-label/ off-label challenge.[33] Children and adults are both humans.[12] The narrative about the fundamental differences between adults and children has helped to obscure this simple fact.

The hope and assumption behind the described regulatory approach is to repeat a successful switch of targets. This switch of targets occurred in pediatric oncology when chemotherapeutic agents, already well-known in the treatment of adult cancers, were used successfully also in pediatric cancers. The regulatory authorities assume that such a switch of targets will also be successful with modern targeted drugs that have been in the meantime developed by life science companies and have revolutionized cancer treatment. Studies in minors are mechanically demanded for drugs that have been successfully investigated in adult patients. But modern targeted cancer drugs are not as unspecific as chemotherapeutic agents. They do not poison the entire body. Instead, they have specific targets. The EMA forces since 2007 companies to commit to clinical studies in minors with other cancer types than the drug has been investigated in adult patients. The EMA is demanding so many clinical studies in its PIPs that there are not enough potential patients on this planet to recruit all of them.[14,15] This is documented even in a publication with an EMA employee as a co-author.[34] Many EMA PIP-demanded "pediatric" studies are initiated by the companies that had to commit to them as a condition for the EMA to even process the approval of their new drug. Many of these studies cannot recruit enough patients. Companies must then submit an application for PIP modification to the EMA. The normal PIP negotiation process extends over a year. Negotiating a PIP modification takes half a year. There are now PIPs that have been modified 14 times. In several cases, the EMA ended up replacing PIPs that required many "pediatric" studies with a waiver, i.e., by dispensing with "pediatric" clinical studies.[13-15]

In the treatment of acute lymphoblastic leukemia (ALL), pediatric oncology faced a plateau of 90% survival for many years. Out of ten minors with ALL nine were cured. Not the tenth. And there was no telling who that one unfortunate patient would be. The breakthrough in overcoming this plateau did not come through enforced regulatory "pediatric" studies, but through innovative science in the context of drug development. Emily Whitehead contracted acute lymphoblastic leukemia (ALL) when she was 5 years old. She relapsed after standard chemotherapy. Her parents were facing the tough decision of either to let her die in peace in a hospice, or to try a new innovative experimental treatment. They opted for the experimental treatment. Blood was withdrawn, Emily's T-cells were re-programmed to fight the malignant ALL cells, and were infused back into her circulation. Thus treated T-cells are called chimeric antigen receptor (CAR) T cells, and the method in general is called CAR-T cell therapy. The FDA approved tisagenlecleucel in 2018 for patients up to 25 years of age. Would Emily have been recruited into one of the uncountable EMA-demanded studies, she would probably be dead. Instead, she is alive and today a healthy young cancer-free woman.[35-17]

In 2019, the FDA published a statement that explained that malignancies in adolescent patients are similar in histology and biologic behaviour to those in adults and therefore recommend participation of adolescents in promising adult cancer studies.[38] Although this is a step away from the children-are-therapeutic-orphans mantra, it is not enough. It is a step away, but the key decision is missing: medicine treats the patient's body, not his administrative or legal status. When a patient's body is adult, it needs adult medicine, not "pediatric" medicine, irrespective of the administrative and/or legal status of the patient.

Since 2020, the FDA demands separate clinical investigation of modern anticancer drugs in children which the FDA deems substantially relevant for pediatric cancer. This is based on the "Research to Accelerate Cures and Equity" (RACE) Act.[39,40] The RACE for Children Act follows the example of the EU with its EMA. All the PIPs and the studies they have triggered so far have not resulted in any clinical progress or success. But these PIPs did have significant results: label changes, more jobs in pediatric oncology research, in regulatory consultancies, in the administrative work around the "pediatric" clinical research machinery, and more.[13-15] It is not by chance that the RACE for Children Act was endorsed by many pediatric cancer research organisations. First publications emphasize that the RACE for Children Act increased the number of pediatric labels.[41,42] But the number of pediatric labels does not translate directly into improved pediatric cancer healthcare.

The RACE for Children Act was also endorsed by many pediatric cancer care organisations that often had been established by parents of children that had passed away with a malignancy. It is heartbreaking to lose a child. The narrative and promise of improving care for children with cancer by a higher number of pediatric labels for new drugs is believed by some or many desperate parents. Diseases against which contemporaneous medicine was helpless have always attracted quacks and crooks, such as for tuberculosis as long as no effective antibiotics existed, and with many other diseases as long as there was no really effective treatment.[43,44] Unfortunately, we are observing the same process in pediatric oncology, this time under the veil of the supposed blessing of more pediatric labels. It is not a conspiracy of individuals, but a systematic challenge of the 21st century. It is an illusion that reflects the changing framework of our society, which has meanwhile become more complex. But an illusion, nonetheless.

It is psychologically understandable that the FDA and the EMA have the desire to play a major role in the progress of science in general and specifically of pediatric medicine and pediatric oncology. But pediatric oncology did not emerge and develop because of pediatric labels. It emerged and developed because the pediatric oncology collaborative groups organized clinical trials to test available medicines. A completely different question is why the Children's Oncology Group (COG) supported the introduction of pediatric legislation and the concept of "pediatric drug development." The COG is the world's largest organization devoted exclusively to pediatric cancer research. The pediatric oncologists in this group are well aware of the deficiencies of many regulatorily demanded clinical studies. But they also live in this world. The pediatric legislation helped them play a much more prominent role on the political stage than before. There are things that cannot be said. One of these things was brought up at a pediatric conference. In a discussion, the COG representative explained that there are studies that the COG members and their centers would simply refuse to participate in. But there are also many "researchers" who are desperately dependent on funds. One option they have is to turn a blind eye. A chain is only as strong as its weakest link. We see here how important it is that Institutional Review Boards (IRBs)/ Ethics Committees (ECs) are aware of this challenge. If they reject a study, the fallible researcher will not risk a dispute that could become public.

The policy of forcing pharmaceutical companies to organize and pay for clinical studies in malignancies in minors has the sad side effect that two schools of academic research have developed. One of these schools is really working on identifying the causes and finding effective therapies. The study that saved the life of Emily Whitehead is a good example for this type of studies and this type of school. The other school has found a way to get guaranteed research contracts by conducting "pediatric" studies that companies must organize and finance as a condition for getting their innovative drugs into the approval process. The second school basks in the light of its alleged fight against childhood cancer. But since the mechanical concept requiring separate drug studies in minors is flawed, the studies conducted on this basis have no scientific merit. It is impossible to strictly distinguish between these two schools. Furthermore, many clinicians are unaware of the regulatory context. If the director of a research facility lands an order to participate in a pediatric study, anyone within that facility who questions the ethics of this study would be putting his job at risk. But when we look at the publications of studies on childhood cancer, we see that again and again the same researchers are involved in conducting one after another of the outlined pointless and harmful childhood cancer studies.[14,15] One excellent example are the pediatric melanoma studies that were demanded by the FDA and the EMA, specifically two studies that had to be terminated because the authorities demanded therapy that was outdated and below standard-of-care. After a few initial patients had been recruited, recruitment dried out, and the studies had to be terminated.[45]

Malignant melanoma

Malignant melanoma is a cancer that origins from cells that produce pigments (μέλας [melas] means black in classical Greek). Almost all melanomas emerge in the skin. If detected early, it can be surgically removed, and the patient is healed. If detected later and if it has already metastasized into different parts of the body, it is very aggressive and lethal.[46] Essentially, there are two types of melanoma: those that develop under the long-term influence of ultraviolet light, and those that can emerge very early also in babies. Melanomas that develop mostly in adults are called "conventional melanoma". As with many other diseases, occasionally also somebody before the 18th birthday contracts a conventional melanoma. Treatment of melanomas has advanced revolutionarily in the last decades with targeted drugs that first were given as single drugs (monotherapy); soon thereafter treatment shifted to giving two drugs simultaneously (combination therapy).

In 2007 the EMA put melanoma on a list of diseases that officially do not exist in children. But in 2008 it revised this decision, referring to a US statistic that reports 1.7 melanomas in 100,000 patients 15–19 years old. It claimed that these numbers are high enough to enable adolescents up to 17 years old to be included in "pediatric" clinical trials. There are two fundamental mistakes in this calculation. First, the discovery of melanoma in an adolescent does not mean that he needs drug treatment. If the melanoma is surgically removed, it is cured. Fortunately, this is the case in the vast majority of all melanomas found in adolescents. Second, the US statistics present 15-19 year olds as a group. Since the incidence increases with age, the proportion of patients who contract a melanoma before the 18th birthday is in the minority even in the 15-19 year-of-age group. The number of juvenile patients with conventional melanoma requiring drug treatment is approximately one-hundredth of the number of patients that EMA thought based on its flawed calculations and assumptions. In addition, the EMA does not differentiate between conventional and non-conventional melanoma. Such a differentiation could be expected from an authority that continuously emphasizes its pediatric expertise. But its expertise is not as deep as it would like it to be. In the meantime, it has also been genetically proven that conventional melanomas are the same disease before and after the 18th birthday.[47,48]

The FDA rewarded "pediatric" studies in patients up to 21 years with one of the first targeted drugs against melanoma, ipilimumab. The EMA issued two PIPs for the first two targeted anti-melanoma drugs, ipilimumab and vemurafenib. Comparable to the approach with cytotoxic agents, the FDA requested and the PIPs demanded studies for the treatment of "pediatric" patients with one drug, respectively. After a few patients had been recruited, physicians refused to refer further patients to the recruiting study centers. Combination treatment had meanwhile become state-of-the-art. Both studies had to be terminated.[13-15,48] Both studies have meanwhile been reported in academic journals[49,50] Both publications elegantly circumvent the true reasons for the study termination by simply reporting that recruitment was low. The fact that the received treatments were below standard-of-care and that patients were thereby harmed is not mentioned. Both publications also mention that the consequence of slow recruitment might be to include adolescents in the future in adult studies. The most important point is that both publications pretend that these studies were normal clinical studies.

Both studies were discussed and criticized in several peer-reviewed publications.[13-15,48] Would the EMA be as scientific as it claims to be, it would have apologized. It did not. Instead, it ignored the literature, and continues to demand inclusion of melanoma patients in a number of further PIPs.[13-15]

We see in the EMA demand for "pediatric" studies an obsession with clinical trials in minors independently of the question if enough patients exist at all and independent of the question if the demanded studies make medical sense. Once flawed EMA decisions are taken and published they are maintained even if it is proven in the literature that they are flawed. It is also interesting to note that the authors of the two academic publications declare no conflicts of interest in having accepted to participate in these studies. Indeed, by the formal criteria of the guidelines of the International Committee of Medical Journal Editors (ICMJE) and of other organizations that control the ethics of academic publications there are not conflicts of interest, see also chapter 9. But there are fundamental conflicts of interest. These two studies should never have started. No Institutional Review Board (IRB)/ Ethics Committee (EC) should have approved them. When they had to be terminated, the involved regulatory authorities, the sponsoring pharmaceutical companies, and the involved researchers should have apologized in public and should have distanced themselves from the regulatory demands for such studies. All this did not happen.

As clinicians, the involved researchers certainly take good care of their patients. But they share the EMA's belief that separate clinical trials with innovative anticancer medicines in people before their 18th birthday advance pediatric oncology. This conviction has the pleasant side effect that it continuously generates new orders in the form of studies that the industry has to finance in order to get their drugs into the EMA approval process.

It is also fascinating to see how companies that have developed effective drugs against conventional melanoma are being forced into allegedly pediatric clinical trials, while the real problem of truly pediatric melanoma that develops without long-term exposure to ultraviolet light has been ignored by the authorities so far. Academic publications discuss also the treatment of truly pediatric, non-conventional melanoma types and make treatment recommendations.[47,51] These recommended treatments are non-approved in children. Should we condemn these recommendations as off-label? Anyone who, for reasons of principle, expresses such thoughts in the presence of the parents of an affected child should consider putting on medieval mail. Otherwise, the mother might scratch out the eyes of the principled person. The father might join her.

Melanoma was the first disease in which the allegedly "pediatric" nature of the disease under study was scientifically examined and criticized. The melanoma studies are an excellent example of the conflict of interest and temptations pediatric researchers are exposed to by regulatory requests for "pediatric" studies. They show that it is not just a question of differing opinions, but of tangible economic interests. Overall, it has degenerated into a power game in which real ethics no longer play a role.

Autoimmune arthritis in minors/ juvenile idiopathic arthritis (JIA)

Medicine today differentiates autoimmune diseases that affect joints into those in adults and those in minors, with different names for diseases that are partially identical. The term JIA came into being when there was a very strong belief in medicine and pharmacology that everything was different with children than with adults: the children-are-not-small-adults mantra. In the beginning, there were seven diseases categorized under JIA, today they are six.[52] The term "JIA" gives the impression that these diseases affect only minors. This impression is wrong. Somebody who is diagnosed with JIA does not switch to an adult type of arthritis in the night of the 16th, 17th or 18th birthday. The disease remains, but the adult rheumatologists use different names, resulting often in wrong treatment. The US Center for Adults with Pediatric Rheumatic Illness (CAPRI) gives a lively expression to this contradiction.[53] Its medical head correctly expresses the opinion that JIA as a correct medical term simply does not exist.[54]

Inflammation is the body's response against injury or infection. In response to an injury, the immune system releases an army of white blood cells to surround and defend the injured area. The production of cytokines and other messenger substances is ramped up and these are released. The results are skin redness, swelling, pain, and more.

Prolonged or chronic inflammations without an external cause, however, are often autoimmune disorders.[55] If joints and surrounding tissue are affected, we speak of arthritis. The term "arthritis" stands for over hundred different types of disease.[56] The most common arthritis is osteoarthritis, a degenerative disease resulting from breakdown of the joint cartilage and the underlying bone. It affects one of seven persons in the US. The most common symptoms are pain and stiffness. Usually the symptoms progress with age.[57] In contrast, rheumatoid arthritis is a chronic autoimmune disorder that primarily affects joints. In rheumatoid arthritis, the own immune system attacks the joints, affecting also the joint cartilage and the bones.[58] Both osteoarthritis and rheumatoid arthritis are diseases of adulthood. However, there are many other – and rare - types of arthritis that can start at an early age. They have in common with pediatric oncology that researchers turned their attention to them when infant mortality had begun to decline in the 20th century. A key difference is that effective drugs had yet to be developed and were not yet available when pediatric rheumatology emerged. For decades, the only anti-inflammatory drug was aspirin. Extracts from the bark of the white willow tree had been used for centuries to treat various fevers and inflammations. In the 19th century, acetyl-salicylic acid was synthetized, was brought on the market, and became the first blockbuster drug.[59] In 1948, a first use of methotrexate was reported in the treatment of childhood leukemia. In the years and decades that followed, methotrexate became one of the most commonly used drugs in the treatment of rheumatoid arthritis.[60] Also in 1948 the first patient with rheumatoid arthritis was treated with cortisone. Soon many rheumatologic patients received cortisone. Oral and intra-articular administration of corticosteroids began in the 1950s. But by 1960 all of the toxic effects of chronic corticosteroid administration had become known. To enable use of lower corticosteroid dosages, additional use of non-steroidal anti-inflammatory drugs (NSAIDs) began in the late 1950s.[61] The discovery of steroids and of disease modifying antirheumatic drugs (DMARDs) such as methotrexate had been a huge step forward in anti-inflammatory treatment, but they have such serious side effects. Especially steroids cannot be safely administered over a long period of time in young people. After World War II, many new non-steroidal anti-inflammatory drugs (NSAIDs) were developed.[62] Methotrexate, NSAIDs and DMARDs were used in the treatment of rheumatic diseases on top of steroids. Some showed low incidence of gastro-intestinal side effects, the principal adverse reaction seen with NSAIDs than seen with their predecessors including aspirin.

Still a generation ago, young patients with chronic arthritis based on autoimmune processes faced a lifetime of misery. The parents were fortunate if they managed to find a rheumatologist to treat them. Furthermore, the available treatments were not very effective and did not prevent pain, disabilities and disfigurement if the facial joints were affected. The outlook of young patients with chronic autoimmune arthritides has improved considerably.[63]

The North American Pediatric Rheumatology Collaborative Study Group (PRCSG) was founded in 1973 and has an over 40-year long track record of successfully supporting the design, conduct, analysis, and publication of trials in close collaboration with industry sponsors. The PRCSG conducted several clinical trials with the then available medicines, which were predominantly NSAIDs and other disease modifying antirheumatic drugs (DMARDs), including methotraxate. In these days, NSAIDs were the cornerstone in the treatment of rheumatoid diseases in minors. The PRCSG leadership was involved in the training of the leadership of the Paediatric Rheumatology International Trials Organisation (PRINTO), an originally European research network that since its inception now includes also centers in Latin America, Asia and Africa. The missions of PRCSG and PRINTO are aligned.[64,65]

PRCSG and PRINTO have done a lot of work in developing adequate methods in conducting clinical trials in young people with rheumatic diseases. Both organizations are clinical organizations that have each tested the drugs that were already on the market. Founded during the period when the children-are-not-little-adults and children-are-therapeutic-orphans mantras were at the peak of their influence, both organizations had the most of pediatric legislation in the US and Europe benefits. A fifteen-year-old patient suffering from one of the diseases subsumed under JIA is physically no more a child. But he is still a child administratively and legally. Representatives of PRINTO have published several articles, together with representatives of the EMA, in which they highly praise the European pediatric regulation.[66,67] As soon as we question the reasons for this, we encounter the fact that all new innovative drugs require "pediatric" studies, which industry has to pay for. There is no other clinical discipline where the flow of money generated by pediatric studies has translated so directly into the praise of the EU pediatric legislation.[14,15] Adolescent patients with autoimmune arthritis are physically old enough to be treated with adult dosages. Significantly younger patients need dosage recommendations appropriate to their age and physical development, but not separate and repeated evidence of the effectiveness of the innovative drugs. The forced repetition of the proof of effectiveness of innovative anti-inflammatory drugs has led to numerous clinical studies from which the research networks made good money. But they did not promote the health care of the patients. The networks adorn themselves with borrowed plumes.

Compared to cancer in minors, the breakthroughs in pediatric rheumatology came much later with innovative drugs including receptor blockers, monoclonal antibodies, and more. All together, these new modern medicines are called biologics or biopharmaceuticals, because they are not chemically synthesized like pharmaceuticals, but isolated from human, animal, plant, fungal, or microbial cells.

The term "juvenile chronic arthritis" was originally used in Europe, and "juvenile rheumatoid arthritis" in North America. In 1995, the International League of Associations for Rheumatology (ILAR) replaced these terms by the term "juvenile idiopathic arthritis" (JIA). JIA is not one single disease, but an umbrella term for several different autoinflammatory diseases that affect joints. The definition for JIA is that the disease is diagnosed before the 16th birthday.

Epilepsy

The treatment of children with epilepsy is still one of the greatest challenges in pediatric healthcare and neurology. Epilepsy is not a specific disease in its own right, but a potential consequence of many different diseases and external factors including stress, alcohol, insomnia, flashing lights in people with low irritability thresholds, accidents, and more. Epileptic seizures range from brief and barely noticeable to long seizures with severe convulsions. Visible convulsions are the most common, but there are other forms, seizures characterized by absences.

Today we know that epilepsy is caused by abnormal synchronized brain activity. Since epileptic seizures cannot be triggered consciously and cannot be suppressed by mere will, it was assumed in the past that supernatural forces and gods took over the control of the individual. Epilepsy is described in many early historical records including the Code of Hammurabi written almost 4,000 years ago. Dealing with epilepsy was associated with superstition. Parents hoped that amulets, rituals and incantations might appease the gods and alleviate the symptoms. The existence of epileptic seizures was widespread in the public consciousness. It was called the "falling sickness" or the "sacred disease" (*morbus sacer* in Latin), and had almost uncountable further names.

Today, thanks to the availability of effective antiseizure medications, epilepsy has lost some of its terror. But also, the treatment of epilepsy fell victim to the children-are-therapeutic-orphans mantra. In 1994, the US National Institute of Health (NIH) organized a conference on the pharmaceutical treatment of epilepsy in children, emphasizing that most new antiseizure medications were not approved in children, had no pediatric pharmacokinetics (PK) or safety data, but were used in children, comparable to drugs in other clinical areas. At the end of the conference, the non-government participants expressed the opinion that medicines efficient for partial-onset seizures (POS) in adults should also be approved in young patients, provided that safety and PK considerations were appropriate.[68]

Since the inception of pediatric legislation, the FDA rewarded and required many "pediatric" studies of antiseizure medications, and the EMA has pestered developers of new innovative antiseizure medications by demanding additional "pediatric" studies in "pediatric investigation plans" (PIPs) since 2007.[14,15,69,70] As part of a PIP negotiation, clinical specialists were asked to provide input on the question of whether new antiseizure medications had really to be re-examined separately in all minors. They examined all studies in minors treated with antiseizure medications in the last forty years and concluded that they worked down to the age of two years.[71,72] With this conclusion, epilepsy is the one major clinical area in which clinicians have brought down the children-are-therapeutic-orphans mantra. They did not do this on their own initiative, but only on special request. But the regulatory authorities reacted. Today the FDA accepts the extrapolation of the efficacy of antiseizure medications from adults to children down to the age of two, while the EMA accepts it down to the age of four years. However, both agencies did not simply accept that antiseizure medications also work in minors. Instead, they claim that it is possible to "extrapolate" their efficacy from adults to minors,[73] as if minors were another species. The FDA claims that the decisions to accept extrapolation evolved with new evolving science and knowledge. But the term of 'extrapolation' of the efficacy of antiseizure medications from adults into minors is misleading. Antiseizure medications work in humans once the central nervous system has reached a minimum of maturity. The question to what degree antiseizure medications work also in newborns and babies is another, very special question that concerns a small fraction of minors, not all of them. The term 'extrapolation' is flawed. Minors are not another species.[12]

Times are changing and unshaken faith in the authorities has weakened. Researchers in child epilepsy complain that parents are increasingly reluctant to allow their children to participate in clinical trials.[74] At this point, the gut feeling of the parents is more correct than the learned opinion of all those who refer to the lack of labels in children.

Essentially, today's medical science, officially accepted by the regulatory authorities, has arrived at what clinicians told the NIH in 1994: antiseizure medications also work in minors. In other words: for several decades, time, money and other resources have been wasted in clinical studies of childhood epilepsy that did not produce anything new beyond repeating what clinicians had known already. What they have shown is that minors are not a different species and that antiseizure medications work for them, too. So far, this has remained an issue of the specific clinical area of pediatric neurology, although it is a challenge at the interface of medicine and regulatory affairs across all medical areas.

Now that the authorities are finally accepting, to some extent, that children are not a different species, we should start thinking about the direction in which research into childhood epilepsy could and should go. A key point should be the interruption of long-lasting seizures, called "status epilepticus". The majority of the literature reports such seizure interruptions in the hospital. But most seizures, including status epilepticus, do not occur in the hospital. They occur at home, at school, or in general during leisure time. Unlike in adults, parents and guardians are almost always present in minors. It is time that we learn to work on ways to better train parents to interrupt status epilepticus themselves, rather than calling the ambulance or taking the convulsing child to the emergency room themselves. This is easier today than in the past, as there are now formulations around that allow application of effective antiseizure medication such as midazolam to the oral mucosa instead of requiring an intravenous application. For decades, rectal diazepam was the only formulation available to be administered by parents. However, its efficacy was often not satisfactory,[75] and the application cumbersome. This is not only a pharmacological and medical challenge, but a much broader challenge that would aim at creating a better social environment to take care of sick children. This will in the future require medical and pharmacological research to seriously improve cooperation with professions, including teachers, social workers, and many more.[14,15,69,70]

Regulatory territorial demands

Injuries of joints occur relatively frequently. One joint that is particularly often affected is the knee. As long as humans are growing, the cartilage in the joints is supplied with blood directly by the circulatory system. With the completion of puberty, this direct supply ceases and the joint cartilage is supplied and nourished by the fluid in the joint capsule. Internal injuries in the knee often damage cartilage structures. As long as young people have not yet reached the end of puberty, even severe cartilage damage can heal by itself surprisingly fast with rest. Even in early adulthood, this no longer works so smoothly, and medical intervention is required. One method of surgical treatment is that cartilage tissue is removed from a less stressed area in a first endoscopic intervention, is sent to a commercial laboratory where the cartilage cells (chondrocytes) are grown into a three-dimensional matrix patch. This patch is then implanted on the injured cartilage in the knee in a second operation. This two-part operation is now a routine procedure in the surgical treatment of knee injuries and allows fast healing. Altogether, this concept is called autologous chondrocyte implantation (ACI). The products used in ACI are regulated by the US FDA as "regenerative medicine advanced therapy" (RMAT),[76] and by the EMA in the EU as "advanced therapy medicinal products" (ATMPs).[77] Both the FDA and the EMA approve products of ACI separately in adults and "children". To get approval in patients before their 18th birthday, both demand separate proof of efficacy in "children" by clinical studies.

Several "pediatric investigation plans" (PIPs) have been issued for chondrocyte products. The striking point about these ACI PIPs is that they require separate "pediatric" studies for patients who have already reached the end of puberty but are still under 18 years of age. This is explicitly described in the PIPs' inclusing criteria.[78-80] The end of puberty can be objectified by X-ray of the bones of the long bones, usually the forearm is used. With the end of puberty, the growth plates close. So, what the EMA is asking for is separate evidence of the effects of chondrocyte patches, classified as medicines, in young people between the physical attainment of puberty and the legal attainment of adulthood at the age of 18. In other PIPs, the EMA demands "pediatric" studies in patients 16-17 years of age,[81] and 15-17 years of age.[82] I call this approach "territorial" because with these PIPs the EMA claims special rights for young people under the age of 18, even if these young people have already a mature body through an objectifiable measurement. People before the 18th birthday ("children") have become a territory where the EMA feels, claims and exercises special rights to apply separate rules. Medically and scientifically, these studies are superfluous and pointless. In one word: nonsense. But as long as the EMA has the power to block registration, as long the general public is not aware of this, and as long as pharmaceutical manufacturers remain in the sleazy corner of alleged money-hungry ruthless actors,[83-90] the EMA can force companies to commit to such pointless studies. The consequence is that manufacturers of ACI products had to run "pediatric" studies with young patients that were physiologically already mature, but not yet administratively, officially and formally.

Knee injuries are becoming more common today because also young people participate in demanding physical sports where such injuries occur relatively frequently.

In 2021, the EMA refused a modification of a PIP mentioned above,[78] with the consequence that the product will never be EU-approved in persons younger than 18 years ("children.").[91] On this basis, surgeons will have to treat their minor patients "off-label". The precise opposite of what the pediatric legislation claimed to try to achieve.

A comparable example from an entirely different medical field is the treatment of perinatal depression, one of the most common complications before or after child birth with potentially horrifying consequences for the mother and the entire family. During pregnancy, the mother's body is flooded with hormones which can contribute to the onset of depression. Symptoms include extreme sadness, low energy, mood swings, fatigue, and more. Potential risks include suicide by the mother, and/ or that the mother kills or injures her own child. Going through perinatal depression is also a risk factor for perinatal depression in the next pregnancy period. The first menstrual period and the potential to become pregnant mark the difference between a prepubertal girl and a young, physically mature woman. Treatment for perinatal depression includes sympathetic psychological support by the family, the boyfriend or husband, healthcare professionals, and, of course, drug treatment. Brexanolone (also called allopreganolone) is FDA-approved for the treatment of perinatal depression in adults.

For registration in young women before the 18th birthday, both the FDA and the EMA demand separate "pediatric" studies. US Study NCT03665038 investigated the safety of brexanolone in young mothers aged 15 to 17 years with postpartum depression.[92] Without such a study, the FDA will not approve brexanolone in adolescent women ("children"). The EMA allopregnanolone/ brexanolone PIP even demands a "pediatric" double-blind, randomised, placebo-controlled trial to show pharmacokinetics, safety, tolerability and efficacy in "postpubescent adolescent girls" with perinatal depression.[93]

These studies also have a territorial claim to special rights towards young women before the age of 18, who are not classified here as human beings but as "children".[12,14,15]

Both examples of territorial claims have the particularly bizarre characteristic that historically the emergence of the children-are-therapeutic-orphans and the children-are-not-little-adults mantras arose with early observations of developmental pharmacology on preterm and term babies.[94-96] Postpubescent adolescents with knee joint injuries as well as young mothers with perinatal depression are no longer vulnerable babies, but bodily mature humans. Whether they also mentally already mature is another question entirely, but it is none of the regulatory agencies' business when it comes to questions of drug safety and efficacy for surgery or the treatment of depression. That the EMA describes the young mothers as "girls" is furthermore an insult that belittles them in an already difficult life situation. Such studies do not consider the young mothers as human beings that need support for their perinatal depression, but abuse them as objects of administration. Does brenaxolone/ allopregnanolone change its mode of action at the 18th birthday? Definitely not. Young mothers and their parents should not consent to participate in such unethical studies, and Institutional Review Boards (IRBs) and/or ethics committees should not approve them.

Bizarre conclusions from pointless studies

Babies cry often when they are hungry, in pain, or feel uncomfortable. But they are not depressed. They cannot speak yet. They cry because there is an understandable reason, and the aim of their crying is that the parents, mostly the mother, should do something. To be depressed is to be sad over a long period of time without a comprehensible reason for this sadness. Depression is a mental state of low mood, aversion to activity, little or no feeling of pleasure in activities that usually bring joy, and more. It is normal to be depressed after an accident, after the loss of a loved one, or after some other heavy blow of fate. But usually, time helps to get over bad experiences. Babies are not depressed, but it can occur in adolescents and even children. Depression requires a minimal degree of maturity of the brain. After accidents, suicide is the most frequent cause of death in today's society in young persons, often caused by an underlying depression. It is therefore important to take a closer look at depression.

Like other challenges in psychiatry, understanding and dealing with depression took detours and went zigzag ways until a reasonable approach emerged. At the beginning of the 20th century, the term depression was uncommon. Instead, the term "melancholy" was used. The prevailing concept was psychoanalysis, established in the early 1890s by Sigmund Freud, based on the assumption of unconscious mental processes that influence human thinking, feeling and acting much more than one realizes. The subconscious contains internal conflicts, several phases of sexuality, and more. In this concept, many internal conflicts that cause problems in adulthood go back to early childhood. Freud theorized that melancholy, like other mental challenges, represented an internal conflict and saw it as a response to either a real or a symbolic loss, such as having failed to achieve a desired goal. A person's unconscious anger over such a loss would lead to self-hatred and self-destructive behavior. In his view, psychoanalysis could help resolve these unconscious conflicts by making them accessible to conscious thinking and thereby reducing self-destructive thoughts and behaviors. Psychoanalysis became very influential and established a dominant position in medicine's dealing with mental challenges.

Effective treatment against "melancholy" did not exist. Psychoanalysis consisted of a weekly conversation with the therapist and lasted for several years. Only well-heeled patients could afford it. An understanding conversation with a depressed person is always helpful up to a certain extent, but when the depression process has reached a pathological stage, that is not enough. All other treatments such as insulin coma, electric shocks, heavy sedatives including opiates, and more expressed helplessness. Only in the 1950s the first antidepressants were introduced, an innovation in the arsenal of medical interventions whose importance can be compared to the introduction of vaccines and antibiotics.[97,98] This introduction of psychoactive drugs reflected also increasing awareness that brain activity and consciousness are based on complex physiological processes in and between the brain cells. When the balance in these processes is disturbed, information processing does no longer work smoothly and can lead to mental challenges, mood disorders, and diseases. Different types of effective antidepressants were gradually developed. An essential cornerstone in the development of drugs for mental disorders, including antidepressants, was the definition of endpoints in clinical studies in order to objectify the type and extent of the disorders and to make measurements and observations in different centers worldwide comparable at all.

Specifically for young persons, there had for a long time been the dogma that depression does not exist in them.[99] When antidepressants were introduced, medical doctors began of course to use also antidepressants to help young patients. But like all other areas of medicine and drug treatment, also the antidepressant treatment of young patients was struck by the children-are-therapeutic-orphans and children-are-not-small-adults mantras. The cornerstone of these mantas was that safety and efficacy of drugs needed to be shown separately in the "pediatric population". With the introduction of pediatric legislation in 1997, the FDA began rewarding studies in "children" under the age of 17 who suffered from depression. Since the reward in the form of a six-month patent extension was worthwhile for the pharmaceutical companies, many studies were carried out on young people with depression in order to prove again that antidepressants also work before the 17th birthday. When a company observed young patients reporting possible suicide in their studies, the FDA sounded the alarm and called a meeting of specialists to discuss the problem of "suicidality" (considering suicide). This meeting resulted in an FDA "black box warning" of suicidality in "children".[100] A black box warning is printed prominently on the label of a drug. In the litigious legal US culture, even a medical doctor who thinks he should prescribe an antidepressant will think three times before actually prescribing it. He could be sued for prescribing a drug off-label. This can massively damage or ruin his career. Worldwide, regulatory authorities took up the FDA warnings.[99] To this day, the assessment of the black box warnings against the use of antidepressants is controversial in the psychiatric literature. Several psychiatric associations warned that these warnings had the potential to do more harm than good.[101-106] The consequence of the black box warning was that "suicidality" in the USA and worldwide decreased. But the number of successful suicides among young people increased. The studies that documented the alleged suicidality were not designed to detect suicidality at all.[107]

The EMA followed the FDA lead and required "pediatric" studies for every new antidepressant.[14,15,108,109]

Antidepressants are like crutches. It is best if you do not need them at all. But when you are depressed, antidepressants, used properly, are a valuable tool. Of course, manufacturers tried to sell as many as possible. These are the laws of the market, and as a doctor you have to make yourself immune to blindly trust in advertising and promises. Antidepressants are not drugs to be prescribed lightly, whether in young, adult, or elderly patients.

The black box warnings against "suicidality" are one of the most bizarre consequences of the children-are-therapeutic-orphans and children-are-not-small-adults mantras. These mantras arose from the observation of toxicities in premature babies.[94-96,108] Its application to young people who were unfortunate enough to contract a disease that becomes more common later in life goes against common sense and medical ethics. Medical care should use all there is to help. Antidepressants are not a miracle cure. They are not guaranteed to help every single patient. Mental illnesses are more complicated than broken bones. But that is no reason to blindly rely on mantras. It takes medical experience, common sense, and a healthy distrust of all mechanical theories that make it too easy when it comes to complex interrelations.

Misogynist studies

The EMA PIP for the antibiotic moxifloxacin demands a "pediatric" clinical study on pelvic inflammatory disease in female adolescents aged 12-17 years by extrapolation of existing adult and pediatric data.[110] These patients are bodily no longer children. To demand such a study is as misogynist as the demanded studies in young mothers with perinatal depression.

Multiple sclerosis

Multiple sclerosis is an inflammatory disease in which the immune system attacks the insulating covers of nerve cells in the brain and spinal cord for unknown reasons. This disrupts the ability of parts of the nervous system to transmit signals, resulting in a range of physical, mental, and sometimes psychiatric challenges. Symptoms can include double vision, blindness in one eye, muscle weakness, trouble with sensation, with coordination, and many more. Multiple sclerosis occurs in several forms, with isolated attacks (relapsing forms), or building up over time (progressive forms). In the relapsing forms of multiple sclerosis symptoms may disappear completely between attacks, although some permanent neurological challenges often remain, especially as the disease advances. The course of multiple sclerosis is not predictable and different from patient to patient. It begins mostly in adults aged twenty to fifty years, but can also begin earlier or later. As in many other clinical areas, also in multiple sclerosis there was for several decades the myth that there is a pediatric vs. an adult of multiple sclerosis. The term "pediatric onset multiple sclerosis" (POMS) is broadly used in the literature.[14,15,111] There is a specialized group, the "International Pediatric Multiple Sclerosis Study Group" (IPMSSG),[112] a global network of neurologists, scientists, clinicians and others that aim at improving understanding and treatment of multiple sclerosis in young patients.

Multiple sclerosis can be treated symptomatically with drugs used also in many other disease areas. Furthermore, specific disease-modifying therapies have been developed, mostly biologics. Disease-modifying biologics shorten the duration of attacks, lower their frequency, and provide symptomatic relief. At present, multiple sclerosis cannot be healed.[113]

Multiple sclerosis is a disease that requires a minimum maturity of the central nervous system. There is no multiple sclerosis in infants, babies and toddlers.

Nevertheless, both the FDA and the EMA approve drugs against multiple sclerosis separately in adults and "children". For ozanimod, approved in adults for the treatment of multiple sclerosis, the FDA demands a clinical study in "children" aged 10 to 17 years that will last until 2033.[114] The EMA PIP for ocrelizumab demands two "pediatric" studies in patients aged 10 to 17 years that should be finalized until 2025.[115]

The IPMSSG has meanwhile come to the conclusion that separate placebo-controlled "pediatric" studies in multiple sclerosis should no longer be performed. The name of the IPMSSG itself is misleading. There is not pediatric multiple sclerosis. Instead, there is multiple sclerosis treated by pediatricians. Nevertheless, the group's position has shifted towards a more reasonable view of the disease. Also the IPMSSG reports a growing hesitancy of parents to allow study participation of their children.[116]

Several "pediatric" studies are performed worldwide with fingolimod, tecfidera, plegridy and other compounds that are already approved for the treatment of multiple sclerosis in adults. All these studies lack medical and scientific sense.

Multiple sclerosis is yet another excellent example for the blur between the different meanings of the term child and for the unfortunate turn the observation of toxicities in preterm newborns has taken towards equating physiologically and administratively/ legally defined children, resulting in "pediatric" studies in patients that bodily are no longer children.

Further questionable studies

The FDA and the EMA demand "pediatric" studies for all new medicines that potentially might be used in patients before their 18th birthday, including for antibiotics, antifungal, and antiviral compounds. The EMA demands separate "pediatric" efficacy studies even for drugs that treat life-threatening disease such as cystic fibrosis where the disease mechanism is at the cellular level and novel drugs like ivacaftor disrupt this disease mechanism in such a way that the affected patients treated can live a completely normal life as long as they take the drug regularly. Other "pediatric" studies demanded by EMA PIPs include topical medications against atopic dermatitis and psoriasis, against allergies, against diabetes, for vaccines, and even for drugs that help in the case of a COVID-19 infection.[13-15,117]

Conclusions

The questionable studies discussed above show that also deeper questions need to be asked. The separation of medicine into two branches, one for adults and one for children, is perfectly fine as far as the administrative and pragmatic question of which medical doctor should look after which patient. Medicine is not a natural science like mathematics or astronomy, but is part of society with all its human strengths and weaknesses. young people also have also different problems than old people. They try sex, legal and illegal drugs, sometimes criminal behavior, and much more. They still lack the wisdom of old age (☺). But if a 15-year-old and a 25-year-old had a car accident, the surgeon should use identical suture material, identical drugs, and exercise the same medical devotion. If an identical disease has different names in adult and pediatric medicine which can lead to different treatments, there is a problem. This is the case with several diseases under the umbrellas term of "juvenile idiopathic arthritis" as opposed to adult rheumatology.[54,118]

Behind apparently self-evident terms such as "child" and the "pediatric population" stand imaginary worlds that can only be understood by looking at history and social dynamics. The blurring of different meanings of the word "child" shows how modern society, through its ever-increasing differentiation, must learn to ensure that unethical research, justified by pseudo-science, can no longer pretend to be real research. This unethical, pointless and often even harmful research hides behind medical hocus-pocus. It is a new worldwide challenge for humanity. There have been many comparable challenges in the past that were overcome. This one will not last forever, either.

References

1. Pediatrics 1999,104,Supplement 3: https://publications.aap.org/pediatrics/issue/104/Supplement_3
2. Blumer JL. Introduction. Pediatrics. 1999 Sep;104(3 Pt 2):582
3. European Society of Developmental, Perinatal Pharmacology https://esdppp.org
4. The Japanese Society of Clinical Pharmacology and Therapeutics https://www.jscpt.jp/eng/
5. Ito S, Nakamura H, Kobayashi T. Pediatric Pharmacology in Japan. Paediatr Drugs 2012 Aug 1;14(4):247-9.
6. US Department of Health and Human Services (DHHS). Pediatric Pharmacology Research Units (PPRU) Network (Historical/For Reference Only). DHHS 2021. https://www.nichd.nih.gov/research/supported/ppru
7. Shirkey H. Editorial Comment: Therapeutic Orphans. J Pediatr 1968 Jan; 72 (1), 119-120
8. Shirkey H. Therapeutic Orphans. Pediatrics 1999 Sep;104(3 Pt 2): 583-4.
9. Christensen ML, Helms RA, Chesney RW. Is pediatric labeling really necessary? Pediatrics. 1999 Sep;104(3 Pt 2):593-7.
10. Philip AG. The evolution of neonatology. Pediatr Res 2005;58(4):799_815 https://www.nature.com/articles/pr2005743.pdf?origin5ppub
11. Jorgensen AM. Born in the USA - The History of Neonatology in the United States: A Century of Caring. NICU currents 2010 Jun;8-12 https://static.abbottnutrition.com/cms-prod/anhi.org/img/Nurse%20 Currents%20NICU%20History%20June%202010.pdf
12. Gillis J, Loughlan P. Not just small adults: the metaphors of paediatrics. Arch Dis Child. 2007 Nov;92(11):946-7 https://www.ncbi.nlm.nih.gov/pmc/articles/PMC2083631/pdf/946.pdf

13. Rose K, Tanjinatus O, Grant-Kels JM, et al. Minors and a dawning paradigm shift in "pediatric" drug development. J Clin Pharmacol 2020, Dec 23.
https://accp1.onlinelibrary.wiley.com/doi/epdf/10.1002/jcph.1806

14. Rose K. Considering the Patient in Pediatric Drug Development. How good intentions turned into harm. Elsevier, London, UK, 2020

15. Rose K. Blind Trust - How parents with a sick child can escape the labyrinth of lies, hypocrisy and false promises of researchers and regulatory authorities. Hammersmith, London, UK, 2022.

16. Krueger G. Hope and suffering: children, cancer, and the paradox of experimental medicine. John Hopkins University Press, Baltimore, MD, USA 2008

17. DeVita VT Jr, Chu E. A history of cancer chemotherapy. Cancer Res. 2008 Nov 1;68(21):8643-53.
http://cancerres.aacrjournals.org/content/68/21/8643.full-text.pdf

18. Athale U, Hijiya N, Patterson BC, et al. Management of chronic myeloid leukemia in children and adolescents: Recommendations from the Children's Oncology Group CML Working Group. Pediatr Blood Cancer. 2019 Sep;66(9):e27827
https://www.ncbi.nlm.nih.gov/pmc/articles/PMC6944522/pdf/nihms-1063361.pdf

19. Subbiah V. Fast-tracking novel drugs in pediatric oncology. Cell Cycle. 2015;14(8):1127-8.
https://www.ncbi.nlm.nih.gov/pmc/articles/PMC4615060/pdf/kccy-14-08-1018049.pdf

20. Children's Hospital of Orange County (CHOC). Side Effects of Chemotherapy and Radiation in Children.
https://www.choc.org/health-topics/side-effects-of-chemotherapy-and-radiation-in-children/

21. Saletta F, Seng MS, Lau LM. Advances in paediatric cancer treatment. Transl Pediatr. 2014 Apr;3(2):156-82.
https://www.ncbi.nlm.nih.gov/pmc/articles/PMC4729100/pdf/tp-03-02-156.pdf

22. Adamson PC. Improving the outcome for children with cancer: Development of targeted new agents. CA Cancer J Cli 2015 May-Jun; 65(3), 212-20

23. Hirschfeld S. History of Pediatric Labeling. https://www.slideserve.com/marlin/history-of-pediatric-labeling; 2012

24. Food and Drug Administration (FDA). Written Requests Issued. Approved Active Moieties to which FDA has issued a Written Request for Pediatric Studies under Section 505A of the Federal Food, Drug, and Cosmetic Act. FDA 2022. https://www.fda.gov/drugs/development-resources/written-requests-issued

25. FDA pemetrexed Written Request. FDA 2001. https://www.fda.gov//media/80043/download

26. Casanova M, Enis Özyar E, Patte C, et al. International randomized phase 2 study on the addition of docetaxel to the combination of cisplatin and 5- fluorouracil in the induction treatment for nasopharyngeal carcinoma in children and adolescents. Cancer Chemother Pharmacol 2016 Feb;77(2):289-98.

27. Kamran SC, Riaz N, Lee N. Nasopharyngeal carcinoma. Surg Oncol Clin N Am 2015;24:547–61.

28. Brennan B. Nasopharyngeal carcinoma. Orphanet J Rare Dis 2006;1:23.

29. FDA docetaxel Written Request. FDA 2007 https://fda.report/media/78577/020499-Docetaxel-Pediatritic-Written-Request.pdf

30. Waarts MR, Stonestrom AJ, Park YC, et al. Targeting mutations in cancer. J Clin Invest. 2022 Apr 15;132(8):e154943. https://www.ncbi.nlm.nih.gov/pmc/articles/PMC9012285/pdf/jci-132-154943.pdf

31. Lee YT, Tan YJ, Oon CE. Molecular targeted therapy: Treating cancer with specificity. Eur J Pharmacol. 2018 Sep 5;834:188-196.

32. EMA: 10-year Report to the European Commission General report on the experience acquired as a result of the application of the Paediatric Regulation. EMA 2017.

https://health.ec.europa.eu/system/files/2020-06/paediatrics_10_years_ema_technical_report_0.pdf

33. Janssen WM. A Historical Perspective on Off-Label Medicine: From Regulation, Promotion, and the First Amendment to the Next Frontiers" Second Washington, D.C. Off-Label Communications, 2009 http://works.bepress.com/william_janssen/19/

34. Hwang TJ, Tomasi PA, Bourgeois FT. Delays in completion and results reporting of clinical trials under the Paediatric Regulation in the European Union: A cohort study. PLoS Med. 2018 Mar 1;15(3):e1002520. https://www.ncbi.nlm.nih.gov/pmc/articles/PMC5832187/pdf/pmed.1002520.pdf

35. Emily's story. Emily Whitehead Foundation 2023. https://emilywhiteheadfoundation.org/our-journey/

36. Emily Whitehead: A Young Girl Beats Cancer with Immunotherapy. https://www.cancerresearch.org/stories/patients/emily-whitehead

37. Maude SL, Laetsch TW, Buechner J, et al. Tisagenlecleucel in Children and Young Adults with B-Cell Lymphoblastic Leukemia. N Engl J Med 2018;378:439-448. https://www.ncbi.nlm.nih.gov/pmc/articles/PMC5996391/pdf/nihms966186.pdf

38. FDA. Considerations for the Inclusion of Adolescent Patients in Adult Oncology Clinical Trials. Guidance for Industry. FDA 2019 https://www.fda.gov/media/113499/download

39. H.R.1231 - RACE for Children Act 115th Congress (2017-2018). https://www.congress.gov/bill/115th-congress/house-bill/1231

40. Drezner N, FDA. FDARA Implementation: Future Pediatric Cancer Drug Development. https://www.fda.gov/media/122696/download

41. Zettler ME. The RACE for children act at one year: progress in pediatric development of molecularly targeted oncology drugs. Expert Rev Anticancer Ther 2022 Mar;22(3):317-321.

42. American Association for Cancer Research (AACR). RACE Act Increased the Number of Cancer Drugs with Required Studies for Use in Pediatric Patients. AACR 2022 https://www.aacr.org/about-the-aacr/newsroom/news-releases/race-act-increased-the-number-of-cancer-drugs-with-required-studies-for-use-in-pediatric-patients/

43. Smith B. Gullible's Travails: Tuberculosis and Quackery 1890-1930. Journal of Contemporary History 1985 Oct,20(4),733-756

44. Kang L, Pederson N. Quackery: A Brief History of the Worst Ways to Cure Everything. Workman Publishing, New York, NY, USA, 2017

45. Rose K, Grant-Kels JM. Pediatric Melanoma – The Whole (Conflicts Of Interest) Story. Int J Womens Dermatol 2018,Nov 19;5(2):110-115. doi: 10.1016/j.ijwd.2018.10.020 https://www.ncbi.nlm.nih.gov/pmc/articles/PMC6451736/pdf/main.pdf

46. Davis LE, Shalin SC, Tackett AJ. Current state of melanoma diagnosis and treatment. Cancer Biol Ther 2019;20(11):1366-1379. https://www.ncbi.nlm.nih.gov/pmc/articles/PMC6804807/pdf/kcbt-20-11-1640032.pdf

47. Pappo AS. Pediatric melanoma: the whole (genome) story. Am Soc Clin Oncol Educ Book 2014;e432-5 https://ascopubs.org/doi/pdf/10.14694/EdBook_AM.2014.34.e432?role=tab

48. Rose K, Senn S. Drug Development: EU Paediatric Legislation, the European Medicines Agency and its Paediatric Committee - Adolescents' Melanoma as a Paradigm. Pharmaceutical Statistics 2014; 13(4): 211-213

49. Geoerger B, Bergeron C, Gore L, et al. Phase II study of ipilimumab in adolescents with unresectable stage III or IV malignant melanoma. Eur J Cancer. 2017;86:358–63.

50. Chisholm JC, Suvada J, Dunkel IJ, et al. BRIM-P: A phase I, open-label, multicenter, doseescalation study of vemurafenib in pediatric patients with surgically incurable, BRAF mutation-positive melanoma. Pediatr Blood Cancer 2018 May;65(5):e26947.

https://www.ncbi.nlm.nih.gov/pmc/articles/PMC5867229/pdf/nihms928012.pdf

51. Bahrami A, Barnhill RL. Pathology and genomics of pediatric melanoma: A critical re-examination and new insights. Pediatr Blood Cancer 2018 Feb;65(2):10.1002/pbc.26792. https://www.ncbi.nlm.nih.gov/pmc/articles/PMC6500729/pdf/nihms-1009468.pdf

52. Arthritis Foundation. Juvenile Idiopathic Arthritis (JIA) https://www.arthritis.org/diseases/juvenile-idiopathic-arthritis

53. Center for Adults with Pediatric Rheumatic Illness (CAPRI) https://www.brighamandwomens.org/medicine/rheumatology-inflammation-immunity/services/pediatric-rheumatology-for-adults

54. Nigrovic PA, Raychaudhuri S, Thompson SD. Review: Genetics and the Classification of Arthritis in Adults and Children. Arthritis Rheumatol. 2018 Jan;70(1):7-17. https://onlinelibrary.wiley.com/doi/epdf/10.1002/art.40350

55. Mahesh G, Kumar KA, Reddanna P. Overview on the Discovery and Development of Anti-Inflammatory Drugs: Should the Focus Be on Synthesis or Degradation of PGE2? J Inflamm Res 2021 Feb 3;14:253–263. https://www.dovepress.com/getfile.php?fileID=66216

56. US Centers for Disease control and prevention (CDC). Arthritis types. 2022. https://www.cdc.gov/arthritis/types/index.html

57. Wikipedia, Osteoarthritis https://en.wikipedia.org/wiki/Osteoarthritis

58. Wikipedia, Rheumatoid Arthritis https://en.wikipedia.org/wiki/Rheumatoid_arthritis

59. Jones AW. Early drug discovery and the rise of pharmaceutical chemistry. Drug Test Anal 2011 Jun;3(6):337-44.

60. Weinblatt ME. Methotrexate in Rheumatoid Arthritis: A Quarter Century of Development. Trans Am Clin Climatol Assoc. 2013; 124: 16–25. https://www.ncbi.nlm.nih.gov/pmc/articles/PMC3715949/pdf/tacca124000016.pdf

61. Benedek TG. History of the development of corticosteroid therapy. Clin Exp Rheumatol 2011 Sep-Oct;29(5 Suppl 68):S-5-12.

62. Rainsford KD. Anti-Inflammatory Drugs in the 21st Century. In: R. E. Harris (ed.), Inflammation in the Pathogenesis of Chronic Diseases, Springer, New York, NY, 2007

63. Stoll ML, Cron RQ. Treatment of juvenile idiopathic arthritis: a revolution in care. Pediatr Rheumatol Online J. 2014 Apr 23;12:13. https://www.ncbi.nlm.nih.gov/pmc/articles/PMC4003520/pdf/1546-0096-12-13.pdf

64. Brunner HI, Rider LG, Kingsbury DJ, Co D, Schneider R, Goldmuntz E, et al. Pediatric Rheumatology Collaborative Study Group - over four decades of pivotal clinical drug research in pediatric rheumatology. Pediatr Rheumatol Online J. 2018 Jul 11;16(1):45.

65. Paediatric Rheumatology International Research Organisation (PRINTO) https://www.printo.it/

66. Ruperto N, Eichler I, Herold R, et al. A European Network of Paediatric Research at the European Medicines Agency (Enpr-EMA). Arch Dis Child. 2012 Mar;97(3):185-8.

67. Ruperto N, Vesely R, Saint-Raymond A, Martini A, for the Paediatric Rheumatology International Trials Organisation (PRINTO). Impact of the European paediatric legislation in paediatric rheumatology: past, present and future. Ann Rheum Dis 2013;72:1893–1896.

68. Sheridan PH, Jacobs MP. The development of antiepileptic drugs for children. Report from the NIH workshop, Bethesda, Maryland, February 17-18, 1994. Epilepsy Res. 1996 Feb;23(1):87-92.

69. Rose K, Neubauer D, Grant-Kels JM. Ethical Issues in Pediatric Regulatory Studies Involving Placebo Treatment. J Pediatr Epilepsy 2020; 9(03): 073-079

70. Rose K, Ettienne EB, Grant-Kels JM, Striano P, Neubauer D, Oishi T. Neurology's vital role in preventing unnecessary and potentially harmful pediatric studies. Expert Review Neurotherapeutics 2022, https://doi.org/10.1080/14737175.2022.2045953

71. Pellock JM, Carman WJ, Thyagarajan V, et al. Efficacy of antiepileptic drugs in adults predicts efficacy in children: a systematic review. Neurology. 2012 Oct 2;79(14):1482-9. https://www.ncbi.nlm.nih.gov/pmc/articles/PMC4098824/pdf/znl1482.pdf

72. Pellock JM, Arzimanoglou A, D'Cruz O, et al. Extrapolating evidence of antiepileptic drug efficacy in adults to children ≥2 years of age with focal seizures: The case for disease similarity. Epilepsia. 2017 Oct;58(10):1686-1696

73. FDA 2019. Drugs for Treatment of Partial Onset Seizures: Full Extrapolation of Efficacy from Adults to Pediatric Patients 2 Years of Age and Older: Guidance for Industry. https://www.fda.gov/media/130449/download

74. Auvin S, French J, Dlugos D, et al. Novel study design to assess the efficacy and tolerability of antiseizure medications for focal-onset seizures in infants and young children: A consensus document from the regulatory task force and the pediatric commission of the International League against Epilepsy (ILAE), in collaboration with the Pediatric Epilepsy Research Consortium (PERC). Epilepsia Open. 2019 Sep 4;4(4):537-543. https://www.ncbi.nlm.nih.gov/pmc/articles/PMC6885693/pdf/EPI4-4-0.pdf

75. Asnis-Alibozek A, Detyniecki K. The unmet need for rapid epileptic seizure termination (REST). Epilepsy Behav Rep 2020 Nov 25; 15:100409.

76. FDA 2019. Expedited Programs for Regenerative Medicine Therapies for Serious Conditions. https://www.fda.gov/regulatory-information/search-fda-guidance-documents/expedited-programs-regenerative-medicine-therapies-serious-conditions

77. Ram-Liebig G, Bednarz J, Stuerzebecher B, et al. Regulatory challenges for autologous tissue engineered products on their way from bench to bedside in Europe. Adv Drug Deliv Rev. 2015 Mar;82-83:181-91 https://mukocell.com/wp-content/uploads/2016/08/ADDRRam.pdf

78. EMA 2018: PIP EMEA-000979-PIP01-10-M01 This PIP version as well as the original PIP version are no longer available on the internet. However, I have conserved a PDF of the M01 version. The EMA has placed the version M02 on the internet, which turns up when you search for the original version or version M01. https://www.ema.europa.eu/en/documents/pip-decision/p/0012/2018-ema-decision-30-january-2018-acceptance-modification-agreed-paediatric-investigation-plan_en.pdf

79. EMA 2019: PIP EMEA-001823-PIP01-15-M01 https://www.ema.europa.eu/en/documents/pip-decision/p/0074/2019-ema-decision-22-march-2019-acceptance-modification-agreed-paediatric-investigation-plan_en.pdf

80. EMA 2018: PIP EMEA-002217-PIP01-17 https://www.ema.europa.eu/en/documents/pip-decision/p/0282/2018-ema-decision-12-september-2018-agreement-paediatric-investigation-plan-granting-waiver_en.pdf

81. EMA 2012: PIP EMEA-000736-PIP01-09 https://www.ema.europa.eu/en/documents/pip-decision/p/0022/2012-ema-decision-27-january-2012-agreement-paediatric-investigation-plan-granting-deferral-granting_en.pdf

82. EMA 2018: PIP EMEA-001264-PIP01-12-M02 https://www.ema.europa.eu/en/documents/pip-decision/p/0161/2018-ema-decision-15-june-2018-acceptance-modification-agreed-paediatric-investigation-plan_en.pdf

83. Angell M. The Truth about the Drug Companies: How They Deceive Us and What to Do about It. Random House Publishers, New York, USA, 2004

84. Angell M. Industry-sponsored clinical research: a broken system. JAMA. 2008 Sep 3;300(9):1069-71.

85. Angell M. Conflicts in serving both non-profit and for-profit medical centres. BMJ. 2015 Oct 21;351:h5491. doi: 10.1136/bmj.h5491.

86. Rosenthal, Elisabeth (2017). An American Sickness: How Healthcare Became Big Business and How You Can Take it Back. Penguin Press. ISBN 9780698407183

87. Gøtzsche PC. Deadly Medicines and Organised Crime: How Big Pharma Has Corrupted Healthcare. Routledge, London, UK, 2013

88. Goldacre B. Bad Pharma: How drug companies mislead doctors and harm patients. HarperCollins Publishers, London, UK, 2012

89. Goldacre B. Bad Science: Quacks, Hacks, and Big Pharma Flacks. Farrar, Straus and Giroux (FSG) Adult, NY, USA, reprint 2010

90. Steinbrook R, Kassirer JP, Angell M. Justifying conflicts of interest in medical journals: a very bad idea. BMJ. 2015 Jun 2;350:h2942

91. EMA 2018: PIP EMEA-000979-PIP01-10-M02 https://www.ema.europa.eu/en/documents/pip-decision/p/0012/2018-ema-decision-30-january-2018-acceptance-modification-agreed-paediatric-investigation-plan_en.pdf

92. A Study to Assess the Safety of Brexanolone in the Treatment of Adolescent Female Participants with Postpartum Depression (PPD). https://clinicaltrials.gov/ct2/show/NCT03665038

93. EMA Allopregnanolone/ brexanolone PIP EMEA-002051-PIP-02-16. EMA 2017 https://www.ema.europa.eu/en/documents/pip-decision/p/0357/2017-ema-decision-1-december-2017-agreement-paediatric-investigation-plan-granting-deferral-granting_en.pdf

94. Burns LE, Hodgman JE, Cass AB. Fatal circulatory collapse in premature infants receiving chloramphenicol. *N Engl 1 Med.* 1959;261:1318-1321

95. Silverman WA, Andersen DH, Blanc WA, et al. A difference in mortality rate and incidence of kernicterus among premature infants allotted to two prophylactic antibacterial regimens. Pediatrics 1956;18:6

96. American Academy of Pediatrics (AAP) 1995 | Committee on Drugs |Guidelines for the Ethical Conduct of Studies to Evaluate Drugs in Pediatric Populations Pediatrics 1995 Feb,95(2),286–294.

97. López-Muñoz F, Alamo C. Monoaminergic Neurotransmission: The History of the Discovery of Antidepressants from 1950s Until Today. Curr Pharm Des. 2009;15(14):1563-86.

98. Hillhouse TM, Porter JH. A brief history of the development of antidepressant drugs: From monoamines to glutamate. Exp Clin Psychopharmacol. 2015 Feb;23(1):1-21. https://www.ncbi.nlm.nih.gov/pmc/articles/PMC4428540/pdf/nihms667554.pdf

99. Varley CK. Treating depression in children and adolescents: what options now? CNS Drugs. 2006;20(1):1-13.

100. FDA 2018. Suicidality in Children and Adolescents Being Treated With Antidepressant Medications. https://www.fda.gov/drugs/postmarket-drug-safety-information-patients-and-providers/suicidality-children-and-adolescents-being-treated-antidepressant-medications

101. Asarnow JR, Mehlum L. Practitioner Review: Treatment for suicidal and self-harming adolescents - advances in suicide prevention care. J Child Psychol Psychiatry. 2019 Oct;60(10):1046-1054.

102. Fornaro M et al. The FDA "Black Box" Warning on Antidepressant Suicide Risk in Young Adults: More Harm Than Benefits? Frontiers in Psychiatry 2019 https://www.ncbi.nlm.nih.gov/pmc/articles/PMC6510161/pdf/fpsyt-10-00294.pdf

103. Martinez-Aguayo JC, Arancibia M, Concha S, et al. Ten years after the FDA black box warning for antidepressant drugs: a critical narrative review. Arch. Clin. Psychiatry (São Paulo) 2016 May/June;43(3). https://www.scielo.br/pdf/rpc/v43n3/0101-6083-rpc-43-3-0060.pdf

104. Spielmans GI, Spence-Sing T, Parry P. Duty to Warn: Antidepressant Black Box Suicidality Warning Is Empirically Justified. Front Psychiatry. 2020 Feb 13;11:18. https://www.ncbi.nlm.nih.gov/pmc/articles/PMC7031767/pdf/fpsyt-11-00018.pdf

105. Gupta S, Gersing KR, Erkanli A, et al. Antidepressant Regulatory Warnings, Prescription Patterns, Suicidality and Other Aggressive Behaviors in Major Depressive Disorder and Anxiety Disorders. Psychiatr Q. 2016 Jun;87(2):329-42.

106. Zito JM, Derivan AT, Kratochvil CJ, et al. Off-label psychopharmacologic prescribing for children: History supports close clinical monitoring. Child Adolesc Psychiatry Ment Health. 2008 Sep 15;2(1):24.
https://www.ncbi.nlm.nih.gov/pmc/articles/PMC2566553/pdf/1753-2000-2-24.pdf

107. Gören JL. Antidepressants use in pediatric populations. Expert Opin Drug Saf. 2008 May;7(3):223-5

108. Rose K, Neubauer D, Grant-Kels JM. Too Many Avoidable Suicides Occur Worldwide in Young Patients. A Review. Rambam Maimonides Med J. 2019, Sep 18.
https://www.rmmj.org.il/userimages/965/1/PublishFiles/977OnlineFirst.pdf

109. Rose K, Grant-Kels JM, Striano P, Ettienne EB, Oishi T, Neubauer D. "Pediatric" Drug Studies Might Be the Largest Abuse in Medical Research in History. It Is Time for Lawyers to Step In. J Law Med 2023,30(1), in press

110. Moxifloxacin PIP EMEA-000492-PIP01-08-M01. EMA 2009.
https://www.ema.europa.eu/en/documents/pip-decision/p/264/2009-european-medicines-agency-decision-23-december-2009-acceptance-modification-agreed-paediatric_en.pdf

111. Wikipedia, Multiple sclerosis
https://en.wikipedia.org/wiki/Multiple_sclerosis

112. International Pediatric Multiple Sclerosis Study Group" (IPMSSG), https://www.ipmssg.org/home.html

113. Goldenberg MM. Multiple Sclerosis Review. P&T 2012 Mar;37(3): 175-84.
https://www.ncbi.nlm.nih.gov/pmc/articles/PMC3351877/pdf/ptj3703175.pdf

114. FDA Ozanimod Approval Package 2020, including pediatric written request
https://www.accessdata.fda.gov/drugsatfda_docs/nda/2020/209899Orig1s000Approv.pdf

115. EMA Ocrelizumab PIP EMEA-000310-PIP03-10-M0. EMA 2021 https://www.ema.europa.eu/en/documents/pip-decision/p/0305/2021-ema-decision-13-august-2021-acceptance-modification-agreed-paediatric-investigation-plan_en.pdf

116. Waubant E, Banwell B, Wassmer E, et al. Clinical trials of disease-modifying agents in pediatric MS: Opportunities, challenges, and recommendations from the IPMSSG. Neurology 2019 May 28;92(22):e2538-e2549. https://www.ncbi.nlm.nih.gov/pmc/articles/PMC6556085/pdf/NEUROLOGY2018940742.pdf

117. Rose K. The COVID-19 Pandemic: A Global High-Tech Challenge at the Interface of Science, Politics, and Illusions. Elsevier, London, UK, 2022 https://www.elsevier.com/books/the-covid-19-pandemic/rose/978-0-323-99149-0

118. Nigrovic PA, Colbert RA, Holers VM, et al. Biological classification of childhood arthritis: roadmap to a molecular nomenclature. Nat Rev Rheumatol. 2021 May;17(5):257-269.

Chapter 8

The Declaration of Helsinki and Research in Minors

Humanity has many facets, one of which is that human history is also a never-ending series of wars. But with increasing international trade, travel, and communication, also efforts for organized international coordination emerged in the 19th century. A series of international sanitary conferences from 1851 on coordinated attempts to contain cholera and other contagious diseases. The Universal Postal Union was established in 1874. The League of Nations was founded after World War I in 1920 as the first worldwide intergovernmental organisation with the aim to maintain world peace. But it failed in preventing World War II.

Wars had and have two sides. They are a place of cruelty where people act out their lowest instincts. And they facilitate social, technical and scientific innovation. War weakens long-established traditional thought patterns and traditions, allowing new ideas to break through. With technological progress and industrialization, also the technology of war advanced. The killing people became increasingly efficient. But it was not just blindly killing people. Also, war medicine advanced, allowing war injuries to be better treated by faster transport to treatment centers, hygienic bandages, topical and systemic drugs, and surgery.[1]

Efforts were made by new branches of science to prove their usefulness, such as the help of psychologists and psychiatrists in selecting recruits and in treating mental war trauma. Preliminary culminations in both faces of war were the two World Wars. They triggered multiple scientific and technical research in the areas of physics, chemistry, encryption, communication, logistics, and more, but also research in the physical and mental capacities and limitations of people under demanding and extreme conditions. In the context of research projects, the rights and interests of the people examined were given little attention, particularly when civilians and often worse prisoners of war fell into the hands of unscrupulous researchers. During World War II, the experimentations by German Nazi and Japanese researchers reached a hopefully preliminary peak of cruelty and ruthlessness.[2-6]

A first international association of medical doctors was established in 1926 with the French name "Association Professionnelle Internationale des Médecins" (APIM). Until World War I, the dominant language used in diplomacy had been French. After World War I, English gradually replaced French as the lingua franca of diplomacy. The treaty of Versailles that terminated World War I was written in English and French. The widespread use of English was further advanced by the prominent international role played by English-speaking nations including the US, UK and the Commonwealth of Nations during and after World War II.[7] The APIM had suspended operations during World War II, but the British Medical Association (BMA) coordinated discussions between medical doctors of the allied nations. Two BMA-sponsored conferences in 1946 and 1947 prepared the replacement of the APIM by a new organisation, now called "World Medical Association" (WMA). The APIM was dissolved, remaining funds went to the new WMA, which was formally established 1947 and has grown until 2021 to 115 national medical associations with many more associate members.[8] The WMA is in official relations with the World Health Organization (WHO) and seeks close collaboration with the UN Special Rapporteur on the right to physical and mental health.[9]

After the horrors of World War II, when the war crimes of Nazi Germany and Japan and the crimes committed in connection with medical experimentation became known, the WMA became a crystallization point in the international debate on ethics in medical research. Already in 1948, the WMA General Assembly had received a report on "War Crimes and Medicine", which led the adoption of the International Code of Medical Ethics in 1949.[9]

The WMA emerged in a time when medical research had started to grow both at the levels of academic research and applied research with the aim to improve treatment as well as to commercialize new achievements and products. During the ensuing decades, academic and commercial research became more closely intertwined, a process which in the US was from the beginning stronger than in continental Europe. Drug approval remained under the responsibility of national regulatory authorities, but drug development and the necessary clinical trials, either coordinated or directly organized by pharmaceutical companies, became increasingly international. The internal language used within large pharmaceutical companies became English. World War II had massively expanded the armamentarium of medicine with the widespread availability of penicillin, soon other classes of antibiotics, followed by new classes of effective drugs. Medicine and the clinical research underlying drug development began to advance at a rate that nobody could have imagined half a century ago. This accelerated development is continuing until today. Experimental human treatment had been tarnished by the recent medical war crimes. But now experimental treatment of people began to save lives, both in adults and children, be it by treatment with antibiotics, by administering insulin to people with type I diabetes mellitus, by treating cancer and other malignancies in adults and children, by treating autoinflammatory diseases such as rheumatoid arthritis with steroids or disease modifying drugs (DMARDs) like methotrexate, and many more areas of clinical medicine.

In 1964 the WMA adopted in Helsinki, Finland, a declaration that would become the first significant effort of the international medical community to establish an ethical framework for research in and experimental treatment of human beings.[10] It became broadly known as the Declaration of Helsinki. Over the ensuing more than 50 years it has become a widely recognized key document. It was partially triggered by the preceding broad abuses of human research subjects.[11] It has been repeatedly updated. Nevertheless, the key principles expressed in the original declaration of 1964 have remained unchanged: that the primary purpose of medical research in humans is to understand the causes, development and effects of diseases and to improve their prevention, diagnosis and treatment. That even the best proven interventions must be evaluated continually through research for their safety, efficacy, and more (§ 6). Furthermore, that participation must be voluntary. This principle is clearly opposed to experiments with people in prisons, in concentration camps, and under other circumstances that limit voluntary and free decision-making.

The emergence of the Declaration of Helsinki reflected several historical circumstances: the rapidly growing range and power of medical treatment options; the awareness of recent crimes in the context of medical research; the wish to coordinate clinical research on an international level; the realization that such a task was beyond the government of one single country; and the desire to advance this process in a peaceful, civilized way.

Physicians have a key role in the direct recruitment and treatment of patients in clinical trials, as well as within the pharmaceutical industry in the planning, conduct, coordination and monitoring of international clinical trials. Neither the WHO nor the WMA have direct governmental authority. But international research needs a framework in which collected data are recognized worldwide.

Also, the spirit and the wording of the Declaration of Helsinki have been exposed to modern currents of thoughts. It now recommends that access to clinical trials for underrepresented groups should be increased so these groups also can benefit from research. It addresses specific issues for countries with limited resources, such as posttrial access to interventions and care for participants from limited resource settings; registration of trials in publicly accessible databases, and the need to publish positive, negative and inconclusive results, emphasizing that science improves through failures and successes.[11] The Declaration of Helsinki has also adapted to medical progress, resulting in recognizing the need to do research in emergency situations where intervention is needed, the patient is unable to give consent immediately and surrogates are not available short-term.[12] It is has also been emphasized that the declaration should address non-physicians.[13] The role of physicians in the wording of the Declaration of Helsinki still reflects a traditional understanding of medical practice that was the norm in past centuries, although in hindsight we see today that it did not correspond to medicine's real treatment power. The role of the medical doctor had then still a quasi-religious quality, something that is still preserved and presented in soap operas, television, and romantic novels, but does not capture well the role of medical doctors in today's healthcare. But that is another story. Anyway, the development of medicines has long outgrown immediate medical action. Medical research and drug development have become multidisciplinary activities which are continuously branching out into more and more rare diseases.

The Declaration of Helsinki does not explicitly mention children. Instead, it addresses potential research subjects that are incapable of giving informed consent, in which case the physician must seek informed consent from the legally authorised representative. Furthermore, when a potential research subject deemed incapable of giving informed consent is able to give assent, the physician must seek that assent in addition to the consent of the legally authorised representative. The potential subject's dissent should be respected.

Individuals incapable of giving informed consent should not be included in a research study without a likelihood of benefit for them unless it intends to promote the health of the group represented by the potential subject. Furthermore, in these patients the research should entails only minimal risk and minimal burden.[10]

The description of children not as children, but as persons uncapable of giving informed consent is a *legal* definition. We have discussed in previous chapters the flaws of the justification of pediatric drug development that are based on the semantic blur between the legal definition of children, i.e., everybody before he comes of age, and the fact that physiologically adolescents have already a body mature enough to be treated by adult drug doses. Specifically in this group, all "pediatric" studies are legally and regulatorily pediatric, but not medically and not scientifically.

The Declaration of Helsinki emerged from the horror of openly cruel and misanthropic research projects during World War II. It attempted to reconcile research in humans and human civilization, and in this it has acquired great merits. The representatives of the medical professions in the WMA are high-ranking physicians who know a lot about clinical treatment and enjoy a high reputation in their own medical world, and on this basis also by the lay public.

The Declaration of Helsinki has become part of a formalized procedure designed to ensure compliance with the official regulations that are the foundations of today's clinical research. The new challenge in pediatric research is that the pediatric studies are *on a formal level* correctly justified. The regulatory authorities demand studies in children that are defined by the 18th birthday, a chronological administrative age limit. The justification of "pediatric drug development" is that children should have the same right as adults to be treated with fully investigated drugs.[14] Otherwise there is allegedly the danger of either administering drugs that do not work at all in children, that they are given in too high doses, or that they might be toxic.[15] These concerns are correct in preterm newborns,[16] but not in all minors up to the night of the 18th birthday. Medications work the same a day, a month, or a year before and after the 18th birthday. The 18th birthday is an administrative and/or legal age limit. The claim that only drugs approved in children are safe and efficient is the imposition of today's drug approval rules on the history of pediatric medicine. But this imposition is flawed. Key pediatric subdisciplines, including pediatric cardiology, pediatric oncology, pediatric neurology, and even neonatology emerged well before separate drug approval in children was even considered. The key to understanding this is that the term "child" has different legal and physiological meanings. When advocates of "pediatric drug development" demand studies in children, they pretend that the 18th birthday, an administrative time limit, corresponds a physiological transformation of the body. But this assumption is simply wrong. The child's body becomes adult during the relatively slow process of puberty. In itself this blur between the administrative/legal and the physiological meaning of the term child is just semantic. But as long as it is not addressed and deciphered, children-are-not-small-adults and children-are-therapeutic-orphans statements appear to be correct. This blur at the interface of medicine and law is a challenge for which the Declaration of Helsinki was not prepared when it was introduced and to which it has not yet adapted.

The *spirit* of the Declaration of Helsinki is very clear: the primary purpose of medical research in humans is to better understand diseases and to improve their prevention, diagnosis and treatment. All interventions should continuously be evaluated and improved, if possible. For the authors of the original version of the Declaration of Helsinki it would have been unimaginable that authorities would demand pointless and/or even harmful studies. That pointless and/or even harmful studies are today demanded by the FDA and the EMA is based on a blur at the interface of medicine and law: all human minors before the 18th birthday are classified as another species for which separate drug approval is required.

Medically and scientifically this does not make sense, at least for adolescents but also for prepubertal children before their 12th birthday. Although separate proof of efficacy in all minors is medically and scientifically pointless, it is correct from a dogmatic regulatory point of view. We can compare such a dogmatic regulatory point of view with the attitude prevailing at the beginning of the Tuskegee Study in 1932: African Americans, in these days still called negroes, were considered as an inferior kind of human being. The Tuskegee Study had been presented at several medical conferences. In these days, medical doctors of colour were not welcome as conference participants.[17,18] Although by the medical standards of the 1960/70s the withholding of antibiotics to African American men with syphilis was unethical, despicable and even criminal, the management of the United States Public Health Service (PHS) was not moved by internal criticism. But the study was terminated within weeks after its key features had been published and criticized in the New York Times. The public's attitude had changed fundamentally during the 40 years since the start of the study. Probably the FDA and the EMA will not dare to defend the overall concept of "pediatric drug development" once the pointlessness of most studies and the harmfulness of many of them is critically discussed in the general public; more so as a relevant degree of these studies are not even truly pediatric, but studies in young, physiologically already mature humans that, however, are classified as "children".

By limiting itself to the legal definition of children, the Declaration of Helsinki has left a weak spot in the continuous need to defend medical research against the creeping in of unethical approaches. Until now, scholarly main teaching has not recognized the distortion behind the apparently scientific justification of research in "children". Really justified additional research in very young children[16] has become a formally correct but content-wise almost completely unfounded demand for separate approval and testing of drugs in "children", regardless of whether these "children" are bodily children any longer, and regardless of reflecting the scientific or medical need for it.

To put it provocatively, the efforts to let children of all ages participate from medical progress occurred successfully hands-on throughout the last century, resulting in almost unbelievable advances on a practical level, including the fight against childhood cancer, the success of pediatric surgery, and many more. However, humanity in modern society has taken a detour in constructing a conceptual foundation that should frame the ethical foundations of this progress. The foundation of medical progress is not only research.

Another foundation is the daily work of physicians, nurses, administrators, and other healthcare professionals, learning from mistakes, and teaching these learnings to the next generation. But the historically new existence and newly established high level of responsibility and authority of the regulatory agencies has led to the over-emphasis on the formal drug approval in "children" and the elimination of common sense in this context. This is certainly not the sole fault of the Declaration of Helsinki. But it shows that the inclusion of minors in medical and therapeutic progress is more difficult on a conceptual level than "just" the practical solution of technical problems that underlay the successful operation of, for example, congenital heart defects or the dosage of drugs. The path initially taken by clinical medicine, i.e., mechanical formulas to estimate doses by body weight or body surface, or dose tables for children, was correct, with the exception of the very young patients. From the learnings of developmental pharmacology about the changed physical characteristics of premature and mature babies, the decision to define "children" *legally* resulted in the *formally* correct demand for research in "children" even where they are de facto bodily no longer children. Medicine treats the body, not the legal status of a patient. In the same breath that developmental pharmacology ushered in the campaign of "pediatric drug development"[19] and "better medicines for children,"[20] it refused to apply its own learnings about the development of the human body from childhood into adulthood (and beyond adulthood) in the context of drug treatment, and specifically of giving correct doses. This is not the fault of the Declaration of Helsinki. But the Declaration of Helsinki reflects an over-reverence of formal legal definitions of children and adults in a place where this leaves room for misunderstandings and flawed medical conclusions.

Many abuses in the past were carried out in secret such as the Mengele twin studies or other studies in German concentration camps or by the Japanese unit 713.[2-6] Others were reported in the scientific literature and were only realized to be unethical when a prominent physician collected them and convinced the editor of a respected journal to publish his critical assessment.[21] The described blur at the interface of medicine and law leads to a situation that formally all "pediatric" studies are correctly justified. But those in adolescents are performed in young people that physiologically are no longer children. They are *allegedly* pediatric studies only. We realize this only if we ask the right questions and openly address the different meanings of the term "child".

This is a new kind of ethical challenge in our modern differentiated society, in which well-established structures and highly respected institutions have developed interests of their own that are just not visible at first glance. Young medical doctors learn what the current authorities teach about treatment, medication, and the framework of clinical research. As so often in life, it will have to be for a new generation of physicians and medical researchers to see through the fog of pseudo-scientific justifications. Mid-term, the Declaration of Helsinki will need several fundamental changes to become once again be a useful tool that researchers can use as a guide. Children should be addressed directly as research subjects, and not through the legalistic paraphrasing of people who cannot give informed consent. The basic needs for therapeutic research in children should be openly addressed: only those studies should be regarded as scientifically and ethically justified that have the potential to improve understanding, diagnosis and treatment of diseases. Achieving pediatric labels for drugs of which we know already that they work in humans is not an ethically acceptable research target. This may be too complex for the current generation of distinguished notables in the WMA. But what is new about this situation? Humanity and society have in history often or always moved forward long before this was properly understood intellectually. Let us hope it will not be centuries before the WMA and the Declaration of Helsinki provide research with a useful guideline for distinguishing reasonable and pseudo-scientific research with minors.

The time has come for the WMA to fulfill its historical responsibility by defining children and their place in medical research in terms of their physical development, and no longer simply in legal terms. Furthermore, the WMA should take a closer look at experimental therapy in adults and children and establish clear rules for where research in children makes sense and where it is pointless. The WMA currently consists of physicians. Maybe the scientific tools and the background knowledge for this already exist in the ranks of its members. Maybe the WMA should adapt its composition to modern times. Or at least it should learn more about the framework of drug development and drug approval and improve its use of common sense.

References

1. Lapage G. Medical Research During War-Time. Nature 1948, Jun 26;161(4104):998-999
https://www.nature.com/articles/161998a0
2. Wikipedia, Unit 713
https://en.wikipedia.org/wiki/Unit_731
3. Russell, Lord of Liverpool. The Knights of Bushido (A Short History of Japanese War Crimes). Cassell & Co, London, UK, 1958
4. Wikipedia, Nazi human experimentation
https://en.wikipedia.org/wiki/Nazi_human_experimentation
5. Nazi Medical Experiments. United States Holocaust Memorial Museum, 2006.
https://encyclopedia.ushmm.org/content/en/article/nazi-medical-experiments
6. Mozes-Kor, E: The Mengele Twins and Human Experimentation. In: Annas G & Grodin M (Eds): The Nazi Doctors and The Nuremberg Code. Oxford University Press, Oxford, UK, 1995
7. Mehtiyev A. The language of diplomacy. California Linguistic Notes 2010,35(2), Spring.
https://english.fullerton.edu/publications/clnArchives/pdf/MethievLgDplmcy.pdf
8. World Medical Association (WMA) 2022. Who we are/ History
https://www.wma.net/who-we-are/history/ .
9. Wikipedia, World Medical Association (WMA)
10. WMA Declaration of Helsinki – Ethical principles for medical research involving human subjects
https://www.wma.net/policies-post/wma-declaration-of-helsinki-ethical-principles-for-medical-research-involving-human-subjects/
11. Ndebele P. The Declaration of Helsinki, 50 years later. JAMA 2013 Nov 27;310(20):2145-6.

12. Shrestha BM. The Declaration of Helsinki in relation to Medical Research: Historical and Current Perspectives. J Nepal Health Res Counc 2012 Aug;10(22):113-7 https://www.researchgate.net/publication/233980544_The_Declaration_of_Helsinki_in_relation_to_Medical_Research_Historical_and_Current_Perspectives

13. Millum J, Wendler D, Emanuel EJ. The 50th anniversary of the Declaration of Helsinki: progress but many remaining challenges. JAMA. 2013 Nov 27;310(20):2143-4. https://www.ncbi.nlm.nih.gov/pmc/articles/PMC4203648/pdf/nihms634500.pdf

14. Ward RM, Benjamin DK Jr, Davis JM, et al. The Need for Pediatric Drug Development. J Pediatr. 2018 Jan;192:13-21.

15. EMA 2004 Evidence of harm from off-label or unlicensed medicines in children EMEA. https://www.ema.europa.eu/en/documents/other/evidence-harm-label-unlicensed-medicines-children_en.pdf

16. Ruggiero A, Ariano A, Triarico S, et al. Neonatal pharmacology and clinical implications. Drugs Context. 2019 Oct 14;8:212608. https://www.ncbi.nlm.nih.gov/pmc/articles/PMC6821278/pdf/dic-8-212608.pdf

17. Washington HA. Medical Apartheid. The Dark History of Medical Experimentation on Black Americans from Colonial Times to the Presen. Anchor Books (Random House), New York, NY, USA 2006

18. Jones JH. Bad Blood. The Tuskegee Syphilis Experiment. The modern classic of race and medicine update with an additional chapter on the Tuskegee Experiment's legacy in the age of AIDS. The Free Press (Simon & Schuster), New York, NY, USA, 1981

19. Mulberg AE, Murphy MD, Dunne J, Mathis LL (Eds.) Pediatric Drug Development: Concepts and Applications. 2nd ed. John Wiley & Sons, Chichester, UK, 2013.

20. European Medicines Agency (EMA) 2015. Better Medicines for Children.

https://www.ema.europa.eu/en/documents/leaflet/better-medicines-children_en.pdf

21. Beecher H. Ethics and Clinical Research. NEJM 1966, 274 (24), 1354-1360

Chapter 9

The International Committee of Medical Journal Editors (ICMJE)

From World War II on medical research, technology, diagnosis and treatment improved fast, accompanied by advances and an expansion of health facilities and technical equipment. This resulted, inter alia, in a growing – and aging – population, a strong increase of chronic diseases because the older people get, the more health challenges they experience, which are not immediately fatal, but are medically manageable. They are called chronic because they last so long. "Χρόνος" (chronos) means "time" in classical Greek. This increase in chronical diseases in turn results in an ever-increasing demand for better health care. Medical and health expenses increased significantly. Ever-increasing care developed into an industry which occupies a considerable amount of capital and labor and has an important position in social and economic life. Health spending increased faster than the gross domestic product (GDP) in the US and many European countries. In 2016, medical spending reached in the US $ US 3.3 trillion, half from private spending, the other half from government spending, financed by taxes. Together with the increasing scale of health service and advances in technical equipment, the division of labor and specialization increased further, too. [1,2] Although the person of the medical doctor still plays a prominent role in hands-on healthcare, healthcare has become a field in which many different professions work closely together. In particular in research, specialists and experts from a wide variety of disciplines are involved.

The scientific and medical literature is an essential background tool in the progress of healthcare. Among the oldest general medical journals that are still published today are the New England Journal of Medicine (NEJM), established in 1812, and the Lancet, established in 1823. Scientific medical journal publication is rapidly increasing in volume and has become the most expanding field of journal publications worldwide. Medical journals are crucial in medical education and sharing of information. This ranks above the use of other sources such as newsletters, textbooks, and monographs. Medical journals have a key role in continuing medical education, more than other methods such as discussions at conferences, personal contact with colleagues, education courses, and more.[3-5]

Academic publishing is undergoing major changes in the transition from the print to the electronic format. An important trend, particularly with respect to journals in the sciences, is open access via the internet. In open access publishing, a journal article is made available for free for anybody using the web by the publisher at the time of publication. Both open and closed journals are sometimes funded by the author paying an article processing charge (APC), shifting fees from the reader to the researcher and their employing institution. This of course presupposes that the author has an institution at his disposal that pays these fees. This in turn only makes the bureaucratization of the scientific community even stronger. There are also many open or closed journals that fund their operations without receiving fees from the authors. And still other journals use these fees for profit in predatory publishing.[6-12]

The publishing of academic journals started in the 17th and expanded in the 18th and 19th century. Medical journals focusing on specific medical issues emerged in the early 20th century. In the beginning, academic publishing was controversial. Often new discoveries were announced as a monograph, reserving priority for the discoverer. Isaac Newton, Gottfried Leibniz, and Galileo Galilei used this approach. Disputes about the priority of a discovery dropped slowly from the 18th to the first half of the 20th century. This decline is probably due to the increasing acceptance of the publication of papers in academic journals. Medical and scientific journals and books are published by commercial companies or organisations that represent healthcare professions such as the American Medical Association (AMA), the American Academy of Pediatrics (AAP), the British Medical Association. There are many more types of publishers. In the 1960/70s, commercial publishers began to buy high ranking scientific journals that had been previously published by non-profit academic societies. When the commercial publishers raised the subscription prices significantly, they lost little of the market as these journals were in high demand. Of the more than 2,000 publishers, the five commercial companies Reed Elsevier, Springer Science+Business Media, Wiley-Blackwell, Taylor & Francis, and SAGE, accounted for half of all articles published in 2013. These companies appear to have high profit margins, making them one of the most profitable industries, especially compared to the smaller publishers, which often operate with lower margins.

Unlike many other industries, in academic publishing the two most important inputs, i.e., the articles and the peer review process, are provided virtually free of charge. At present, a crisis in academic publishing is broadly discussed, based on a pressure of budget cuts at universities and increased costs for journals. Papers on academic work are usually published in an academic journal that contains original research results or reviews existing results. Papers undergo a process of peer review by one or more peer reviewers, referees who are regarded as on the same hierarchical level as the submitting corresponding author. These peer reviewers check the content of the submitted manuscript if it is suitable for publication by the respective journal. Submitted papers may undergo a series of reviews, revisions, and re-submissions before finally being accepted or rejected. This process usually takes several months. Thereafter there is often a delay of months or even over a year before the accepted manuscript is published.

Some journals, particularly newer ones, publish now in electronic form only. Paper journals are now generally made available in electronic form as well, both to individual subscribers, and to libraries. Almost always these electronic versions are available to subscribers immediately upon publication, or even before. Sometimes they are also made available to non-subscribers, be it immediately by open access or after a time embargo of months or even years, in order to protect against loss of subscriptions.

Peer review is a central concept for academic publishing. The peer reviewers must find a manuscript sufficiently high in quality to merit publication. Furthermore, reviewers are usually familiar with the sources consulted by the author(s), which helps against plagiarism. The process of academic publishing has two phases: peer review and production. The peer review process is increasingly managed online. Manuscripts undergo one or several rounds of review in which the author must modify the manuscript following the reviewers' comments. This is repeated until the editor is satisfied, and the work is accepted. The production process then takes an article through copy editing, typesetting, inclusion in a specific issue of a journal, printing and/ or online publication. Copy editing ensures that the article conforms to the journal's house style; that all references are correct; that the text is consistent and legible; and that mistakes and typos in English are corrected. Often this involves substantive editing and negotiating with the authors.[13,14]

For two centuries, medical journals have mediated the production and dissemination of medical knowledge, their histories inextricably entwined with that of the medical system and with the progress of science alltogether.[15,16] Despite the emergence of rivals unimaginable a generation ago, the journal and its peers maintain substantial influence on both the medical profession and society.[17,18]

In the following, we outline how the scientific justifications for clinical studies with minors and the publication of these studies in medical journals have so far elegantly circumvented the otherwise very strict control mechanisms of the medical and scientific literature business.

The essential element in the self-understanding of science and in the opinion that the general public has of science is the belief that science is a testable and objectifiable system of opinions and knowledge, in contrast to different religious beliefs, political opinions, and philosophical assumptions. Within this basic understanding, the honesty of the scientists involved is an indispensable prerequisite. Science should be value-neutral and free of conflicts of interest, and where actual or potential conflicts of interest exist, they should be clearly stated so that the independent reader can form his or her own opinion. Science is felt and seen as a large global community in which other rules apply than in politics, for example, where every person with some life experience knows that what politicians say is not necessarily what they mean. And where every person with some life experience also knows that politicians always promise the blue sky before the election. Once they are elected and have power over the administrative machinery of the state or part of the state, it remains to be seen to what extent they actually try to implement what they have promised.

Science is not just what it claims to be. Science has become a complex - and expensive - system in which there is not only the alleged neutrality or objectivity of the scientists. Scientists do not live on air and love alone. They need employment, and their position in research and teaching is also a position of power. Science could not exist without the framework of security provided by today's state. But science and the institutions represented in it are not simply state structures. To a certain extent they are also independent of the state. The security mechanisms in place today reflect the excesses and mistakes of the past and the effort to counter them with elements of sincerity and honesty and to make those elements controllable as well.

Today's "International Committee of Medical Journal Editors" (ICMJE) was originally known as the Vancouver Group, after the location of its first meeting in Vancouver, Canada. This group issued in 1979 the Uniform Requirements for Manuscripts Submitted to Biomedical Journals ("Uniform Requirements" or "URMs"). All this goes back to 1968 when the secretary to a terribly important kidney specialist grew tired of retyping his papers to change the format of references when a paper had been rejected by one journal and had to be submitted to another journal with different requirements. Encouraged by a medical librarian, she asked the editors of several high level medical journals if they could not use the same format for references. These editors and others met at a clinical research conference and agreed to use the formats used by the US National Library of Medicine. Eighteen journals signed this agreement. In the early 1970s, editors of high level medical journals discussed if they could also agree on international standards for manuscripts. In 1978 they established an international steering committee in Vancouver, Canada, and later re-named it to the International Committee of Medical Journal Editors (ICMJE). For a while, the ICMJE was often also called the Vancouver group.

In its early years, the controversies surrounding the "Uniformed Requirements" involved discussions on reference formats, for example the citing of references by the author's family name plus the year of the publication, plus a list of all references ordered alphabetically by the respective first authors' family names at the end of the paper ["Harvard system"], versus the numerical system with a sequential numbers for each new reference and a list in this order at the end of the publication. (This book uses the latter system.) Other controversies were about units of measure and abbreviations. But by the middle 1980s the ICMJE shifted its focus to ethical issues, including listing people as authors when the work was done by others; duplicate publication; and scientific fraud. In 1987 the ICMJE decided to issue these requirements as separate documents. The ethical issues that caused the most prolonged debates over the last 25 years were authorship criteria, editorial freedom, duplicate publication, scientific fraud, conflicts of interest, and some other subjects such as advertising discussed at individual meetings.[19]

Publications are the means by which progress in career development or at least a maintenance of the respective career in the scientific community is secured. The current rules on authorship criteria, editorial freedom, duplicate publication, scientific fraud, conflicts of interest, and some other subjects reflect the importance of publications for individual career development, but also their importance for the evaluation of new drugs and therapeutic approaches. A dark side of scientists is that they are often a bit more unworldly than, for example, marketing managers in industry. It was common for decades for the marketing departments of pharmaceutical companies to pay ghostwriters to write papers that professors would then submit and eventually publish under their own names. Co-authors were added to the list of authors as a courtesy, even though they had not contributed anything significant.

After a series of revisions, the ICMJE guidelines were given in 2013 their current name of "Recommendations for the Conduct, Reporting, Editing, and Publication of Scholarly Work in Medical Journals".[20-23] They are guidelines concerning the ethics, preparation and formatting of manuscripts submitted to biomedical journals for publication. Most leading biomedical journals demand compliance with the ICMJE recommendations. As of January 2020, 5570 journals worldwide claim to follow the ICMJE recommendations.[24]

The recommendations' purpose is to establish best practice and ethical standards in the conduct and reporting of research and other material published in medical journals. They reflect the fact that in academia, publications are the essential element that decides one's career. The semi-serious joke "publish or perish" describes the pressure to publish in order to succeed in an academic career. Such institutional pressure is generally strongest at research universities. Publications bring attention to scholars and their sponsoring institutions and can promote continued funding and careers. The value of published work is often determined by the prestige of the academic journal it is published in. Journals are measured by their impact factor, the average number of citations of articles published in a specific journal.[25]

Historically, many pharmaceutical companies attempted to represent their product as well as possible in the literature and in oral presentations at medical conferences by directly bribing key opinion leaders and/ or leading authors, by donating to their institutions, by wining & dining at medical conferences, by lavish gifts, by covering travel expenses for the authors and their spouses, and much more. There is a lot of money in health care and the medical system. Not only innocent angels and white knights work in academia and not only villains in the area of business that in the industry is called "medical marketing". Healthcare has evolved into a complex and expensive system that is increasingly exposed to dimensions such as politics, financial investment, competition for philanthropic donations, tax breaks, competition for the most capable and productive employees, and many more. This also has the consequence that white knights and villains can be on both sides. Naive workers in academia and industry can have children with health problems and be shaken by the edifice of lies they find behind the facade of academic research. In the effort to allow only academics the ability to search for truth,[26-33] there is more effort to strengthen one's social position in competition with other institutions than the most ardent protagonists admit.[34-36]

Part II B of the ICMJE recommendations discusses disclosure of financial and non-financial relationships & activities and conflicts of interest. It emphasizes the importance of public trust in the scientific process and the credibility of published articles. It explains that potential for conflict of interest and bias exists when professional judgment concerning a primary interest, such as patients' welfare or the validity of research, may be influenced by a secondary interest, such as financial gain. Furthermore, that perceptions of conflict of interest are as important as actual conflicts of interest. Direct financial relationships are described as the most easily identifiable, the ones most often judged to represent potential conflicts of interest and thus the most likely to undermine the credibility of the journal, the authors, and science itself. It also lists other interests that may represent or be perceived as conflicts, such as personal relationships or rivalries, academic competition, and intellectual beliefs.[22] The ICMJE has developed a disclosure of interest form that is regulatory updated and is used by many journals to document actual or perceived conflicts of interest to ensuring independent authorship free of conflicts of interest.[37]

The movement of "pediatric drug development" and the ensuing clinical studies in minors represent a new challenge for medical journals, their editors, and with this also the ICMJE and further committees, groups and institutions dedicated to the maintenance of ethics in medical publishing. The studies on minors required by the regulatory authorities, who are often physically no longer children and in most cases represent nothing more than a repetition of the demonstration of the effectiveness and safety of new drugs, are not only pointless, superfluous and therefore unethical, but often harm also the young patients by exposing them to placebo or to treatment below standard-of-care, as explained in detail in Chapter 7.

But the demand for these studies is not based on individual bribes. Rather, we have a structural conflict of interest here that is essentially the same as that underpinned the maintenance of the Tuskegee study when Peter Buxton, a non-involved US Public Health Service (PHS) employee, began to express doubts about the admissibility and ethics of the study and asking the PHS management to terminate it. PHS employees were allowed to attend the autopsies performed on the bodies of African Americans who had died of the syphilis that had intentionally not been treated with antibiotics. They published about their observations during these autopsies. During the decades the Tuskegee study took place, nobody involved in the publications about this study ever asked critical questions.[38-41] The participating scientists were respected employees of a respected institution. They secured their jobs and careers with such publications. This did not include individual bribery. But there was a structural conflict of interest.

That the studies in "pediatric drug development" are required by the authorities and are justified by leaders of the AAP and developmental pharmacology does not mean that they are ethically correct and acceptable. The conflicts of interest that underlie them are structural and a new challenge in the balance of power of science, pseudo-science, regulatory authorities, and public trust in the authorities. The "pediatric" studies outlined in chapter 7 reflect a coalition of academic scientists, regulatory authorities, and initially also pharmaceutical companies that first benefited from the "pediatric" studies beginning in 1997. Pharmaceutical companies profited through the US patent extension. FDA employees profited by raising their academic profile and speaking at numerous scientific meetings. "Pediatric" researchers profited by building and securing their careers. The only ones that did not benefit from these studies were and are the young patients themselves and their families. Both children and adults belong to the human race. Emphasising predominantly that children are not small adults carries the danger to unconsciously negate all that is to be gained through a vision which takes in human beings throughout their lives.[34,35,42]

The publication that claimed that nasopharyngeal carcinoma (cancer of the nose and/or the windpipe) is a "pediatric" disease was based on US pediatric exclusivity. The study compared the addition of docetaxel to chemotherapy with cisplatin and 5-fluouracil in "children" aged up to 21 years.[43] Nasopharyngeal carcinoma occurs relatively frequently also in minors, but it is definitely not a pediatric disease.[44,45] The company that produced docetaxel got an FDA written request.[46] The motivation to finance this study was to get a patent extension. All those involved in this study profited, with the exception of the young patients and their families. But nobody was bribed. Everything was done by the book.[34,35,47] The conflicts of interest were of a structural nature that is not yet captured by the ICMJE recommendations. Half a century ago, nobody could have imagined this new type of conflicts of interest. They reflect the billions that today are flowing into "pediatric" clinical research. The European Commission estimates the costs of European Union pediatric investigation plans (PIPs) at € 2.1 billion per year.[48,49] Over the 17 years the European pediatric regulation is in force, this amounts to about € 36 billion. Not just peanuts. Justified by the allegedly improved healthcare for minors. Once these studies will be discussed in the public, it will become much more difficult to pretend that they are really based on science.

In a matter as complex as the ICMJE guidelines, it would be impossible not to be criticized.[50-53]

The weak point in the ICMJE guidelines and their definition of conflicts of interest on which we focus here is that on the one hand, the "pediatric" studies are *formally* correctly justified. But the term "child" has several meanings. By systematically confusing these meanings, semantic confusion becomes intentional deception. It has often been critically mentioned that a relevant percentage of drugs in administratively defined minors in not approved in these minors.[54-56] However, this in itself is *not* a medical or scientific issue.[34,35] Today, new medicines have to go through the drug development process. But historically, pediatric medicine did not emerge and develop through the development of special medications for children (with one exception), but through their systematic use and testing in underage patients. The one exception was the development of lung surfactant to treat respiratory distress syndrome in preterm newborns that are not yet able to produce the surfactant needed to keep the lungs running on their own.[57,58] The warning call that drugs are not approved for "children" retrospectively imposes a situation that exists today on the history of pediatric medicine that developed different circumstances. It thereby produces a fundamentally flawed impression of the role of the regulatory authorities in the emergence of pediatrics. "Pediatric drug development" also reflects the regulatory authorities' efforts to inflate, exaggerate, and misrepresent their role in the emergence of the medical discipline of pediatrics.

It is probably the first time in modern history that an entire branch of science is engaging in a systematic deception. Most pediatricians who accept participation in research projects do so to raise additional funds for their institution. They are probably unaware of the depth of this systematic deception. But that does not make this deception any better. It is not the first time in the history of science that science's internal control mechanisms have been blind to their own weaknesses.

The ICMJE will have to expand its description of conflicts of interest in a new version of its recommendations and will have to add a new chapter on "pediatric" clinical studies.

There are a number of additional groups that aim at controlling the ethics of research.

The Committee on Publication Ethics (COPE) is a nonprofit organization with the mission to define best practice in the ethics of scholarly publishing and to assist editors and publishers in this. COPE was established in 1997 by a small group of medical journal editors in the UK. In 2022 COPE has over 13,000 members worldwide from all academic fields. COPE's first guidelines were developed in 1999 and were published as Guidelines on Good Publication Practice in the Annual Report in 1999. On their basis, the first edition of Code of Conduct for Editors was published on the first COPE website in 2004, with an editorial in the British Medical Journal (BMJ). The COPE code of conduct was replaced in 2017 with a simplified description of expectations as COPE's Core Practices, with links to COPE's detailed guidance.[59,60]

COPE has links with the Council of Science Editors, the European Association of Science Editors, the International Society of Managing and Technical Editors,[61] the World Association of Medical Editors,[62,63] the Open Access Scholarly Publishers Association,[64,65] the Directory of Open Access Journals,[66,67] the International Association of Scientific, Technical, and Medical Publishers (STM),[68,69] and the Association of Learned and Professional Society Publishers.[70,71]

The Council of Science Editors (CSE), formerly the Council of Biology Editors (CBE; 1965–2000) and originally the Conference of Biology Editors (CBE; 1957–1965), is a US-based non-profit organization that supports editorial practice among scientific writers. In 2008, the CSE adopted the slogan "CSE: Education, Ethics, and Evidence for Editors (E4)".[72,73]

The European Association of Science Editors (EASE) is a non-profit membership organisation for people interested in science communication and editing. Founded in 1982, in France, EASE now has an international membership.[74,75]

The existence of the listed groups shows that science and its publication structures are not a state-run business that is easy to understand. To the contrary. Nevertheless, all these groups will have to adapt their guidelines and recommendations to research and publications to clinical research in minors and "pediatric drug development".

References

1. Phelps CE. Health Economics. Routledge, 6th edition, New York, NY, USA 2018

2. Wikipedia, Health Economics
https://en.wikipedia.org/wiki/Health_economics

3. Garba S, Ahmed A, Mai A, et al. Proliferations of Scientific Medical Journals: A Burden or A Blessing. Oman Med J. 2010 Oct; 25(4): 311–314. https://www.ncbi.nlm.nih.gov/pmc/articles/PMC3191655/pdf/OMJ-D-10-00052.pdf

4. Loscalzo J. The future of medical journal publishing: the journal editor's perspective: looking back, looking forward. Circulation 2016; 133:1621–1624

5. Huang WW, Feldman SR. The proliferation of online for-profit medical journals. J Am Acad Dermatol 2016 Sep;75(3):656-657

6. Albert KM. Open access: implications for scholarly publishing and medical libraries. J Med Libr Assoc. 2006 Jul; 94(3): 253–262.
https://www.ncbi.nlm.nih.gov/pmc/articles/PMC1525322/pdf/i1536-5050-094-03-0253.pdf

7. Thomas SP. No Laughing Matter: Proliferation of Predatory Journals. Issues Ment Health Nurs 2020 Apr;41(4):269-270.
https://www.tandfonline.com/doi/epdf/10.1080/01612840.2020.1720448

8. Roberts WC. Proliferation of Online Medical Journals. Am J Cardiol. 2016 Feb 15;117(4):699-700. doi: 10.1016/j.amjcard.2015.10.049

9. Grudniewicz A, Moher D, Cobey KD, et al. Predatory journals: No definition, no defence. Nature 2019 Dec;576(7786):210-212
https://www.nature.com/articles/d41586-019-03759-y

10. Leena G, Jeevan KVJ. Disrupting predatory journals. Current Science 2022 Feb,122(4)
https://www.currentscience.ac.in/Volumes/122/04/0396.pdf

11. Beall's List of Potential Predatory Journals and Publishers
https://beallslist.net/

12. (New) List of Predatory Journals – 2023
https://www.openacessjournal.com/blog/predatory-journals-list/

13. Forgues B, Liarte S. Academic Publishing: Past and Future. M@n@gement 2013, 16(5),739-756.
https://www.cairn.info/revue-management-2013-5-page-739.htm

14. Wikipedia, Academic publishing
https://en.wikipedia.org/wiki/Academic_publishing

15. Goda Naujokaitytė. Number of scientists worldwide reaches 8.8M, as global research spending grows faster than the economy. 14 Jun 2021
https://sciencebusiness.net/news/number-scientists-worldwide-reaches-88m-global-research-spending-grows-faster-economy

16. Gastfriend E. 90% of All the Scientists That Ever Lived Are Alive Today.
https://futureoflife.org/guest-post/90-of-all-the-scientists-that-ever-lived-are-alive-today/

17. Podolsky SH, Greene JA, Jones DS. The Evolving Roles of the Medical Journal. N Engl J Med 2012; 366:1457-1461
https://www.nejm.org/doi/pdf/10.1056/NEJMp1113567?articleTools=true

18. Ziman JM. The Proliferation of Scientific Literature: A Natural Process. Science 1980 Apr;208(4442),369-371
DOI: 10.1126/science.7367863

19. Huth EJ, Case K. The URM: Twenty-five Years Old. Science Editor 2014, Jan-Feb;27(1),17-19
https://www.icmje.org/recommendations/archives/summary78-04.pdf

20. International Committee of Medical Journal Editors (ICMJE).
https://www.icmje.org/

21. ICMJE, History of the Recommendations
https://www.icmje.org/recommendations/browse/about-the-recommendations/history-of-the-recommendations.html

22. ICMJE. Recommendations for the Conduct, Reporting, Editing, and Publication of Scholarly Work in Medical Journals. ICMJE 2022.
https://www.icmje.org/icmje-recommendations.pdf

23. Van der Weyden MB. The ICMJE and URM: Providing Independent Advice for the Conduct of Biomedical Research and Publication. Mens Sana Monogr. 2007 Jan-Dec; 5(1): 15–25.

24. Wikipedia, ICJME recommendations https://en.wikipedia.org/wiki/ICMJE_recommendations

25. Wikipedia, Publish or perish https://en.wikipedia.org/wiki/Publish_or_perish

26. Angell M. The Truth about the Drug Companies: How They Deceive Us and What to Do about It. Random House Publishers, New York, USA, 2004

27. Angell M. I academic medicine for sale? New Engl J Med. 2000 May 18;342(20):1516-8

28. Angell M. Industry-sponsored clinical research. A broken system. JAMA 2008 Sep 3;300(9):1069-71

29. Rosenthal, Elisabeth (2017). An American Sickness: How Healthcare Became Big Business and How You Can Take it Back. Penguin Press. ISBN 9780698407183

30. Gøtzsche PC. Deadly Medicines and Organised Crime: How Big Pharma Has Corrupted Healthcare. Routledge, London, UK, 2013

31. Goldacre B. Bad Pharma: How drug companies mislead doctors and harm patients. HarperCollins Publishers, London, UK, 2012

32. Goldacre B. Bad Science: Quacks, Hacks, and Big Pharma Flacks. Farrar, Straus and Giroux (FSG) Adult, NY, USA, reprint 2010

33. Steinbrook R, Kassirer JP, Angell M. Justifying conflicts of interest in medical journals: a very bad idea. BMJ. 2015 Jun 2;350:h2942

34. Rose K. Considering the Patient in Pediatric Drug Development. How good intentions turned into harm. Elsevier, London, UK, 2020

35. Rose K. Blind Trust - How parents with a sick child can escape the labyrinth of lies, hypocrisy and false promises of researchers and regulatory authorities. Hammersmith, London, UK, 2022.

36. Rose K, Grant-Kels JM, Striano P, Ettienne EB, Oishi T, Neubauer D. "Pediatric" Drug Studies Might Be the Largest Abuse in Medical

Research in History. It Is Time for Lawyers to Step In. J Law Med 2023,30(1), in press

37. ICMJE Disclosure of interest form. Updated February 2021 https://www.icmje.org/disclosure-of-interest/

38. Washington HA. Medical Apartheid. The Dark History of Medical Experimentation on Black Americans from Colonial Times to the Present. Anchor Books (Random House), New York, NY, USA 2006

39. Jones JH. Bad Blood. The Tuskegee Syphilis Experiment. The modern classic of race and medicine update with an additional chapter on the Tuskegee Experiment's legacy in the age of AIDS. The Free Press (Simon & Schuster), New York, NY, USA, 1981

40. US Centers for Disease Control and Prevention (CDC). The Syphilis Study at Tuskegee Timeline https://www.cdc.gov/tuskegee/timeline.htm

41. Heintzelman CA. The Tuskegee Syphilis Study and Its Implications for the 21st Century. The New Social Worker Careers Magazine Fall 2003, Vol. 10, No. 4 https://www.socialworker.com/feature-articles/ethics-articles/The_Tuskegee_Syphilis_Study_and_Its_Implications_for_the_21st_Century/

42. Gillis J, Loughlan P. Not just small adults: the metaphors of paediatrics. Arch Dis Child 2007 Nov;92(11):946-7 https://www.ncbi.nlm.nih.gov/pmc/articles/PMC2083631/pdf/946.pdf

43. Casanova M, Enis Özyar E, Patte C, et al. International randomized phase 2 study on the addition of docetaxel to the combination of cisplatin and 5- fluorouracil in the induction treatment for nasopharyngeal carcinoma in children and adolescents. Cancer Chemother Pharmacol 2016 Feb;77(2):289-98.

44. Petersson F. Nasopharyngeal carcinoma: A review. Semin Diagn Pathol. 2015 Jan;32(1):54-73.

45. Brennan B. Nasopharyngeal carcinoma. Orphanet J Rare Dis. 2006 Jun 26;1:23. https://www.ncbi.nlm.nih.gov/pmc/articles/PMC1559589/pdf/1750-1172-1-23.pdf

46. FDA. Written Requests Issued. Approved Active Moieties to which FDA has issued a Written Request for Pediatric Studies under Section 505A of the Federal Food, Drug, and Cosmetic Act. FDA 2022. https://www.fda.gov/drugs/development-resources/written-requests-issued

47. Rose K. Pediatric Oncology At The Crossroads: A Call for Change. Editorial. Pharmaceut Med 2020 Oct 7. https://rdcu.be/b8drm

48. EU Commission. Report from The Commission To The European Parliament And The Council. State of Paediatric Medicines in the EU – 10 years of the EU Paediatric Regulation. 2017. https://eur-lex.europa.eu/legal-content/EN/TXT/PDF/?uri=CELEX:52017DC0626&from=en

49. EU Commission. State of Paediatric Medicines in the EU. 10 years of the EU Paediatric Regulation. Report from the Commission to the European Parliament and the Council. COM (2017) 626.2017.

50. Wilson G. Developmental Pharmacology. Anaesthesia & Intensive Care Medicine 2021;22(9),587-593

51. Van den Anker JN. Developmental Pharmacology. Dev Disabil Res Rev 2010;16(3):233-238

52. Van den Anker JN, Reed MD, Allegaert K, et al. Developmental Changes in Pharmacokinetics and Pharmacodynamics. J Clin Pharmacolog 2018 Oct;58(Suppl 10) S10–S25 https://accp1.onlinelibrary.wiley.com/doi/epdf/10.1002/jcph.1284

53. Smits A, Annaert P, Cavallaro G, et al. Current knowledge, challenges and innovations in developmental pharmacology: A combined conect4children Expert Group and European Society for Developmental, Perinatal and Paediatric Pharmacology White Paper. Br J Clin Pharmacol. 2022 Dec;88(12):4965-4984. https://www.ncbi.nlm.nih.gov/pmc/articles/PMC9787161/pdf/BCP-88-4965.pdf

54. Aranda JV, Soyka LF. Developmental Pharmacology and Therapeutics - Who Needs It? Dev Pharmacol Ther 1980;1:1–5

55. Ward RM, Benjamin DK Jr, Davis JM, Gorman RL, Kauffman R, Kearns GL, et al. The Need for Pediatric Drug Development. J Pediatr. 2018 Jan;192:13-21.

56. Rocchi F, Paolucci P, Ceci A, et al. The European paediatric legislation: benefits and perspectives. Ital J Pediatr 2010 Aug 17;36:56. https://www.ncbi.nlm.nih.gov/pmc/articles/PMC2933611/pdf/1824-7288-36-56.pdf

57. Sardesai S, Biniwale M, Wertheimer F, et al. Evolution of surfactant therapy for respiratory distress syndrome: past, present, and future. Pediatr Res. 2017 Jan;81(1-2):240-248. https://www.nature.com/articles/pr2016203

58. Halliday HL. Surfactants: past, present and future. J Perinatol. 2008 May;28 Suppl 1(Suppl 1):S47-56. https://www.ncbi.nlm.nih.gov/pmc/articles/PMC7104445/pdf/41372_2008_Article_BFjp200850.pdf

59. Committee on Publication Ethics (COPE) www.publicationethics.org

60. Wikipedia, Committee on Publication Ethics https://en.wikipedia.org/wiki/Committee_on_Publication_Ethics

61. International Society of Managing and Technical Editors (ISMTE) https://www.ismte.org/

62. World Association of Medical Editors (WAME) https://www.wame.org

63. Wikipedia, World Association of Medical Editors (WAME) https://en.wikipedia.org/wiki/World_Association_of_Medical_Editors

64. Open Access Scholarly Publishers Association (OASPA) https://oaspa.org/

65. Wikipedia, Open Access Scholarly Publishers Association (OASPA) https://en.wikipedia.org/wiki/Open_Access_Scholarly_Publishing_Association

66. Directory of Open Access Journals (DOAJ) https://doaj.org/

67. Wikipedia, Directory of Open Access Journals (DOAJ) https://en.wikipedia.org/wiki/Directory_of_Open_Access_Journals

68. International Association of Scientific, Technical, and Medical Publishers (STM) https://www.stm-assoc.org/

69. Wikipedia, STM https://en.wikipedia.org/wiki/International_Association_of_Scientific,_Technical,_and_Medical_Publishers

70. Association of Learned and Professional Society Publishers (ALPSP), https://www.alpsp.org/

71. Wikipedia, Association of Learned and Professional Society Publishers (ALPSP) https://en.wikipedia.org/wiki/Association_of_Learned_and_Professional_Society_Publishers

72. Council of Science Editors (CSE). https://www.councilscienceeditors.org

73. Wikipedia, Council of Science Editors https://en.wikipedia.org/wiki/Council_of_Science_Editors

74. European Association of Science Editors (EASE) https://ease.org.uk

75. Wikipedia, European Association of Science Editors https://en.wikipedia.org/wiki/European_Association_of_Science_Editors

Chapter 10

The Council for International Organizations of Medical Sciences (CIOMS)

The Council for International Organizations of Medical Sciences (CIOMS) is an international non-governmental organization of 40 international, national, and associate member groups that represent the biomedical science community. It was jointly established by the World Health Organization (WHO) and United Nations Educational, Scientific and Cultural Organization (UNESCO) in 1949 as a successor to the International Medical Congress that had organized 17 conferences from 1867 on until the outbreak of World War I. The CIOMS's main goal is advancing public health by publishing guidelines on ethics, product development, and safety in medical research, such as the 2016 International Ethical Guidelines for Health-Related Research Involving Humans.[1-3] On this basis, the CIOMS represents the currently prevailing doctrines that define the ethics of medical research, teaching and therapeutic practice.

In the CIOMS guidelines of 2016, number 17 discusses research involving children and adolescents. It may come as no great surprise to the reader that this guideline does not make a distinction between the legal and physiological meanings and definitions of children and adolescents vs. adults.

On the one hand the basic definition of children is legal, but on the other hand it explains in the first paragraph that children and adolescents have distinctive physiologies and health needs and therefore merit special consideration by researchers and research ethics committees. Furthermore, the first paragraph explains that their distinctive physiologies and emotional development may also place them at increased risk of being harmed in the conduct of research, and that they may not be able to protect their own interests due to their evolving capacity to give informed consent with without appropriate support. The first paragraph concludes that specific protections to safeguard children's rights and welfare in research are therefore needed.[3]

The difference between the legal and the physiological definition of what a child is fundamental in assessing the need and value of what currently is called "pediatric drug development," a concept that currently results in thousands of questionable clinical studies with minors worldwide. The legal age limits do not correspond to physiological changes of the body. This was in the past much less important as there were few effective drugs, and as during World War II and the years thereafter the learnings of developmental physiology and pharmacology did not yet exist.[4-8] Furthermore, the administrative organization of the society was at a much lower level than today. Documents proving name and date of birth were not introduced and widely used until the 20th century.

The CIOMS guideline altogether has a high focus on social vulnerability, having in mind that a lot of clinical research is performed also in developing countries where many people live in poverty. The CIOMS's focus on social vulnerability as well as harm reduction or prevention corresponds broadly with other international normative documents, including the UNESCO's Universal Declaration on Bioethics and Human Rights, which recognises vulnerability as part of the human condition, but emphasizes that special vulnerability imposes a moral obligation on the state to protect the persons concerned.[9,10] Article 7 of the UNESCO declaration discusses persons without the capacity to consent.[9]

The guidelines by CIOMS, the UNESCO declaration, and further declarations, guidelines, conventions and more fail to differentiate between two fundamentally different issues. There is a lot of social inequality in every single country and between different countries worldwide. There is also the desire of many well-meaning people to reduce or eliminate social inequality. The many international conventions, declarations and more address these social inequalities and certainly speak from the heart of many well-meaning people. But the world does not change through benevolence and declarations alone.

There will always be a tension between observations and worldviews. But the discussion about the medical need of clinical studies with children should not be justified politically, but scientifically. If we take a closer look at these justifications, they are not scientific, but pseudo-scientific. Representatives of developmental pharmacology and regulatory agencies claim that the non-approval of more than half of the drugs used in children is evidence that children are a neglected group.[11-13] The twist in this argument is the implicit assertion that children as a neglected group are medically underserved compared to adults. Not in the third world, but in general. And that claim is simply wrong. Children in the developed world have never been better cared for medically than they are today.

Even in the developing countries child health care is no longer what it was a century or two ago. Child mortality has plummeted, and even in the poorest countries a large proportion of children are now vaccinated against a range of diseases that previously killed many children or severely affected their future quality of life. Part of the reason for the high pressure from asylum seekers heading to Europe and North America from relatively poor countries is that the health services in these poor countries have been improved, also through philanthropic activities, to such an extent that the population numbers have increased massively. But these countries lack the social and economic structures to accommodate and care for this massively increased number of residents. So they do what seems logical to the individual: they seek their fortune in distant countries where television and social media suggest there is a chance to have a good life. Psychologically nothing different compared to what people from Europe did when the European countries exported their culture and their settlers all over the world.

If we conclude from the claim that children are a neglected group that they are also poorly cared for medically, then there are only two possibilities; either this claim is correct, or it is not. But are Europe's or North America's streets littered with underserved and/or dead children? Definitely not. The other possibility is that there is something wrong with the approval of drugs for children. Unfortunately, that is exactly the case. Scientifically and physiologically, the body of a 17-year-old is no longer a child's body. And a ten-year-old's body is no longer a baby's body anymore. The regulatory definition of children through rigid chronological age limits results in the demand for child studies for which there is no scientifically valid justification.

Advocates of "pediatric drug development" claim they are bringing a little more equity to medical research and drug development. But this argument is flawed. It equates arbitrarily the legal definition of children and adolescents with different physical characteristics, as if children and adolescents were another species than adults. From this then follows the demand for the repetition of drug studies in "children", and often additionally or sometimes alternatively the demand for extrapolation from adults to minors (classified as "children").

We need to keep two issues apart. The criticism of social inequality by organisations such as CIOMS, UNESCO, & more is an issue about which different opinions exist. Our modern society could not live without different opinions. But above all, the criticism of social inequality is a political issue. The shaky foundations of "pediatric drug development" and the flawed justifications of pointless or exaggerated "pediatric" studies in minors that often are legally still children but physiologically no longer is fundamentally different. Furthermore, the children-are-not-small adolescents mantra is correct for preterm newborns, less correct for school age children, and no longer correct for adolescents. Mankind must learn to apply the learnings of developmental physiology and developmental pharmacology to the requirements of drug development.[4,5] The official declarations, guidelines & more by CIOMS, UNESCO and others reflect the official recognition of a teaching that reflects the initial findings in developmental physiology and pharmacology more than half a century ago. But the fact that these official bodies and their declarations, guidelines, & more are official and are represented by people who had to struggle through the slog of careers in their respective organizations until they could represent their countries and organisations on a global stage does not make these declarations, guidelines & more right.

The debate will never end whether our world order is unjust, whether it was right that Europe has expanded since the end of the Middle Ages, that it has colonized almost the entire world, and much more. Having this debate is perfectly correct and necessary in the study of politics, and/or history. It is a debate that can also be conducted during an election campaign. But the CIOMS and its declarations are not an election campaign. The CIOMS claims to represent science and ethics. The CIOMS documents mix ethics, morale, politics and moralistic appeals. They have such a focus on moralizing accounts of injustice in the world that really burning scientific questions are swept under the rug and stay there.

The debates on science, history and ethics have found a new stage at the level of international diplomacy, which is even less in touch with reality than the debates on science in individual countries. Noble declamations sound beautiful. They move little or nothing immediately. But they have the side effect of putting erroneous concepts, such as "pediatric drug development," under a moral cloak. This makes these concepts more durable. This is unfortunate, because it cements unethical pseudo-scientifically based studies, and it will take longer for criticism of them to reach the higher world of international diplomacy. Furthermore, it also helps maintain structures that hamper and stall exploration of truly burning issues.

References

1. Council for International Organizations of Medical Sciences (CIOMS) https://cioms.ch/
2. Wikipedia, Council for International Organizations of Medical Sciences (CIOMS) https://en.wikipedia.org/wiki/Council_for_International_Organizations_of_Medical_Sciences
3. International Ethical Guidelines for Health-related Research Involving Humans. Prepared by the Council for International Organizations of Medical Sciences (CIOMS) in collaboration with the World Health Organization (WHO). CIOMS, Geneva 2016 https://cioms.ch/wp-content/uploads/2017/01/WEB-CIOMS-Ethical Guidelines.pdf
4. Burggren W. Developmental Physiology: Grand Challenges. Front Physiol. 2021 Jun 10;12:706061. https://www.ncbi.nlm.nih.gov/pmc/articles/PMC8225327/pdf/fphys-12-706061.pdf
5. Kearns GL, Abdel-Rahman SM, Alander SW, Blowey DL, Leeder JS, Kauffman RE, et al. Developmental pharmacology--drug disposition, action, and therapy in infants and children. N Engl J Med. 2003 Sep 18;349(12):1157-67.
6. Rose K. Considering the Patient in Pediatric Drug Development. How good intentions turned into harm. Elsevier, London, UK, 2020. https://www.elsevier.com/books/considering-the-patient-in-pediatric-drug-development/rose/978-0-12-823888-2 and https://www.sciencedirect.com/book/9780128238882/considering-the-patient-in-pediatric-drug-development
7. Rose K. Blind Trust - How parents with a sick child can escape the labyrinth of lies, hypocrisy and false promises of researchers and regulatory authorities. Hammersmith, London, UK, 2022. https://www.book2look.com/book/mMqwf6ap9C

8. Rose K, Tanjinatus O, Grant-Kels JM, et al. Minors and a dawning paradigm shift in "pediatric" drug development. J Clin Pharmacol 2020, Dec 23.
https://accp1.onlinelibrary.wiley.com/doi/epdf/10.1002/jcph.1806

9. UNESCO. Universal Declaration on Bioethics and Human Rights. UNESCO, Paris, 2005
https://en.unesco.org/about-us/legal-affairs/universal-declaration-bioethics-and-human-rights

10. Ho CW. CIOMS guidelines remain conservative about vulnerability and social justice. Indian J Med Ethics. 2017 Jul-Sep;2(3):175-179.
https://ijme.in/wp-content/uploads/2017/06/253the175_cioms_guidelines_remain.pdf

11. Wilson G. Developmental Pharmacology. Anaesthesia & Intensive Care Medicine 2021;22(9),587-593

12. European Medicines Agency (EMA). Evidence of harm from off-label or unlicensed medicines in children. EMEA/126327/2004. EMA 2004.
https://www.ema.europa.eu/en/documents/other/evidence-harm-label-unlicensed-medicines-children_en.pdf

13. European Medicines Agency (EMA). History of the Paediatric Regulation. EMA 2007.
https://www.ema.europa.eu/en/documents/other/european-paediatric-initiative-history-paediatric-regulation_en.pdf

Chapter 11

Institutional Review Boards (IRBs) and Ethics Committees (ECs)

Today's level of medical care would be impossible if new vaccinations, medicines and medical devices were not continuously further developed and systematically tested for their safety and efficacy. Without a thorough knowledge of human anatomy and physiology and the basic disease mechanisms, it would be impossible to prepare, run, evaluate and report clinical studies that aim at improving prevention and treatment of diseases This basic understanding was and is gained in systematic observations, which do not only work to improve existing therapies, but also strive for a more in-depth understanding of physical processes, including the mental processes that accompany them. Because medical care is already at a high level, most new medicines only offer the potential for incremental improvements compared to existing care. However, there are exceptions such as the COVID-19 pandemic that would not have been overcome so quickly without innovative effective vaccines. Furthermore, the aging of the population means that more and more health problems have to be treated that do not appear until old age, including most forms of cancer and other malignancies, autoimmune diseases, degenerative diseases of the central nervous system, of the musculoskeletal system, and of further body parts and body functions. There are also rare diseases for which there is still no cure or for which there is currently only symptomatic treatment. And illnesses that reflect the fact that many more people are now surviving accidents that previously would have killed them. Spinal cord injuries can have devastating consequences, including hemiplegia, paraplegia and tetraplegia. Paraplegia and tetraplegia are among the major unsolved health care problems. There are small incremental improvements in therapy. In the near or distant future, it may or may not be possible to restore many more of these patients to their former functioning. Incremental advances in clinical and basic research are being studied extensively.[1,2] The trials that test potentially better treatments are collectively called clinical research and are by far the most laborious and expensive part of drug development. Three main interest groups and questions come together in clinical research. On the one hand there are the people who take part as study subjects. On the other hand there are the people and institutions that try to develop new treatments, organize the clinical and other trials to prove their safety and efficacy, report the results to the public, and try to mobilize further funds to continue with this research. The third pillar in this triangle is the regulatory authorities that emerged only in the 20th century as a relevant quantity.

Before World War II and more so in the 19th century, research with human subjects barely resembled research today. There were no multicenter randomized placebo-controlled clinical studies. Research was largely based on observation, discovery, publication, and the attempt to draw conclusions. This approach has been described as "gentlemen scientists" tinkering and seeking to understand the human body.[3]

Most reviews of the role of ethics committees and IRBs address the abuses committed by researchers in Nazi Germany during World War II and by academic researchers in the western world after World War II, including the Willbrooks study and the Tuskegee study.[4-9] After the Tuskegee study had become known and condemned by critical press reports, the US government set up the "National Commission for the Protection of Human Subjects of Biomedical and Behavioral Research", which in turn issued recommendations to the US congress regarding the ethical conduct of human subjects research and wrote the Belmont Report.[3,10] Over time, a system of ethical codes, principles, and regulations emerged to prevent these abuses and to ensure that the rights and welfare of research participants are protected and honored.[4]

Since World War II, the development and continuous improvement and fine-tuning of therapeutic interventions has become a huge machinery with scientists, treating physicians, and clinical centers that treat patients and recruit study subjects; the life science industry that finances clinical studies; and the contract research organisations, i.e. companies that carry out the necessary studies.[11] In addition, all those involved receive continuous input from basic research and academic science.

In the US, "Institutional Review Boards" (IRBs) must approve any clinical study before the planned project can go ahead. In Europe, these are called "Ethics Committees" (ECs). Around the world, IRBs/ECs have become a permanent fixture without which clinical research projects cannot begin. IRBs/ECs have acquired the power of the state to decide if scientific projects can proceed. Few control mechanisms have such great power to make decisions.[12,13]

IRBs/ECs are also the local and/or national level institutions designed to provide a last line of defence against abuse in clinical research. But most of the reviews that present and describe their function reflect the level of science half a century ago, when IRBs/ECs were established in the face of Nazi crimes and the unethical academic research projects exposed by critical publications.

Among the most potent myths surrounding clinical research are the many reports of greedy, money-hungry drug companies and the noble struggle of the academic researchers who represent pure science.[14-21]

Critical papers address what is perceived as an expansive mission and bureaucracy of IRBs/ECs, who have been criticized as dysfunctional and more concerned with protecting the institution than research participants. Others claim that IRBs/ECs are overburdened and overreaching. Frequently discussed issues include excessive paperwork, inflexible interpretation of regulatory requirements, attention to inconsequential details, and expanding obligations of IRBs that seem to have little to do with protection of research participants. Fear of regulatory admonition has fueled a focus on compliance with regulations. Some perceive excessive regulation as seriously affecting or stifling research productivity and adding cost without adding meaningful protections for participants. Clinical researchers complain that the IRB/EC review process is inefficient and delays their research for what they perceive as minor modifications. The public hears about problems and fears that research might be unsafe and existing protections ineffective or inadequate. Driven by concerns about redundancy and delay, the concept of single or central IRB/EC reviews for multicenter studies has emerged. Over the decades since IRBs/ECs were codified into regulations, IRB/EC review and oversight has developed and matured as part of a robust system providing substantial protections for the health, rights, and welfare of research subjects. However, research methods and opportunities have evolved, the domains of oversight have expanded, and the research enterprise has grown and diversified. The rules, norms, procedures, and even articulation of the goals of IRB review have not kept pace.[6]

An additional key element of IRBs/ECs is that the ethical integrity in the conduct of health care research is essential for maintaining the public trust, and that the potential for a conflict of interest is minimized.[22] Participants in IRBs/ECs are rightly held in high esteem by the public.

Health care academics make up a large proportion of IRB/EC members. One particular conflict of interest that is less frequently addressed is the fact that academic research has far less funding available compared to industry-funded research. In addition,

IRB/EC members represent local hands-on institutions. Whether we call the resulting feelings envy, or inferiority complex, or whatever, not all feedback from IRBs/ECs healthcare institutions is based on wisdom only. The feedback is often a mixture of justified concerns and sensible suggestions, but also the feedback from know-it-alls from local healthcare academics; a desire to have a say in the scientific design of large international studies; and making the same suggestions over and over again that companies cannot possibly fulfil, e.g., limiting the right of the study organizer to terminate the study prematurely. Some IRBs/ECs are notorious for not being inclined to approve clinical projects in their geographical area, so research companies give them a wide berth. Such IRBs/ECs are even proud of their attitude, which unfortunately reflects an also existing arrogance of the academic world towards the rest of the world in general and towards applied clinical research in particular.[12,13]

Clinical development has become such an industrialized international process that the individual IRB/EC member is not necessarily optimally prepared to give qualified feedback based solely on hands-on experience. We have the same process with IRBs/ECs that we see in all areas of society: everything becomes more complicated and unmanageable, and yet there must be safeguards at every level to prevent abuse.

The peculiarity of pediatric clinical research is that all involved academic specialists claim that they want only what is best for the "pediatric population"; but that a large part of the research projects, their organization and their financing by the life science industry are enforced by the authorities and carried out and justified by academic researchers and advocacy groups such as the American Academy of Pediatrics (AAP),[23] the European Society for Developmental and Perinatal Pharmacology (ESDPPP);[24] and others, are often superfluous, clinically pointless, and/or massively exaggerated.[25-29] In the past, in view of past Nazi crimes and other abuses, it was repeatedly emphasized that children should be protected *from* research. The next phase was the emphasis on protecting and helping children *through* research. IRBs/ECs will not be able to avoid dealing with this question in a targeted and in-depth manner.

Science has become a global process in which millions of highly qualified employees make a career. The jobs in science and their counterparts in industry, in the supervisory authorities, and in the executing contracting companies (clinical research organisations, CROs)[9] are well paid and enjoy a high social reputation. It is not always immediately apparent at first glance whether the project in which a scientist is involved is really worthwhile. In this jungle, "pediatric drug development" has created a unique ecological niche. Its projects have to be financed by industry, they lead to ongoing publications; they are established and defended by the leading scientists. And yet they are unethical. IRBs/ECs have the power not to approve unethical projects and to terminate ongoing projects if they have concluded that they are either useless or even harmful to patients. Why have IRBs/ECs hardly intervened against "PDD" so far? Unfortunately, the answer is quite simple. Mainstream official science, in coalition with government and initially together with industry, has spawned a movement that bears the official stamp of validity. But not everything that is officially sanctioned is ethical.

There are now many handbooks, reviews, and overviews to prepare or guide current or prospective members of IRBs/ECs.[28-36] They reflect the fact that IRBs/ECs have become an integral part of the medical R&D machinery, with more and more operational regulations, rules, and additional considerations.

Justifications for "pediatric drug development" are published continuously and repeatedly by respected academic and scientific journals. These publications are not intended for scientific discussion. Rather, they justify the current state of affairs by repeating the same claims over and over, including that children are therapeutic orphans, that the "pediatric population" is a neglected population because fewer drugs are approved than adults, and so on. These claims come in scientific guise, but unfortunately they are just pseudo-science.[39-43] They reflect the temptation of pseudo-scientific projects that guarantee secure salaries and high social recognition, but which, on closer inspection, are worthless and pointless.

The discussed challenges reflect the contradiction between the existing continuous improvement of medical and therapeutic possibilities and the desire to further accelerate this process through research on one hand, and the fact on the other hand that the scientific process has become so complex that it also offers space for projects and areas that do not contribute anything substantial, but nevertheless enjoy official recognition, are supported by clinical institutions, with its reports accepted by medical and scientific journals, and so on.

IRBs/ECs will have to face this challenge. Many IRB/EC handbooks oscillate between on the one hand complex and difficult dilemmas of clinical practice that occur every day and often do not have an easy solution, and on the other hand explaining the framework of clinical research and development which is indeed becoming more and more complicated and difficult to understand. In this difficult ocean of confusing impressions, there is a very simple question for research projects that should always be asked first: does the project in question make sense? Research projects submitted by pharmaceutical companies and CROs are usually well prepared at the level of statistical assumptions, reference to current literature and existing regulations, and many other formally comprehensible criteria. But the simplest IRB/EC member should always stubbornly ask the basic question of whether the respective project makes sense. If a question is to be answered that is not really a question, such as whether antibiotics, antivirals or other medications work before the 18th or 12th birthday, then the IRB/EC verdict should be a resounding "NO". The Declaration of Helsinki has no special exception paragraphs for research projects that only meet regulatory requirements without having medical sense. Such projects are unethical. They should be rejected, and if they are already running, suspended. To see that a given study is pointless does not require to have studied medicine, pharmacology, philosophy, or history. A sound common sense and a healthy self-confidence are sufficient. The submitting company may need one or several "pediatric" studies for regulatory purposes. But if such a study is pointless, it should be rejected. This is a new type of challenge for IRBs/ECs. At least it makes life less boring.

References

1. Kirshblum S, Snider B, Eren F, et al. Characterizing Natural Recovery after Traumatic Spinal Cord Injury. J Neurotrauma. 2021 May 1; 38(9):1267-1284. https://www.ncbi.nlm.nih.gov/pmc/articles/PMC8080912/pdf/neu.2020.7473.pdf

2. Rouanet C, Reges D, Rocha E, et al. Traumatic spinal cord injury: current concepts and treatment update. Arq Neuropsiquiatr. 2017 Jun;75(6):387-393. https://www.scielo.br/j/anp/a/D5MZLCn7xRcMg67mxFgbGmr/?lang=en

3. Spellecy R, Busse K. The History of Human Subjects Research and Rationale for Institutional Review Board Oversight. Nutr Clin Pract. 2021 Jun;36(3):560-567.

4. McNair L. Ethical and regulatory oversight of clinical research: The role of the Institutional Review Board. Exp Biol Med (Maywood). 2022 Apr;247(7):561-566. https://www.ncbi.nlm.nih.gov/pmc/articles/PMC9014527/pdf/10.1177_15353702221078216.pdf

5. Enfield KB, Truwit JD. The purpose, composition, and function of an institutional review board: balancing priorities. Respir Care. 2008 Oct;53(10):1330-6. https://rc.rcjournal.com/content/respcare/53/10/1330.full.pdf

6. Grady C. Institutional Review Boards: Purpose and Challenges. Chest. 2015 Nov;148(5):1148-1155. https://www.ncbi.nlm.nih.gov/pmc/articles/PMC4631034/pdf/chest_148_5_1148.pdf

7. Mondragón Barrios L, Martínez Levy GA, Díaz-Anzaldúa A, et al. Rethinking Benefits in Health Research, Reflections of an Ethics Committee. Yale J Biol Med. 2022 Sep 30;95(3):389-398. eCollection 2022 Sep. https://www.ncbi.nlm.nih.gov/pmc/articles/PMC9511940/pdf/yjbm_95_3_389.pdf

8. Wikipedia, Ethics committee
https://en.wikipedia.org/wiki/Ethics_committee

9. Wikipedia, Institutional Review Board
https://en.wikipedia.org/wiki/Institutional_review_board

10. The Belmont Report. The National Commission for the Protection of Human Subjects of Biomedical and Behavioral Research, 1979
https://www.hhs.gov/ohrp/regulations-and-policy/belmont-report/index.html and
https://www.hhs.gov/ohrp/sites/default/files/the-belmont-report-508c_FINAL.pdf

11. Wikipedia, Contract Research Organisation (CRO)
https://en.wikipedia.org/wiki/Contract_research_organization

12. Jacobs N. Ethics by Committee: A History of Reasoning Together about Medicine, Science, Society, and the State. University of Chicago Press, Chicago, IL, USA, 2022

13. Jacobs N. "An Official Conscience and Warranting Agency": Institutional Isomorphism and the Rise of Dutch Ethics Review in the 1970s and 1980s. Eur J Hist Med Health 2021 Oct;*78*(2),287-309.

14. Angell M. The Truth about the Drug Companies: How They Deceive Us and What to Do about It. Random House Publishers, New York, USA, 2004

15. Angell M. Industry-sponsored clinical research: a broken system. JAMA. 2008 Sep 3;300(9):1069-71.

16. Angell M. Conflicts in serving both non-profit and for-profit medical centres. BMJ. 2015 Oct 21;351:h5491. doi: 10.1136/bmj.h5491.

17. Rosenthal, Elisabeth (2017). An American Sickness: How Healthcare Became Big Business and How You Can Take it Back. Penguin Press. ISBN 9780698407183

18. Gøtzsche PC. Deadly Medicines and Organised Crime: How Big Pharma Has Corrupted Healthcare. Routledge, London, UK, 2013

19. Goldacre B. Bad Pharma: How drug companies mislead doctors and harm patients. HarperCollins Publishers, London, UK, 2012

20. Goldacre B. Bad Science: Quacks, Hacks, and Big Pharma Flacks. Farrar, Straus and Giroux (FSG) Adult, NY, USA, reprint 2010

21. Steinbrook R, Kassirer JP, Angell M. Justifying conflicts of interest in medical journals: a very bad idea. BMJ. 2015 Jun 2;350:h2942

22. Shekelle PG, Ruelaz A, Miake-Lye IM, et al. Maintaining Research Integrity: A Systematic Review of the Role of the Institutional Review Board in Managing Conflict of Interest [Internet]. Washington (DC): Department of Veterans Affairs (US); 2012 May. https://www.ncbi.nlm.nih.gov/books/NBK98419/pdf/Bookshelf_NBK98419.pdf

23. American Academy of Pediatrics (AAP) www.aap.org

24. European Society for Developmental and Perinatal Pharmacology (ESDPPP) www.esdppp.org

25. Rose K. Considering the Patient in Pediatric Drug Development. How good intentions turned into harm. Elsevier, London, UK, 2020. https://www.elsevier.com/books/considering-the-patient-in-pediatric-drug-development/rose/978-0-12-823888-2 and https://www.sciencedirect.com/book/9780128238882/considering-the-patient-in-pediatric-drug-development

26. Rose K. Blind Trust - How parents with a sick child can escape the labyrinth of lies, hypocrisy and false promises of researchers and regulatory authorities. Hammersmith, London, UK, 2022. https://www.book2look.com/book/mMqwf6ap9C

27. Rose K, Tanjinatus O, Grant-Kels JM, et al. Minors and a dawning paradigm shift in "pediatric" drug development. J Clin Pharmacol 2020, Dec 23. https://accp1.onlinelibrary.wiley.com/doi/epdf/10.1002/jcph.1806

28. Rose K, Neubauer D, Grant-Kels JM. Rational Use of Medicine in Children – The Conflict of Interests Story. A Review. Rambam Maimonides Med J. 2019 Jul 18; 10(3): e0018. Review. doi:10.5041/RMMJ.10371. https://www.rmmj.org.il/userimages/928/2/PublishFiles/953Article.pdf

29. Rose K, Grant-Kels JM, Striano P, Ettienne EB, Oishi T, Neubauer D. "Pediatric" Drug Studies Might Be the Largest Abuse in Medical Research in History. It Is Time for Lawyers to Step In. J Law Med 2023,30(1), in press

30. Amdur RJ, Bankert EA (authors). Institutional Review Board Member Handbook. Jones and Bartlett Publishers, Burlington, MA, USA, 2011

31. Bankert EA, Gordon BG, Hurley EA, et al. Institutional Review Board: Management and Function, 3rd Edition and Institutional Review Board: Member Handbook, 4th Edition. Public Responsibility in Medicine & Research (Prim&r), Jones & Bartlett Learning, Burlington, MA, USA 2021

32. Farber Post L, Blustein J (Eds.). Handbook for Health Care Ethics Committees. Johns Hopkins University Press, Baltimore, MD, USA, 2021

33. Hester DM. Ethics by Committee: A Textbook on Consultation, Organization, and Education for Hospital Ethics Committees. Rowman & Littlefield, Lanham, MD, USA, 2007 https://www.researchgate.net/publication/282251925_Ethics_By_Committee

34. Hester DM, Schonfeld T (Eds.). Guidance for Healthcare Ethics Committees. 2nd edition, Cambridge University Press, Cambridge, UK, 2022

35. Blokdyk G (Author). Ethics committee. A complete guide. Practical Tools for Self-Assessment. 5STARCooks, UK, 2021

36. Eckstein S (Ed.). Manual for Research Ethics Committees: Centre of Medical Law and Ethics, King's College London. 6th edition, Cambridge University Press, Cambridge, UK, 2011

37. Rosenfeld SJ. Institutional Review Board Assessment - Balancing Efficiency and Quality. Ochsner J. 2020 Spring;20(1):50-55. https://www.ncbi.nlm.nih.gov/pmc/articles/PMC7122259/pdf/TOJ-19-0075_50Rosenfeld.pdf

38. Flege MM, Thomsen SF. Institutional review boards' attitudes towards remuneration in paediatric research: Ethical considerations. J Paediatr Child Health. 2017 Dec;53(12):1149-1151. doi: 10.1111/jpc.13711.

39. Van den Anker JN. Developmental Pharmacology. Dev Disabil Res Rev 2010;16(3):233-238

40. Van den Anker JN, Reed MD, Allegaert K, et al. Developmental Changes in Pharmacokinetics and Pharmacodynamics. J Clin Pharmacolog 2018 Oct;58(Suppl 10) S10–S25 https://accp1.onlinelibrary.wiley.com/doi/epdf/10.1002/jcph.1284

41. Ward RM, Benjamin DK Jr, Davis JM, et al. The Need for Pediatric Drug Development. J Pediatr 2018 Jan;192:13-21. https://www.ncbi.nlm.nih.gov/pmc/articles/PMC7942021/pdf/nihms-1601167.pdf

42. European Medicines Agency (EMA). Evidence of harm from off-label or unlicensed medicines in children. EMEA/126327/2004. EMA 2004. https://www.ema.europa.eu/en/documents/other/evidence-harm-label-unlicensed-medicines-children_en.pdf

43. European Medicines Agency (EMA). History of the Paediatric Regulation. EMA 2007. https://www.ema.europa.eu/en/documents/other/european-paediatric-initiative-history-paediatric-regulation_en.pdf

Chapter 12
Gillick Competence

The term "Gillick competence" has become well established in medical law and medical literature.[1,2] For a person under 16 years of age, having achieved Gillick competence means that she or he has now the right to decide or consent to their own medical treatment without parents having to give permission or even knowing about it. The term is based on a decision of the UK House of Lords, acting as the supreme British Court, in 1985. A circular of the British Department of Health and Social Security (DHHS) had advised medical doctors on contraception for young women under 16. It stated that prescribing a contraception was at the doctor's discretion and could be done also in under-16s without parental consent. This was litigated by a Victoria Gillick, a British activist and campaigner and a Roman Catholic mother of 10 children (five sons, five daughters). She had begun her campaign in 1980 in response to the mentioned DHSS circular. The House of Lords decided that 'parental rights' do not exist other than to safeguard the best interests of a minor; that in certain circumstances a minor can consent to treatment; and that in these circumstances a parent has no power to veto it. A minor deemed Gillick competent can also prevent his parents viewing his medical records. Medical staff will not disclose his medical records unless his consent to disclosure is manifest. The principle of Gillick competence is legally binding in practically all countries of the British Commonwealth, but not in the USA.[2,3] A minor under 16 has the legal competence to consent to medical examination and treatment if he has sufficient maturity and intelligence to understand the nature and implications of that treatment. This competence to make healthcare decisions depends on (1) his maturity, taking account of his experiences and his ability to manage influences on his decision making, balancing information, peer pressure, family pressure, fear and misgivings; (2) his intelligence, i.e. his understanding; his ability to weigh risk vs. benefit, to consider long term factors such as effect on family life, schooling, & more.[1]

The Gillick competence is broadly discussed in the literature with more than 100 PubMed entries when the search term "Gillick competence" is entered.[4,5] Two opposing positions have emerged, one emphasizing the strong desire to provide for autonomy in health care that is expressed frequently in contemporary bioethics; the other emphasizing that the Gillick competence adds a burden upon children and adolescents that is unwarranted and through which damage is done to integral human relationships. However, the author of this juxtaposition emphasizes that they are not in opposition and not even in simple contradiction, but are oriented against each other in a way in which they feed off and depend on one another, and in some respects overlap.[6]

The Gillick competence emerged with the discussion of contraception and the right of young people to make decisions about their sexuality without parental interference. But it not limited to the prescription of contraceptives. Instead, it regards the entire range of possible medical interventions. British jurisdiction does no longer cover the US, but also in the US the autonomy of young persons is discussed in many dimensions, including for example the right of minors to consent to donor stem cells for the treatment for a wide range of diseases for which a sibling needs a stem cell transplantation. The AAP supports this right explicitly also for minors.[7] Of course there are also voices that warn against making such a decision at an early age and argue that it is better to wait until the potential cell donor has grown up and can now give this consent as an adult. The only condition under which these authors also consent to cell donation by minors is if the recipient sibling would likely suffer from serious complications or die without the transplantation and no tissue-matched unrelated or related donors are available. They also argue that the removal of stem cells always involves a certain risk.[8] Other medical areas in which the Gillick competence can play a role is the use of puberty blockers in gender dysphoria, the distress a person experiences if his personal sense of his gender and his physiological gender do not match.[9] Puberty blockers postpone puberty and give more time to consider possible surgical, hormonal, and other interventions. Another area where the Gillick competence applies is the right of a young, underage woman to consent to the termination of her pregnancy.[10]

During the COVID-19 pandemic, courts in Australia, New Zealand, England and Canada decided in several cases, often in the context of parenting disputes, that minors should be vaccinated against the corona virus. They found it generally to be in the best interests of children to receive COVID-19 vaccinations. Here, too, the Gillick competence applies. A final judgment on this complex issue has not yet been made.[11]

The question of whether the Gillick competence also applies to the consent of minors to participate in clinical studies is controversial. In general, there is agreement that it should not be considered applicable for use in research. But there are two exceptional situations in which it might be legitimately applied: (1) when the research is likely to trigger significant advantages for the participants while exposing them to relatively minor risks, and (2) when it is likely to generate great societal benefit, pose minimal risks for the participants, and yet raise parental objection. In such cases, Gillick competency should be assessed by somebody without interest or involvement in the research to prevent a biased assessment and to exclude conflicts of interest.[12]

The principle of Gillick competence is particularly important in our context. It shows that a healthy understanding of the need for autonomy for young people has found its way into today's judicial thinking. The changed social attitudes towards the role and self-responsibility of young people are a reality today. To put it provocatively: The Gillick competence shows that the increasing recognition of reality has also found its way into legal thinking. And it shows that a stubborn insistence on chronological age limits as a basis for inclusion and exclusion into clinical trials, classifying those after the 18th birthday as "adult" and those before the 18th birthday as "pediatric", does not do justice to today's understanding of human dignity and complexity. The classification of young mothers as "children" by the European Medicines Agency (EMA) that demands placebo-controlled clinical trials to again show the safety and efficacy of brexanolone/ allopreganolone in the treatment of perinatal depression also before the 18th birthday is a clear abuse of these young mothers.[13] These studies are not only pointless as the 16th or 18th birthdays are not physiological, but administrative time limits. The abuse and the insulting of young women by the execution machinery of clinical trials should be classified as doing harm. The contrary of what the Declaration of Helsinki demands. See also chapter 7.

References

1. Griffith R. What is Gillick competence? Hum Vaccin Immunother. 2016;12(1):244-7. https://www.ncbi.nlm.nih.gov/pmc/articles/PMC4962726/pdf/khvi-12-01-1091548.pdf
2. Wikipedia, Gillick competence https://en.wikipedia.org/wiki/Gillick_competence
3. Wikipedia, Victoria Gillick https://en.wikipedia.org/wiki/Victoria_Gillick
4. PubMed https://pubmed.ncbi.nlm.nih.gov/
5. PubMed entries for "Gillick competence" https://pubmed.ncbi.nlm.nih.gov/?term=gillick+competence
6. Zimmermann N. Gillick Competence: An Unnecessary Burden. New Bioeth. 2019 Mar;25(1):78-93.
7. American Academy of Pediatrics. Children as Hematopoietic Stem Cell Donors. Pediatrics 2010;125(2):392-404. https://publications.aap.org/pediatrics/article/125/2/392/72261/Children-as-Hematopoietic-Stem-Cell-Donors?autologincheck=redirected
8. Chan TK, Tipoe GL. The policy statement of the American Academy of Pediatrics -- children as hematopoietic stem cell donors -- a proposal of modifications for application in the UK. BMC Med Ethics. 2013 Oct 31;14:43 https://www.ncbi.nlm.nih.gov/pmc/articles/PMC4228464/pdf/1472-6939-14-43.pdf
9. Thornton J. Court upholds Gillick competence in puberty blockers case. Lancet. 2021 Oct 2;398(10307):1205-1206.
10. Moreton KL. Gillick reinstated: judging mid-childhood competence in healthcare law: an NHS Trust v ABC & A Local Authority [2014] EWHC 1445 (Fam). Med Law Rev. 2015 Spring;23(2):303-14.
11. Freckelton I. Vaccinating Children: The COVID-19 Family Law Jurisprudence. J Law Med. 2022 Aug;29(3):645-662.

12. Hunter D, Pierscionek BK. Children, Gillick competency and consent for involvement in research. J Med Ethics. 2007 Nov;33(11):659-62. https://www.ncbi.nlm.nih.gov/pmc/articles/PMC2598111/pdf/659.pdf

13. EMA Allopregnanolone/ brexanolone PIP EMEA-002051-PIP-02-16. EMA 2017 https://www.ema.europa.eu/en/documents/pip-decision/p/0357/2017-ema-decision-1-december-2017-agreement-paediatric-investigation-plan-granting-deferral-granting_en.pdf

Chapter 13

New Conflicts of Interest in Medical Research

The first paragraph of the preamble to the EU pediatric regulation explains that drugs have to undergo extensive studies to ensure their safety and efficacy. The second paragraph then explains that such studies may not have been done in the "pediatric population" and that many drugs currently used to treat the "pediatric population" have not been approved. "Market forces alone have proven insufficient to stimulate adequate research into, and the development and authorisation of, medicinal products for the pediatric population."[1] In the following, the pediatric regulation promises to do what market forces failed to achieve.

An uneasiness with market forces has accompanied the industrialization and the changing societal structures of the emerging new society. In the context of economics, the market is a system in which parties engage according to supply and demand. The antithesis to a market-oriented society is not that supply and demand decide what is produced, offered, sold and used, but what an authority orders to be produced and distributed. Although this counter-concept completely disavowed itself with the collapse of the Soviet Union and other workers' and peasants' paradises, it still lingers as an idea in the minds of intellectuals and bureaucrats in the West.

The people who have the power to decide about production and consumption will always promise that everything will improve under their benevolent rule. But once they have the power, they will not give up their power willingly. The Soviet Union ultimately failed because it was unable to meet the basic needs of the people.[2-4] The market does that much better. The market also works in pediatrics and neonatology, two sub-sciences that have made phenomenal advances over the last half century. And yet, the promise to do even better has persuaded lawmakers to give regulatory agencies the power to order clinical trials in minors ("children"). And just as the simplest things didn't work in the Soviet Union back then, since 1997 the US regulatory authorities have mostly rewarded hundreds of clinical trials in minors, and the EU authorities ordered even more. In science, research, medicine and drug registration, the US and the EU differ in that the boundaries between academic research and applied research are much more flexible in the US. The FDA works closely with academic researchers and their professional representatives. Open arrogance would not last long in the United States. The EMA, on the other hand, has been much more isolated in Europe since it was founded in 1995. The working language of EMA is English, which is currently only spoken by the general public in Ireland. The aloofness of the EMA explains why it is sticking to demands in many areas that have long since become obsolete on an international scientific level, such as the demand for "pediatric" studies on malignant melanoma or perinatal depression.

In the lives of people who work in scientific research, there are two principles that contradict each other. On the one hand, there is strong competition between researchers. It's impossible for everyone to be the best. On the other hand, there is the desire for social security, a desire that scientists and researchers share with all those who have to work for a living. But if there is a lot of social security for the individual scientist, why should he make any effort at all? Every society has to find its balance in this question. But in "pediatric drug development" a special solution was found for a special group of alleged researchers: the payment of pointless studies that "explore" what we already know about drugs again in younger people. But this "exploration" is nothing but an official repetition. In adolescents, the same doses of virtually all drugs are found in separate "pediatric" studies as in adults.[5] And yet such studies continue to be demanded, more so by the European Medicines Agency (EMA) than by the FDA.[6-8] This works as long as the general public can be successfully fooled into believing that these are serious research activities, because everything is allegedly different in "children."

The jobs in the FDA, the EMA, and the EU national regulatory authorities are well paid. In Europe, someone who once works for an authority will hardly ever leave. Job security is much higher than in industry, and on top of that, EMA employees hardly pay any taxes. All of this does not in itself explain "pediatric drug development," but it provides sufficient background to get an idea of something that at first sight seems too absurd and bizarre to be reality. At least the FDA accepts today that antiseizure medications work for adults down to two years of age,[9] within the face-saving exercise of "extrapolation of efficacy".[10] The EMA has reduced the age limit down to four years in its most recent draft guideline.[11]

Without support from academia, regulatory agencies could not demand decades of pointless and damaging "pediatric" studies. There are some specific areas in the world of clinical pediatric medicine that openly benefit from pseudoscientifically based studies, notably the juvenile rheumatology and childhood cancer research associations. But it was on the general level that the AAP officially endorsed the Shirkey-founded children-are-therapeutic-orphans mantra.

The tricky challenge here is that it is not about direct bribery. It is a mixture of pomposity, fundraising for research projects, and reverence for government institutions that first claimed and now continues to defend the supposed need for "pediatric" studies. A new kind of conflict of interest that so far has gracefully sidestepped the control mechanisms in clinical research discussed in previous chapters.

The idea that everything is different in children arose with the observation of toxicities in premature babies and the scientific processing of these observations by pediatrics and developmental pharmacology. But what was correctly observed and analyzed in terms of toxicities in preterm infants,[12-14] encountered several new societal structures and patterns of perception: the "pediatric population" was now seen as a population block open to administrative setups and metrics such as compulsory education and intelligence measurements. Drug development had transitioned from a private business to something subject to a new governmental oversight and control that was historically new in its depth. Pediatric medicine and developmental pharmacology were new entities that needed recognition and funding. The companies involved in drug development were subject to an unprecedented barrage of fundamental criticism as greedy and ruthless monster companies.[15-22] The regulatory authorities developed from relatively small administrative institutions into extremely powerful power structures. Academic science, medicine, and the regulatory authorities were at a pinnacle of societal acclaim.

In this mixture of societal realities and perceptions, the children-are-therapeutic-orphans concept was born. It spread the moral obligation to care more about "children". It was successful in getting the message across that the "pediatric population" was severely underserved; and it managed to convince the lawmakers by throwing into the balance the recognition of science and academic research.

Conflicts of interest in academic research were well known. But the discussion about conflicts of interest in academic research has remained for decades on the level of bribery of the individual scientist or clinician by wealthy pharmaceutical companies. Such bribery has indeed taken place. They were almost commonplace. Any impartial observer witnessing the level of care provided for clinicians at a conference for cardiology or gastroenterology in the 1990s was easily persuaded that these companies knew no boundaries.

It is new in the history of modern science that official doctrines are based on pseudo-scientific principles and yet are sold as pure science for more than half a century. That in itself is already unethical. Even more unethical is it that these doctrines result in clinical trials that are medically and scientifically pointless and often even harm the young patients. This doctrine and the studies that follow from it not only reflect that science and health care play an enormous economic role in our modern society. In addition, various myths persist that we have discussed in varying contexts throughout the book. One is the myth of scientists, doctors and regulators as the white knights, flying the banner of humanity against malicious, money-hungry forces in the pharmaceutical industry.

The myth of selfless medicine sanctioned by God runs through European history, mixed with religious ideas, and led to today's state-sanctioned medicine and the associated drug approval. Professions that competed with medicine were either marginalized, like midwives, or integrated into medicine, like surgeons, dentists, and pharmacists.

There are also opposite developments. Women used to be excluded from science, culture and medicine. They are fighting for their place and are doing this quite well in the developed world. With the demise of the international scientific communication based on the Latin language and the rise of modern vernacular written culture, also midwives have meanwhile built up their international and scientific communication culture. The International Confederation of Midwives (ICM) supports, represents and works to strengthen professional associations of midwives on a global basis. At present, ICM has over 100 members, representing midwifery associations in around 100 countries.[23,24] Midwifes are still in competition with the medical profession,[25] but there is also organized cooperation, different country by country.

Academic science has taken a powerful place in our society. Moralizing appeals to the well-being of children are part of the tradition of child advocacy that has emerged since the 19th century. For the worldwide largest and most powerful professional representation of pediatricians, the American Academy of Pediatrics (AAP), to team up the academic profession of developmental pharmacology, and make demands that amount to getting pediatric researchers commissioned for decades is certainly an understandable temptation. But that does not make it right to follow this temptation. To the contrary. It is fascinating to see how the interplay of moralizing appeals to the child's well-being and the weighing of scientific reputation combined in a process that convinced US lawmakers that the "pediatric population" was under-provisioned medically and pharmaceutically and that this deficit would have to be remedied by clinical studies in "children", even if these "children" were physiologically already mature. Pharmaceutical companies benefited from patent extensions in the USA.

The adoption of pediatric legislation by the European Union (EU) was a next step, resulting in more and more pointless studies in minors. Protected by the bad image of the pharmaceutical industry, senseless and harmful studies have been requested by the European Medicines Agency (EMA) in its bizarre pediatric investigation plans (PIPs) for more than fifteen years. Hundreds of PIP-demanded studies are actually carried out worldwide. Many of them struggle to recruit participants. As drug development is increasingly focusing on rare diseases, parents of children with rare diseases are faced with a scientific world that claims they only want the best for their children.

Our Western society will sooner or later recognize and process these conflicts of interest. Illusions can fool most people's perceptions for a while, but not forever, and not for all people. Just as no one today trusts researchers so blindly that research projects on children could also be carried out without the consent of the parents, many safety mechanisms today are based on events that happened decades or more ago and caused great excitement at the time. The Institutional Review Boards (IRBs) and Ethics Committees (ECs) have the power and authority to reject proposed study projects and to suspend ongoing study projects. But of course they first have to recognize the hidden conflicts of interest in "pediatric drug development".

As in many other areas of life, research institutions and the ideas and teachings associated with them tend to fossilize and become fixed in traditional frameworks. This is all the more the case where public administration still has a life of its own that often assumes Kafkaesque proportions.

The term "Kafkaesque" is used to describe concepts and situations in which bureaucracies overpower people, often in a surreal, nightmarish milieu that evokes feelings of senselessness. The term has transcended the literary realm to apply to real-life occurrences and situations that are incomprehensibly complex, bizarre, or illogical.[26] There are Kafkaesque elements in "pediatric drug development" especially as long as one does not see through that there are tangible interests and conflicts of interest behind seemingly bizarre and senseless demands from the authorities. However, this changes once we manage to see through the official smokescreens.

References

1. Regulation (EC) No 1901/2006 Of The European Parliament And Of The Council of 12 December 2006 on medicinal products for paediatric use and amending Regulation (EEC) No 1768/92, Directive 2001/20/EC, Directive 2001/83/EC and Regulation (EC) No 726/2004 https://eur-lex.europa.eu/legal-content/EN/TXT/PDF/?uri=CELEX:32006R1901&from=EN
2. Walker EW. Dissolution: Sovereignty and the Breakup of the Soviet Union (The Soviet Bloc and After) Rowman & Littlefield, Lanham, Maryland, 2003
3. Wikipedia, Dissolution of the Soviet Union https://en.wikipedia.org/wiki/Dissolution_of_the_Soviet_Union
4. Harari YN. Sapiens. A Brief History of Humankind. Vintage Classics, New York, NY, USA, 2019
5. Momper JD, Mulugeta Y, Green DJ, et al. Adolescent dosing and labeling since the Food and Drug Administration Amendments Act of 2007. JAMA Pediatr. 2013 Oct;167(10):926-32. https://jamanetwork.com/journals/jamapediatrics/fullarticle/1723817
6. Rose K, Grant-Kels JM, Striano P, Ettienne EB, Oishi T, Neubauer D. "Pediatric" Drug Studies Might Be the Largest Abuse in Medical Research in History. It Is Time for Lawyers to Step In. J Law Med 2023,30(1), in press
7. Rose K. Blind Trust - How parents with a sick child can escape the labyrinth of lies, hypocrisy and false promises of researchers and regulatory authorities. Hammersmith, London, UK, 2022.
8. Rose K. Considering the Patient in Pediatric Drug Development. How good intentions turned into harm. Elsevier, London, UK, 2020.
9. FDA 2019. Drugs for Treatment of Partial Onset Seizures: Full Extrapolation of Efficacy from Adults to Pediatric Patients 2 Years of Age and Older: Guidance for Industry. https://www.fda.gov/media/130449/download

10. Sun H, Temeck JW, Chambers W, et al. Extrapolation of Efficacy in Pediatric Drug Development and Evidence-based Medicine: Progress and Lessons Learned. Ther Innov Regul Sci 2017;2017:1-7 https://www.ncbi.nlm.nih.gov/pmc/articles/PMC5587157/pdf/nihms901908.pdf

11. EMA. Guideline on clinical investigation of medicinal products in the treatment of epileptic disorders. Draft. EMA 2018. https://www.ema.europa.eu/en/documents/scientific-guideline/draft-guideline-clinical-investigation-medicinal-products-treatment-epileptic-disorders-revision-3_en.pdf

12. Burns LE, Hodgman JE, Cass AB. Fatal circulatory collapse in premature infants receiving chloramphenicol. *N EngI 1 Med.* 1959;261:1318-1321

13. Silverman WA, Andersen DH, Blanc WA, et al. A difference in mortality rate and incidence of kernicterus among premature infants allotted to two prophylactic antibacterial regimens. Pediatrics 1956;18:6

14. American Academy of Pediatrics (AAP) 1995 | Committee on Drugs |Guidelines for the Ethical Conduct of Studies to Evaluate Drugs in Pediatric Populations Pediatrics 1995 Feb,95(2),286–294.

15. Angell M. The Truth about the Drug Companies: How They Deceive Us and What to Do about It. Random House Publishers, New York, USA, 2004

16. Angell M. Industry-sponsored clinical research: a broken system. JAMA. 2008 Sep 3;300(9):1069-71.

17. Angell M. Conflicts in serving both non-profit and for-profit medical centres. BMJ. 2015 Oct 21;351:h5491. doi: 10.1136/bmj.h5491.

18. Rosenthal, Elisabeth (2017). An American Sickness: How Healthcare Became Big Business and How You Can Take it Back. Penguin Press. ISBN 9780698407183

19. Gøtzsche PC. Deadly Medicines and Organised Crime: How Big Pharma Has Corrupted Healthcare. Routledge, London, UK, 2013

20. Goldacre B. Bad Pharma: How drug companies mislead doctors and harm patients. HarperCollins Publishers, London, UK, 2012

21. Goldacre B. Bad Science: Quacks, Hacks, and Big Pharma Flacks. Farrar, Straus and Giroux (FSG) Adult, NY, USA, reprint 2010

22. Steinbrook R, Kassirer JP, Angell M. Justifying conflicts of interest in medical journals: a very bad idea. BMJ. 2015 Jun 2;350:h2942

23. International Confederation of Midwifes. https://www.internationalmidwives.org/

24. Wikipedia, International Confederation of Midwives https://en.wikipedia.org/wiki/International_Confederation_of_Midwives

25. Wagner M. A global witch-hunt. Lancet. 1995 Oct 14;346(8981):1020-2

26. Wikipedia, Franz Kafka https://en.wikipedia.org/wiki/Franz_Kafka

Chapter 14
Neonatology

Neonatology is the medical specialty that takes care of newborn infants who are ill and need special care, predominantly because of prematurity, low birth weight, birth defects, infections, breathing difficulties, or oxygen deprivation during the birth process long enough to have damaged the brain. Neonatology takes place in neonatal intensive care units (NICUs). One of the causes that eventually led to the concept of children as therapeutic orphans originated in toxicities caused by antibiotics that were given to preterm newborns in the 1940/50s and were described in the literature to warn other medical doctors so they would not repeat the same mistakes.[1-3]

Neonatology is one of the many medical sub-disciplines where true revolutions have taken place during the last century. For a baby with a bodyweight of 1 kg the chance of survival changed from 5% a hundred years ago to 95% during the 20th century.[4,5] This makes neonatology a very successful discipline of pediatric medicine. The term "neonatology" emerged in 1961,[6] making it one of the youngest pediatric sub-disciplines.

Comparable to pediatric oncology, neonatology was not primarily advanced by the development of new medicines, but by the administration of medicines and technical devices used in general medicine. The two major exceptions were the introduction of the incubator, and the development of lung surfactant to prevent and treat respiratory distress syndrome. Neonatal respiratory distress syndrome is a disease and challenge unique to newborn infants. It is caused by a deficiency of lung surfactant, which in a normal timely birth is produced by the baby itself from shortly before the birth on. Until neonatal respiratory distress syndrome was better understood, it was not known why premature infants often died from respiratory failure. The first clinical trials with lung surfactant were not performed by pharmaceutical companies, but by clinicians and pediatric researchers. Lung surfactant was the first drug developed specifically for the treatment of neonates. It reduced neonatal mortality by about 50%.[7-9]

There are many ethical challenges in neonatology. Parents hope that their child will survive. But what if major disabilities are to be expected? There have also been several unwanted tragedies in neonatology. For a while, the most common cause of blindness was the administration of highly concentrated oxygen. Blindness caused by too highly concentrated oxygen and toxicities by antibiotics in preterm newborns occurred in hands-on daily practice, not during clinical trials for regulatory purposes. Eventually, this and other errors were corrected.[10-11] Key steps in advancing the care of newborns were the introduction of thermoregulation by incubators, parenteral nutrition, administration of steroids to mothers at risk of a premature birth to trigger the earlier production of lung surfactant by the infant itself, and eventually the application of lung surfactant, first derived from animals, today produced artificially by chemical and/or recombinant technologies.[4,5,7-9,12-15] Furthermore, as all other areas of medicine and pediatrics, also neonatology profited from advances in antibiotic, antifungal, and later on more advanced anti-inflammatory treatments, and other newly available effective drugs in general.

Another commonality between neonatology and pediatric oncology is that the regulatory authorities played no role in the pioneering decades of these disciplines. Reviews of the history of neonatology do not even mention the role of the FDA, the EMA, or the EMA's predecessors in Europe.[4,5,7-9]

Beyond drug development, fundamental cultural challenges occurred in medicine, including neonatology. Parents were initially only allowed to see their child through a glass partition to prevent infections. Hospital patients were expected to conform to the strict rules represented by the medical and nursing staff. The regimented ward with patients laying straight and neatly covered up by sheets, blankets and bedcovers was assumed to be normal and right.[16] Eventually, more was learned about the key role of establishing an emotional bond between the mother and her child and the importance of physical contact between mother and child, a characteristic shared by man himself with apes and their young children.[17i] Over the years, the former strict attitude of medical doctors and healthcare professionals in neonatal care and hospital care in general relented.[4,5]

Many publications complain about the lack of studies in the "pediatric population" and specifically in neonates.[18-26] As in all other parts of medicine and clinical research, we must also here ask whether these complaints and demands are made out of compassion towards the newborns; out of a professional desire to secure more research funds for neonatology; out of the wish to emphasize the importance of the regulatory authorities; their power; their desire to play a major role also in this area; or out of the desire to secure the respective lucrative "pediatric" jobs.[12-15,27] There is a fundamental flaw in the expressed wish for more clinical studies in neonates. If only a few infants at risk would survive, this demand would be reasonable. But neonatology is a very successful discipline. The demand for more drugs approved also in neonates is a regulatory, not a medical demand. It is not made to improve medical care for infants at risk, but is a demand based on loyalty to the ideology of "pediatric drug development" and the concept of children as therapeutic orphans. Of course, these demands are made in the name of therapeutic improvement in the care of infants and babies at risk. That does not make them any more honest.

Most FDA/EMA requested/ demanded "pediatric" studies are medically pointless or exaggerated. This applies even more to neonatology where the dose of drugs may have to be corrected a few hours after a first application in the morning of the same day. The body of the preterm newborn develops very fast.

Specifically in clinical studies submitted to Institutional Review Boards (IRBs)/ Ethics Committees (ECs) it is fundamentally important to clarify whether the respective study is planned to improve the medical care of the small patients, or whether it is a study that primarily serves approval purposes without really advancing the therapeutic situation. Aside from major breakthroughs like the introduction of lung surfactant, the use of incubators, and more, neonatologists have advanced their discipline primarily through incremental improvements in hands-on care, not by regulatory drug studies. If the respective study documentation does not adequately address why the study is being sponsored by a pharmaceutical company, then IRBs/ECs should look closer. Just a summary justification that medicines must also be approved for newborns is not sufficient. Many antibiotics, antifungals, and other effective drugs are routinely used without being specifically approved in neonates or preterm newborns. If the respective study is based on an EMA "pediatric investigation plan" (PIP), then double caution is called for. Also neonates should not be used as guinea pigs to satisfy dogmatic demands of regulatory authorities or to allow researchers to leave a footprint in pediatric research.

References

1. Silverman WA, Andersen DH, Blanc WA, Crozier DN. A difference in mortality rate and incidence of kernicterus among premature infants allotted to two prophylactic antibacterial regimens. Pediatrics. 1956;18:614
2. Burns LE, Hodgman JE, Cass AB. Fatal circulatory collapse in premature infants receiving chloramphenicol. *N EngI 1 Med.* 1959;261:1318-1321
3. AAP 1995: Guidelines for the Ethical Conduct of Studies to Evaluate Drugs in Pediatric Populations, Committee on Drugs. American Academy of Pediatrics, Pediatrics, 1995 Feb;95(2):286-94
4. Jorgensen AM. Born in the USA – The History of Neonatology in the United States: A Century of Caring. https://static.abbottnutrition.com/cms-prod/anhi.org/img/Nurse%20 Currents%20NICU%20History%20June%202010.pdf
5. Philip AG. The evolution of neonatology. Pediatr Res. 2005 Oct;58(4):799-815. https://www.nature.com/articles/pr2005743.pdf?origin=ppub
6. Vidyasagar D. "Half a Century of Evolution of Neonatology: A Witness's Story" : Dr. K. C. Chaudhuri Lifetime Achievement Award Oration Delivered at AIIMS, New Delhi on 7th September 2014. Indian J Pediatr. 2015 Dec;82(12):1117-25. doi: 10.1007/s12098-015-1838-8
7. Obladen M. History of surfactant up to 1980. Biol Neonate 2005;87(4):308-16.
8. Bae CW. History of Pulmonary Surfactant Replacement Therapy for Neonatal Respiratory Distress Syndrome in Korea. J Korean Med Sci. 2019 Jul 1; 34(25): e175. https://www.ncbi.nlm.nih.gov/pmc/articles/PMC6597488/pdf/jkms-34-e175.pdf
9. Halliday HL. The fascinating story of surfactant. J Paediatr Child Health 2017 Apr;53(4):327-333 https://onlinelibrary.wiley.com/doi/epdf/10.1111/jpc.13500

10. Patz A. The Role Of Oxygen In Retrolental Fibroplasia. Trans Am Ophthalmol Soc. 1968;66:940-85. https://www.ncbi.nlm.nih.gov/pmc/articles/PMC1310320/pdf/taos00033-0953.pdf
11. Tasman W, Patz A, McNamara JA, et al. Retinopathy of prematurity: the life of a lifetime disease. Am J Ophthalmol. 2006 Jan;141(1):167-74.
12. Rose K. Considering the Patient in Pediatric Drug Development. How good intentions turned into harm. Elsevier, London, UK, 2020
13. Rose K. Blind Trust - How parents with a sick child can escape the labyrinth of lies, hypocrisy and false promises of researchers and regulatory authorities. Hammersmith, London, UK, 2022.
14. Rose K, Neubauer D, Grant-Kels JM. Rational Use of Medicine in Children – The Conflict of Interests Story. A Review. Rambam Maimonides Med J. 2019 Jul 18; 10(3): e0018. Review. doi:10.5041/RMMJ.10371. https://www.rmmj.org.il/userimages/928/2/PublishFiles/953Article.pdf
15. Rose K. The Challenges of Pediatric Drug Development. Curr Ther Res Clin Exp. 2019, https://doi.org/10.1016/j.curtheres.2019.01.007
16. Youngson R, Schott I. Medical Blunders. Robinson, London, UK, 1996
17. Harari YN. Sapiens. A Brief History of Humankind. Penguin Random House, London, UK, 2014
18. Bucci-Rechtweg CM, Ward RM. Tiny and Forgotten: A Call for Focused Neonatal Policy Reform. Ther Innov Regul Sci. 2019 Sep;53(5):615-617.
19. Stiers J, Ward RM. Newborns, One of the Last Therapeutic Orphans to Be Adopted. JAMA Pediatr 2014 Feb;168(2):106-8.
20. Barrett JS, Bishai R, Bucci-Rechtweg C, et al. Challenges and Opportunities in the Development of Medical Therapies for Pediatric Populations and the Role of Extrapolation. Clin Pharmacol Ther. 2018 Mar;103(3):419-433. doi: 10.1002/cpt.1000. Epub 2018 Jan 31.
21. Dotta A, Braguglia A, Salvatori G. Pharmacological research in neonatology. J Matern Fetal Neonatal Med. 2011 Oct;24 Suppl 1:44-6.

22. Sivanandan S, Jain K, Plakkal N,et al. Issues, challenges, and the way forward in conducting clinical trials among neonates: investigators' perspective. J Perinatol. 2019 Sep;39(Suppl 1):20-30. doi: 10.1038/s41372-019-0469-8

23. Wang J, Avant D, Green D, et al. A Survey of Neonatal Pharmacokinetic and Pharmacodynamic Studies in Pediatric Drug Development. Clin Pharmacol Ther. 2015 Sep;98(3):328-35.

24. Smith AM, Davis JM. Challenges and opportunities to enhance global drug development in neonates. Curr Opin Pediatr. 2017 Apr;29(2):149-152.

25. Giacoia GP, Taylor-Zapata P, Zajicek A. Drug Studies in Newborns: A Therapeutic Imperative. Clin Perinatol 2012 Mar;39(1):11-23.

26. O'Hara K, Martin JH, Schneider JJ. Barriers and Challenges in Performing Pharmacokinetic Studies to Inform Dosing in the Neonatal Population. Pharmacy (Basel). 2020 Feb 5;8(1):16. https://www.ncbi.nlm.nih.gov/pmc/articles/PMC7151681/pdf/pharmacy-08-00016.pdf

27. Rose K, Grant-Kels JM, Striano P, Oishi T, Neubauer D, Ettienne EB. "Pediatric" Drug Studies Might Be the Largest Abuse in Medical Research in History. It Is Time for Lawyers to Step In. J Law Med 2023,30(1), in press

Chapter 15

Conclusions and Outlook

This book touches on a contemporary fundamental ethical challenge that does not fit the mold of ordinary disclosures. We are used to it being revealed that politicians or alleged philanthropists are evading taxes; that politicians systematically channel off public funds to their accounts through intricate channels; that famous and powerful men touch young and attractive women improperly or do worse; and the like. As so often in life, reality is even more phantastic than a crime writer or a good science fiction author could invent.

Revelations can only work if the investigative journalist or the curious & critical scientist can even imagine a connection in what he or she is looking at. That something as sacrosanct and precious as the healthcare of children with such a prominent position in the public sphere is exploited for a shameless end in itself goes beyond the imagination of any honest person at first. This is also the reason why it has not been noticed until now. The best strategy for uncovering a secret in the past was a hiding place on a desert island. But there are fewer and fewer desert islands, and what else could one hide there besides gold or diamonds? In addition, the days of piracy, when buccaneers appropriated some of the riches that the colonial powers had taken from their colonies are long gone. Today, the best way to hide something questionable is to find a strategy or method to put it in the direct view of the public so that everyone sees it, everyone has heard about it, and everyone assumes that someone makes sure that everything has its correctness. A good place for this is issues at the interface of sciences which are already complex in and of themselves. This book discusses medicine and law as the top two branches, with the specific sciences of developmental physiology and developmental pharmacology, all of pediatric medicine, drug approval, the drug development process, the economy of drug development, and much more. All of these sciences and processes are complicated in and of themselves. Beyond that, the specialists involved spare no effort to strengthen the impression of venerableness and indubitability.

Welcome to the 21st century where everybody claims to be honest, where politicians make promises of everything under the sun, at least as long as they want to be elected, and where once in office they do not always deliver. Does this sound like something you have heard before? Correct. Human nature has never changed and will never change. There will always be a tension between what politicians and officials say and what they do; between what they say and what they really want. This is really nothing new. But what is really new is that there is not something dirty going on in secret or without the knowledge of the public, but it is documented on the Internet so openly that anyone can gain access to this data. All "pediatric investigation plan" (PIP) decisions are published by the European Medicines Agency (EMA) on its website. You have just to enter the PIP number into google, e.g., EMEA-002051-PIP02-1 for allopregnanolone to read about the demanded "pediatric" studies in young mothers younger than 18 years with perinatal depression. The description of study 1 is verbatim "Double-blind, randomised, placebo-controlled trial to evaluate pharmacokinetics, safety, tolerability and efficacy of allopregnanolone in post-pubertal adolescent girls with postpartum depression."[1] The Food and Drug Administration (FDA) regularly publishes lists for which drugs they have requested or mandated truly pediatric and/or allegedly pediatric studies.[2] Both the FDA and the EMA publish regular reports on the alleged successes of pediatric drug development.[3-7] Let us hope that eventually the decoding of these reports will move one or the other person, parent or scientist to question the whole thing critically.

Medicine, science, and medical healthcare are continuously improving. Not only due to incremental personal learnings of the medical doctor, nurse, pharmacists, and other health care professional during their individual life, but to a very relevant degree through scientific progress. But scientific progress is not achieved by every single scientist on this earth. There is true progress, and there is the age-old dream of almost everybody to have a secure job with a good salary and a high social standing. With "pediatric drug development" we see how an entire branch of science has created a pseudo-problem, justified and continues to justify it pseudo-scientifically, and has managed through the detour of legislation to have laws enacted that result in an unlimited flow of "pediatric" studies on new drugs that the pharmaceutical industry must organize and pay for. The pinnacle of this charade is that the pediatric researchers, along with the regulatory officials, can pose as the magnanimous researchers who coerce at least some worthwhile studies from the profit-hungry industry.

The term "junk science" describes the use of statements that appear to be based on solid science. The term is used to describe scientific data, research, or analysis as spurious or fraudulent. It is often invoked in political and legal contexts where facts and scientific results have a great amount of weight in making a determination. The term "junk science" is used as the opposite of the expressions "sound science" or "solid science." Three books discuss "junk science" in depth.[8-10] The term was used at least from 1985 on, i.e. years before the first book was published in 1991.[8,11-13] The first book describes the challenges caused by admitting junk science into US courtrooms.[8,12,13] Pseudo-evidence based on junk science has resulted in many innocent people being found guilty in court, leaving them in prison for years or even decades.[8,10] A weakness of the litigious American legal system is that a villain is sought for almost everything, even when in fact none exists. Years after the thalidomide disaster, the antinausea drug pyridoxine/doxylamine, a combination of pyridoxine hydrochloride (vitamin B_6) and doxylamine succinate, sold in the US under the brand name Bendectin, was accused to cause malformations in babies as well.[14] These allegations were never really scientifically proven, but they created such a bad investment climate for developing morning sickness drugs that Bendectin was pulled from the market and pharmaceutical companies stopped developing new drugs in this area.[8,11,14] The car Audi in its US version "Audi 5000" was accused of sudden unintended and uncontrollable acceleration, resulting in serious accidents. When the US National Highway Transportation Safety Board and similar agencies in Canada and Japan investigated the accidents, carefully considering and rejecting possible causes, they all reached the same conclusion that the accidents had occurred when people had mistakenly stepped on the gas instead of the brake.[8,12,13,15] Other potentially useful products may never be introduced at all for fear of liability. Rising health insurance costs are fueled partially by large malpractice verdicts, some based on spurious scientific reasoning. Medical doctors may base treatment decisions not on the best available medical information but on a standard of care defined by malpractice verdicts.

"Pediatric drug development" has become a new variation of junk science, particularly where claims are made that common sense can quickly debunk as nonsense, such as EMA's claim that off-label treatment of children is always harmful.[16] The entire discipline of pediatrics and many of its sub-disciplines evolved off -label, decades before the term off-label even existed.[17-21]

The decisive difference to the use of "junk science" in courtrooms is that the concept of "pediatric drug development" has been given an official character through legislation, so that criticism of it must initially fail.

A recent publication discusses the current state of progress of science in general. Theories of scientific and technological change see discovery and invention as processes where previously accumulated knowledge allows next generation researchers to stand on the shoulders of their predecessors and continue contributing to the growth of knowledge and wisdom. Despite the current exponential growth in the volume of scientific publications and the growing scientific and technological knowledge, progress appears to be slowing in several major fields. The authors find that papers and patents are increasingly less likely to break with the past to push science and technology into new directions. They see this universally across research and science. They call this overall a decline in disruptiveness and link it to a narrowing in the use of previous knowledge and in an increasing tunnel view. They also see the observed decline as unlikely to be driven by changes in the quality of published science, citation practices or field-specific factors. They conclude that the slowing rates of disruption may reflect a fundamental shift in the nature of science and technology.[22] The weakness of this paper is that it only describes symptoms, but not their human roots and with that the real reasons of this development. On the one hand, the causes are easy to describe: they reflect the fact that all researchers are real people (and not robots), are human, and are therefore also exposed to human temptations. These temptations cannot be captured by simple schemes. Open bribery has really become more difficult, with pretty good mechanisms to prevent it. But as the defense mechanisms have become more complicated, the characteristics of temptation have become more complicated as well, reflecting a more complicated human society. Reputation; public esteem; the official seal of the value of "pediatric" research, even when the people being studied are physically not even children; all of this has condensed into a new social and psychological entity characterized by perpetual emphasis on the moral imperative to perform clinical trials in "children" and its high moral and ethical value.[23,24] This has lulled public perception for a while. On the other hand, long-lasting but nevertheless temporary deception has happened many times in history. It is easy to overcome once it has been identified and once that identification has found its way into the public discussion and consciousness. Then the discussion will start about which strategies and recommendations should be applied to overcome this. The basic strength of our Western culture is that it accepts criticism and does not imprison critics or even burn them at the stake as has often happened in history. Galileo Galilei escaped such a fate, but not Giordano Bruno.[25-27]

This book presents a different analysis compared to the one by Park et al.[22] and comes to different conclusions. I agree with Park et al. that the process of science and development has reached a critical point. It is not simply a slow decline in disruptiveness compared to earlier discoveries that might be perceived as an irreversible process. Instead, in the current process of research, development, and the growth of science there is a reluctance to call a spade a spade. There are underlying reasons for this reluctance. But to overcome them is not an unsurmountable obstacle. These reasons and obstacles are not purely scientific in nature. They are more linked to human nature. Everyone has an idea of what a child is. As we have seen, pediatric drug development has exploited a gap in the precise definition of what a child is to force unethical, pointless, and/or grossly overblown clinical trials in minors. All under the guise of pure science. Just as everyone has a rough idea of what children are, the societal debate still works with vague terminology. Everyone knows the motivations that lead to taboos, to look the other way, and to shrug. That is why inconvenient truths do not surface as quickly as desirable. Once such dams had been broken in the MeToo debate about improper behavior towards women, persons such as Harvey Weinstein could no longer hide behind their fame and strong social influence. Improper behaviour which can range from patriarchal remarks to violent rape.[28,29] In the debate about clinical trials involving minors, we are not there yet. But we address important points in this book.

The mentioned decline in disruptiveness will hopefully move for all life sciences towards a point where the debate will focus on the fundamental questions of research outlined in this book. Hopefully, it will then draw implications for scientific publications, scientific careers, and the relationship between medicine and the community, between medical doctors and parents of ill children. I call this a node in development. As soon as this node/ knot dissolves, the development of knowledge and science will take off again. It's like everyone's personal career. The biggest obstacle is usually the person themselves, not the environment. The ancient Greeks already knew this: know thyself (gnôthi seautón/γνῶθι σεαυτόν).[30] Our western society is balanced and strong enough to survive the mirror that we hold up here and to draw reasonable conclusions. Who would have thought that one day the world's largest lodging business would be an institution that does not own a single home?[31,32] Or that one of the largest transport organizations in the world that does not own a single car itself?[33,34] As for the reported and bemoaned decline in disruptiveness, I hope that the core ideas of this book are disruptive enough.

More than ever science penetrates a growing number of areas of society. Not only in the development of drugs, but also in the development of medical devices; in the advancement of aeronautics and aerospace; in the development of cars, trains and ships; in the development of weapons, of communication, and more. The weapons of World War II were already lethal, cruel, and horrifying. But we see today how Russia, which inherited from the former Soviet Union a vast stockpile of weapons and the military tradition of Soviet times, both outdated, shows a military performance massively inferior than expected and feared before its invasion of Ukraine, thanks to the West's advanced long-range, high-precision artillery and the flexibility and cohesion of Ukraine's numerically inferior armed forces. Without the advanced weapons provided by the West, and without the cohesion of Ukraine's population, including the armed forces, Putin's murderous troops would have invaded Kiev long ago. The challenge we are seeing right now is that growth in knowledge, technology and applied science in Western countries and societies, is not sufficiently flowing back into academic science.

Areas that are necessary to be addressed here include the trade unions, which in many countries have reduced the university structures to rigid skeletons; the labor laws of many countries, which have a similar effect not only on the people who work in research, but also on those who work in academic administration; the popular belief in the sacredness of academic knowledge; the desire of many scientists to be able to communicate with scientists from other countries on an equal footing and to be perceived as such; even if they have little to contribute, they are treated politely. But science is also based on competition, and not everyone can be the best. There are many more factors. Many of the touched elements are political in nature, have grown over decades, and have reached a level of traditionality that they will not change overnight. But there are a number of areas where conscious action can trigger changes quickly.

Progress in overcoming obstacles to scientific progress always has two phases. The first phase is that the existing challenges are clearly identified. The second phase is finding the right steps to start overcoming.

Just a quick reminder: it took seven years until Peter Buxtun, who worked at the US Public Health Service (PHS) and had risked his job during this time span trying to convince management to end the Tuskegee Syphilis Study, realized he was being stonewalled. Once he realized that, the step to inform a journalist was relatively short. It was now a matter of weeks before the study was unveiled on the front page of a national US newspaper. The study had been known in medical circles, but not beyond. What had changed in the forty years since it had begun were science, the industrial production of antibiotics, and the mood of public opinion. Allowing sick African Americans to die of syphilis untreated was no longer ignored with a shrug.[35-37]

Whoever wants to obtain scientific positions in the academic world has to prove himself in scientific research. With this, positions in science have two sides: individual career, and really advancing science and producing new wisdom. The more university careers lead to permanent positions in which the position holders only have to repeat what they have learned decades ago or developed themselves, the more academic science threatens to become a rigid skeleton in which young ideas have little space.

One operative conclusion is that a new gigantic operational task is expecting IRBs/ECs. US and EU pediatric legislation were and are justified by emphasizing that a relevant percentage of the population is younger than 18y. IRBs/ECs will need special training and a high-level worldwide debate about the potential conflicts of interest behind alleged "pediatric" clinical research projects. This training will have to include regulatory affairs, specifically about pediatric laws, and the questionable studies they have triggered over the last decades. It will be a painful experience for science and all structures that should control, but do not sufficiently.

The International Council of Medical Journal Editors (ICMJE) will have to train its members about the questionable characteristics of "pediatric" studies. It will take a few years until the last pediatric professor and the last head of a pediatric department hopeful have learned that accepting study projects that carry the FDA or EMA seal but are scientifically questionable, pointless or even harmful, will not advance their future career. This will help dramatically to push down the number of "pediatric" study projects that are approved worldwide.[38,39]

The Council for International Organizations of Medical Sciences (CIOMS) is yet another place where terribly important scientists and professors meet regularly to discuss terribly important issues and then come to terribly important (and sadly most of the time pretty banal) conclusions. As an international non-governmental organization of international, national, and associate member groups representing the biomedical science community that was jointly established by the World Health Organization (WHO) and the United Nations Educational, Scientific and Cultural Organization (UNESCO), it is even more shielded from the public than the EMA.[40,41] It would be nice and desirable if also the CIOMS would address this challenge and take a clear position.

A further key area is not only the management of scientific publications, but also the appreciation, more precisely the lack of appreciation, towards applied science performed in industry. European academic careers are separated from academia by an almost unbridgeable gulf. You learn different things in industry than in academia, and you apply your learnings in a different way. Common sense plays a much bigger role in the industry. This gulf between industry and academia is much wider and deeper in Europe than in the US. The more academy hesitates to open up here, it is increasingly becoming a museum-like place where pre-chewed knowledge is repeated. This applies to all key areas of science, including specifically medicine, pharmacology, engineering, law and related disciplines.

As discussed above, innovation will need two phases. Phase 1 is prepared with this book and other publications. This phase will need a broad discussion in academic and non-academic circles. This is a very controversial issue. In this regard, the coming years and decades will certainly not be boring. Of course those institutions, pediatric sub-disciplines, and individuals who have profited substantially and continue to do so will put up a fierce resistance.

But the listed examples of pointless and harmful allegedly "pediatric" studies cannot be ignored in the long run. The pediatric legislation has now been in existence for 25 years (US) and 15 years (EU). The process of dealing with these laws has not really started yet. There are still many – biased – supporters. Several critical peer-reviewed papers have been published, but most of them still limited to specific clinical areas.[42-46] There is no point in simply condemning as bad something that has been around for decades.

The next question will of course be how to modify pediatric legislation. This will be a gigantic task, and it will be made more difficult by the fact that politicians will be reluctant to share responsibility for questionable clinical studies. For once, the industry cannot be made the scapegoat. The driving force was a rather informal coalition of AAP, clinical pharmacology, other pediatric advocacy groups, and regulatory agencies. But the key question will be what is really necessary for the approval of drugs for minors. This could be the subject of another book, but here are some basic elements. Of the three major areas of pediatric legislation - child-friendly formulations, preclinical studies on young animals, clinical studies - the requirement for child-friendly formulations is the only one that really makes sense. Of course, the authorities have often made excessively exaggerated demands also here, but in principle it is gratifying when drug developers have to make an effort to offer formulations suitable for children at an early stage. The focus of this book is clinical trials in minors. Separate efficacy & safety studies in adolescents should disappear altogether. Adolescents should be routinely included as subjects in pivotal adult studies. Dose finding is necessary in younger patients. With the modern methods of pharmacokinetics and pharmacodynamics, these dosages can now be calculated in advance. Relatively small confirmatory studies are sufficient to verify these dosages. If the authorities have serious security concerns, security data can be recorded in registries. With their limited number of study participants, the approval studies never identify the rare side effects that can always occur with new drugs. The one age group where I cannot offer no easy recommendations is neonates and preterm neonates.

As we have learned from the saga of "pediatric drug development", it is dangerous to give the approval authorities a free hand. They exaggerate like any small child who is offered the choice of whatever it likes in a children's toy store. It would take a truck to take home all the toys it wants, and you would need a new house to put them all at home. A reasonable approach will be found for neonatology once the pseudo-scientific justification of "pediatric" studies are discredited and demystified in the public and the scientific discussion.

At worst the result of this discussion would be tighter and even more pointless controls. But if we manage to keep the discussion reasonable, it will improve research in minors towards more humane and meaningful clinical investigations.

References

1. EMA allopregnanolone PIP EMEA-002051-PIP02-16. EMA 2017 https://www.ema.europa.eu/en/documents/pip-decision/p/0357/2017-ema-decision-1-december-2017-agreement-paediatric-investigation-plan-granting-deferral-granting_en.pdf

2. FDA List of Determinations Including Written Request. Pediatric Exclusivity Determinations Made under Section 505A of the Federal Food, Drug, and Cosmetic Act (the Act), as amended by the FDA Amendments Act of 2007 (FDAAA. FDA 2023. https://www.fda.gov/drugs/development-resources/list-determinations -including-written-request

3. FDA, The Pediatric Exclusivity Provision. Status Report to Congress, January 2001. https://www.fda.gov/downloads/Drugs/DevelopmentApprovalProces s/DevelopmentResources/UCM049915.pdf

4. FDA, Best Pharmaceuticals for Children Act and Pediatric Research Equity Act. Status Report to Congress, July 2016. https://www.fda.gov/downloads/ScienceResearch/SpecialTopics/Pedi atricTherapeuticsResearch/UCM509815.pdf

5. State of Paediatric Medicines in the EU. 10 Years of the EU Paediatric Regulation. Report from the Commission to the European Parliament and the Council. COM (2017) 626. https://ec.europa.eu/health/sites/health/files/files/paediatrics/docs/201 7_childrensmedicines_report_en.pdf

6. Report From The Commission To The European Parliament And The Council. State of Paediatric Medicines in the EU - 10 years of the EU Paediatric Regulation. European Commission, 2017. https://www.europarl.europa.eu/RegData/docs_autres_institutions/co mmission_europeenne/com/2017/0626/COM_COM(2017)0626_EN.pdf

7. EMA, 10-year Report to the European Commission General Report on the Experience Acquired as a Result of the Application of the Paediatric Regulation. EMA 2017.

https://health.ec.europa.eu/system/files/2020-06/paediatrics_10_years_ema_technical_report_0.pdf

8. Huber P. Galileo's Revenge: Junk Science In The Courtroom. Basic Books, New York, NY, USA, 1991
9. Agin D. Junk Science: An Overdue Indictment of Government, Industry, and Faith Groups That Twist Science for Their Own Gain. St. Martin's Griffin, New York, NY, USA, 2007
10. Fabricant C. Junk Science and the American Criminal Justice System. Akashic Books, Brooklyn, New York, NY, USA, 2022
11. Wikipedia, Junk science https://en.wikipedia.org/wiki/Junk_science
12. McDermott MA. Booknote. Galileo's Revenge: Junk Science in the Courtroom. Harvard J Law Technol, 1992;6(Fall Issue):207-211 https://jolt.law.harvard.edu/assets/articlePDFs/v06/06HarvJLTech207.pdf
13. Baughman JF. Galileo's Revenge: Junk Science in the Courtroom. Michigan Law Review,1992;90(6):1614-1623. https://repository.law.umich.edu/cgi/viewcontent.cgi?params=/context/mlr/article/2319/
14. Wikipedia, Pyridoxine/doxylamine https://en.wikipedia.org/wiki/Pyridoxine/doxylamine
15. Wikipedia, Audi 100 https://en.wikipedia.org/wiki/Audi_100
16. Evidence of harm from off-label or unlicensed medicines in children. EMA 2004. https://www.ema.europa.eu/en/documents/other/evidence-harm-label-unlicensed-medicines-children_en.pdf
17. Plate V. The Impact of Off-Label, Compassionate and Unlicensed Use on Health Care Laws in preselected Countries. https://bonndoc.ulb.uni-bonn.de/xmlui/bitstream/handle/20.500.11811/4152/1936.pdf

18. Rose K, Grant-Kels JM, Striano P, Ettienne EB, Oishi T, Neubauer D. "Pediatric" Drug Studies Might Be the Largest Abuse in Medical Research in History. It Is Time for Lawyers to Step In. J Law Med 2023,30(1), in press

19. Rose K. Abuse of Minors in Clinical Studies: A Worldwide Ethical Challenge for the 21st Century. Ethics International Press, Bradford, UK, July 2023
https://ethicspress.com/products/abuse-of-minors-in-clinical-studies

20. Rose K. Blind Trust - How parents with a sick child can escape the labyrinth of lies, hypocrisy and false promises of researchers and regulatory authorities. Hammersmith, London, UK, 2022.
https://www.book2look.com/book/mMqwf6ap9C

21. Rose K. Considering the Patient in Pediatric Drug Development. How good intentions turned into harm. Elsevier, London, UK, 2020.
https://www.elsevier.com/books/considering-the-patient-in-pediatric-drug-development/rose/978-0-12-823888-2 and
https://www.sciencedirect.com/book/9780128238882/considering-the-patient-in-pediatric-drug-development

22. Park M, Leahey E, Funk RJ. Papers and patents are becoming less disruptive over time. Nature 613, 138–144 (2023).
https://www.nature.com/articles/s41586-022-05543-x

23. Gang A, Lopez M, Raphael JL. Protecting the American Dream: a Pediatric Imperative. Pediatrics 2021 Feb;147(2):e20200370

24. Guidelines for the ethical conduct of studies to evaluate drugs in pediatric populations. Committee on Drugs, American Academy of Pediatrics. Pediatrics 1995 Feb;95(2):286-94.

25. Wikipedia, Galileo Galilei
https://en.wikipedia.org/wiki/Galileo_Galilei

26. Rowland ID. Giordano Bruno: Philosopher / Heretic. University of Chicago Press, Chicago, IL, USA, 2009

27. Wikipedia, Giordano Bruno
https://en.wikipedia.org/wiki/Giordano_Bruno

28. Wikipedia, MeToo movement
https://en.wikipedia.org/wiki/MeToo_movement

29. Wikipedia, Harvey Weinstein sexual abuse cases
https://en.wikipedia.org/wiki/Harvey_Weinstein_sexual_abuse_cases

30. Wikipedia, Know thyself
https://en.wikipedia.org/wiki/Know_thyself

31. Airbnb
www.airbnb.com

32. Wikipedia, Airbnb
https://en.wikipedia.org/wiki/Airbnb

33. Uber
www.uber.com

34. Wikipedia, Uber
https://en.wikipedia.org/wiki/Uber

35. Wikipedia, Tuskegee Syphilis Study
https://en.wikipedia.org/wiki/Tuskegee_Syphilis_Study

36. Washington HA. Medical Apartheid: The Dark History of Medical Experimentation on Black Americans from Colonial Times to the Present. Anchor Books, New York, NY, USA, 2008

37. Brandt, Allan M. 1978. Racism and research: The case of the Tuskegee Syphilis study. The Hastings Center Report 8(6): 21-29.
https://dash.harvard.edu/handle/1/3372911

38. International Committee of Medical Journal Editors
https://www.icmje.org/

39. Wikipedia, ICMJE recommendations
https://en.wikipedia.org/wiki/ICMJE_recommendations

40. Council for International Organizations of Medical Sciences (CIOMS),
https://cioms.ch/

41. Wikipedia, Council for International Organizations of Medical Sciences (CIOMS)

https://en.wikipedia.org/wiki/Council_for_International_Organizations_of_Medical_Sciences

42. Nigrovic PA, Raychaudhuri S, Thompson SD. Review: Genetics and the Classification of Arthritis in Adults and Children. Arthritis Rheumatol. 2018 Jan;70(1):7-17. https://onlinelibrary.wiley.com/doi/epdf/10.1002/art.40350

43. Nigrovic PA, Colbert RA, Holers VM, et al. Biological classification of childhood arthritis: roadmap to a molecular nomenclature. Nat Rev Rheumatol. 2021 May;17(5):257-269.

44. Pellock JM, Carman WJ, Thyagarajan V, et al. Efficacy of antiepileptic drugs in adults predicts efficacy in children: a systematic review. Neurology. 2012 Oct 2;79(14):1482-9. https://www.ncbi.nlm.nih.gov/pmc/articles/PMC4098824/pdf/znl1482.pdf

45. Pappo AS. Pediatric Melanoma: The Whole (Genome) Story. Am Soc Clin Oncol Educ Book 2014;e432-5 https://ascopubs.org/doi/pdf/10.14694/EdBook_AM.2014.34.e432

46. Waubant E, Banwell B, Wassmer E, et al. Clinical trials of disease-modifying agents in pediatric MS: Opportunities, challenges, and recommendations from the IPMSSG. Neurology 2019 May 28;92(22):e2538-e2549. https://www.ncbi.nlm.nih.gov/pmc/articles/PMC6556085/pdf/NEUROLOGY2018940742.pdf